A Book Of

MERCHANT BANKING AND FINANCIAL SERVICES

For

MBA Semester - III (Finance Specialisation - Core Subject)
Course Code : 306
As Per Pune University's Revised Syllabus
Effective from June 2014

Meera Govindaraj
M.Com., M.B.A. (Finance)

Sudhakar B. Kulkarni
Certified Financial Planner

MERCHANT BANKING AND FINANCIAL SERVICES

ISBN 978-93-5164-047-9

First Edition : July 2014

© : **Authors**

The text of this publication, or any part thereof, should not be reproduced or transmitted in any form or stored in any computer storage system or device for distribution including photocopy, recording, taping or information retrieval system or reproduced on any disc, tape, perforated media or other information storage device etc., without the written permission of Authors with whom the rights are reserved. Breach of this condition is liable for legal action.

Every effort has been made to avoid errors or omissions in this publication. In spite of this, errors may have crept in. Any mistake, error or discrepancy so noted and shall be brought to our notice shall be taken care of in the next edition. It is notified that neither the publisher nor the authors or seller shall be responsible for any damage or loss of action to any one, of any kind, in any manner, therefrom.

Published By :
NIRALI PRAKASHAN
Abhyudaya Pragati, 1312, Shivaji Nagar,
Off J.M. Road, PUNE – 411005
Tel - (020) 25512336/37/39, Fax - (020) 25511379
Email : niralipune@pragationline.com

Printed By :
Repro Knowledgecast Limited,
Thane

DISTRIBUTION CENTRES
PUNE

Nirali Prakashan
119, Budhwar Peth, Jogeshwari Mandir Lane
Pune 411002, Maharashtra
Tel : (020) 2445 2044, 66022708, Fax : (020) 2445 1538
Email : bookorder@pragationline.com

Nirali Prakashan
S. No. 28/27, Dhyari,
Near Pari Company, Pune 411041
Tel : (022) 24690371
Email : dhyari@pragationline.com
bookorder@pragationline.com

MUMBAI
Nirali Prakashan
385, S.V.P. Road, Rasdhara Co-op. Hsg. Society Ltd.,
Girgaum, Mumbai 400004, Maharashtra
Tel : (022) 2385 6339 / 2386 9976, Fax : (022) 2386 9976
Email : niralimumbai@pragationline.com

DISTRIBUTION BRANCHES

NAGPUR
Pratibha Book Distributors
Above Maratha Mandir, Shop No. 3, First Floor,
Rani Jhanshi Square, Sitabuldi, Nagpur 440012,
Maharashtra, Tel : (0712) 254 7129

BENGALURU
Pragati Book House
House No. 1, Sanjeevappa Lane, Avenue Road Cross,
Opp. Rice Church, Bengaluru – 560002.
Tel : (080) 64513344, 64513355,
Mob : 9880582331, 9845021552
Email:bharatsavla@yahoo.com

JALGAON
Nirali Prakashan
34, V. V. Golani Market, Navi Peth, Jalgaon 425001,
Maharashtra, Tel : (0257) 222 0395
Mob : 94234 91860

KOLHAPUR
Nirali Prakashan
New Mahadvar Road,
Kedar Plaza, 1st Floor Opp. IDBI Bank
Kolhapur 416 012, Maharashtra. Mob : 9855046155

CHENNAI
Pragati Books
9/1, Montieth Road, Behind Taas Mahal, Egmore,
Chennai 600008 Tamil Nadu, Tel : (044) 6518 3535,
Mob : 94440 01782 / 98450 21552 / 98805 82331, Email : bharatsavla@yahoo.com

RETAIL OUTLETS
PUNE

Pragati Book Centre
157, Budhwar Peth, Opp. Ratan Talkies,
Pune 411002, Maharashtra
Tel : (020) 2445 8887 / 6602 2707, Fax : (020) 2445 8887

Pragati Book Centre
Amber Chamber, 28/A, Budhwar Peth,
Appa Balwant Chowk, Pune : 411002, Maharashtra,
Tel : (020) 20240335 / 66281669
Email : pbcpune@pragationline.com

Pragati Book Centre
676/B, Budhwar Peth, Opp. Jogeshwari Mandir,
Pune 411002, Maharashtra
Tel : (020) 6601 7784 / 6602 0855

PBC Book Sellers & Stationers
152, Budhwar Peth, Pune 411002, Maharashtra
Tel : (020) 2445 2254 / 6609 2463

MUMBAI
Pragati Book Corner
Indira Niwas, 111 - A, Bhavani Shankar Road, Dadar (W), Mumbai 400028, Maharashtra
Tel : (022) 2422 3526 / 6662 5254, Email : pbcmumbai@pragationline.com

www.pragationline.com   info@pragationline.com

Preface ...

Financial Services and financial markets are a vital part of the economy which act as intermediaries between the savers of funds and users of funds. Over a period of time a lot of changes have taken place in the financial sector mainly due to changing demands and ever developing technology. Contribution of the financial sector in GDP is increasing with every passing year. Also because of globalisation and liberalisation need of financial services is constantly increasing for cross border as well as domestic financial transactions.

The current scenario in financial services is very complex even for seasoned professionals. It is not surprising that many students may find it difficult. The purpose of this book is to acquaint the students about the basics of various financial services and their intricacies. The major change observed nowadays is that those who need funds are directly raising the same from the retail investor through public offer both for equity and debt. It is also seen that the role of financial intermediaries is getting diluted in some ways but getting stronger in some other ways. The Merchant Banker plays a pivotal role in issue management. The role of a Merchant Banker is discussed at length in this book. Financial markets are broadly regulated by SEBI and RBI and the respective role regulator is also explained in this book.

Financial Services comprise of many financial products and services and these products are delivered by different financial institutions and agencies. The role of these institutions and agencies is also explained with the regulations. Considering the number of players in the market, competition is increasing day by day along with expectations of the end users. Competition is mainly seen in the insurance, banking, broking and mutual fund business. Due to competition, innovation in product and delivery system is taking place from time to time, however the innovation has to be within the framework of rules and regulations and that is the real challenge faced by the various players in the market.

We thank Shri Dinesh bhai Furia and Shri Jignesh Furia of Nirali Prakashan for giving us an opportunity to write this book. We also would like to express our gratitude towards the staff of Nirali Prakashan for their hard work and constant support in the process of publishing this book.

Last but not the least our sincere appreciation and gratitude to our esteemed readers. Do feel free to share your views on this book. We look forward to it.

Authors

Syllabus ...

1. Meaning, Scope, Participants and Instruments

Definition of Merchant Banking and Its Scope, Procedure for Registration of Merchant Banking, Operational Guide Lines by SEBI for Merchant Bankers, Code of Conduct for Merchant Bankers, Indian Financial System and Its Participants.

BSE, NSE and Over the Counter Exchange of India – History, Role, Functions, Trading Operations and Settlement of Transactions, Regulations of Stock exchanges.

Money Market – Structure of Money Market, Money Market Instrument, Indian Money Market, Features and Defects, Players in the Indian Money Market, The Reforms in Indian Money Market.

Capital Market Instruments – Preference Share. Equity Shares, Non-voting Shares, Convertible Cumulative Debentures (CCD), Preference Shares, Fixed Deposits, Warrants, Debentures and Bonds, Global Depository Receipts, American Depository Receipts, Global Debt Instruments.

2. Public Issue Management and Regulations

Public Issue Management – Functions, Mechanism, Role of Issue Manger, Activities Involved in Public Issue.

Various Methods of Marketing of New Issues – Pure Prospectus Method, Offer for Sale Method, Private Placement Method, Initial Public Offer Method, Rights Issue Method, Bonus Issue Method, Book Building Process, Stock Option Method, Bought out Method – Meaning, Feature, Advantages, Limitations, Practical Example.

Prospectus – Prospectus for Public Offer – Its Importance, Difference between Regular Prospectus and Abridged Prospectus, Letter of Offer, Disclosures in Prospectus, Abridged Prospectus and Letter of Offer, Types of Prospectus – Red Herring Prospectus, Information memorandum, Shelf Prospectus.

Underwriting – Definition, Types – Firm, Sub-underwriting, Joint Underwriting, Syndicate Underwriting, Advantages, Variants of Underwriting – Offer for Sale, Bought out Deals, Private Placements.

Post Issue Activities – Meaning, Activities Involved like Allotment, Price Fixation, Dispatch of Certificated etc. Pricing Models – Net Asset Value, Profit Earning Capacity Value, Average Market Price.

3. Services Offered by Merchant Bankers

Mergers and Acquisition Services – Merger, Acquisition, Takeover, Hostile Merger, Stepwise Procedure for Amalgamation, Strategies Adopted to Avoid Hostile Merger – Divestiture, Crown Jewels, Poison Pill, Greenmail, White Knight, Golden Parachutes, Street Sweep, Bear Hug, Brand Power, Poison Put, Pac Man Defense, White Squire.

Types of Mergers – Horizontal, Vertical, Diagonal, Forward, Reverse, Forward Triangular, Reverse Triangular, Conglomerate, Congeneric, Negotiated, Arranged, Unopposed, Defended, Competitive, Tender Offer.

Valuation Method – Net Assets, Discounted Cash Flow Method, Methods of Financing – Ordinary Share, Debt and Preference Shares, Deferred Payment, Tender Offer.

Buy Back of Shares, Delisting of Shares, Issue of Debentures – SEBI Guidelines.

Portfolio Management Services – Meaning, Scope, Registration of Portfolio Manager, Duties, Responsibilities, Rights, Contents of Agreement between Client and Portfolio Manger, Reports to be Furnished, Code of Conduct (Regulation 13 of SEBI Regulation on Portfolio Managers).

Credit Syndication Services – Meaning, Institutions Offering Syndicated Loans, Types, Procedure, Project Appraisal, Documentation and Security, Sanction of a Loan.

4. Financial Services : Part - I

Meaning, Scope and Evolution of Financial Services.

Introduction of Various Financial Services – Leasing, Hire Purchase, Factoring, Forfeiting, Bill Discounting, Consumer Finance, Housing Finance, Insurance, Credit Cards, Credit Ratings, Mutual Funds and Venture Capital.

Leasing – Definition, Meaning, Types, Process, Advantages, Limitations, Financial Implications.

Hire Purchase – Meaning, Scope, Difference between Hire Purchase and Leasing. Calculation of Interest, Methods of Interest Calculation.

Factoring, Forfeiting, Bills Discounting – Meaning, Definitions, Scope Advantages and Limitations.

Insurance – Meaning, Overview, Types – Life and General – Advantages, Scope of Growth in India.

5. Financial Services : Part - II

Consumer Finance – Meaning, Types, Documents and Security, Players in the Market – Banks, NBFC, Co-operative Banks, Role of Consumer Finance in Growth of Economy.

Housing Finance – Major Institutions Involved, Types, Rate of Interest, Advantages, Scenario in India.

Credit Ratings – Origin, Definition, Advantages, Credit Rating Agencies – Global and Indian, Symbols, CRISIL, ICRA, Equity Ratings, Scope in India, CIBIL.

Mutual Funds – Definition, Products, SEBI Requirements for Asset Management Company (AMC), Association of Mutual Funds Industry (AMFI), Evaluating Mutual Fund, Growth in India.

Venture Capital – Definition, Types, Stages Exit Mechanism, Advantages, Limitations, Growth in India.

Contents ...

1. **Merchant Banking and Financial Services:**
   Meaning, Scope, Participants and Instruments 1.1 – 1.44

2. **Public Issue Management and Regulations** 2.1 – 2.40

3. **Services Offered by Merchant Bankers** 3.1 – 3.48

4. **Financial Services : Part - I** 4.1 – 4.36

5. **Financial Services : Part - II** 5.1 – 5.32

   Case Studies C.1 – C.4

Chapter 1...

Merchant Banking and Financial Services: Meaning, Scope, Participants and Instruments

Contents ...

- 1.1 Merchant Banking
    - 1.1.1 Introduction
    - 1.1.2 Definitions
    - 1.1.3 Scope of Merchant Banking
    - 1.1.4 SEBI (Merchant Bankers) Rules and Regulations
- 1.2 Indian Financial System and its Participants
    - 1.2.1 Introduction
    - 1.2.2 Components of the Indian Financial System
- 1.3 Stock Exchange
    - 1.3.1 Introduction
    - 1.3.2 History of Stock Exchanges
    - 1.3.3 Bombay Stock Exchange (BSE)
    - 1.3.4 National Stock Exchange (NSE)
    - 1.3.5 Over the Counter Exchange of India (OTCEI)
    - 1.3.6 Trading Operations and Settlement of Transactions
    - 1.3.7 Regulations of Stock Exchanges
- 1.4 Money Market
    - 1.4.1 Introduction
    - 1.4.2 Requirements of Money Market
    - 1.4.3 Structure of Money Market
    - 1.4.4 Developments in Indian Money Market
    - 1.4.5 Money Market Instruments
- 1.5 Capital Market
    - 1.5.1 Introduction
    - 1.5.2 Importance of Capital Market
    - 1.5.3 Capital Market Instruments
- Points to Remember
- Questions for Discussion

Learning Objectives
- To define the merchant banking and its scope
- To understand SEBI regulations, operational guidelines and code of conduct
- To understand Indian Financial System viz. capital market and money market
- To understand the concept of Indian Financial System
- To know the participants in Indian Financial System
- To understand the regulatory frame work
- To explain the functions of stock exchanges and their role in economy
- To understand historical perspective of stock exchanges in India
- To understand the regulations related to stock exchanges
- To understand the basics of money market, Need of money market, Developments in money market, Different instruments of money market
- To be able to describe equity linked security and fixed income security
- Discuss the regulation pertaining to issue of different kinds of securities

1.1 Merchant Banking

1.1.1 Introduction

Merchant Banks play a pivotal role in capital markets. Public savings is the main source in financing big projects and crores of rupees are raised every year from the market either through equity or debt. Merchant banks act as a conduit between corporates and investors.

In addition, merchant banks offer a package of services ancillary to the promotion and development of industry. These are mostly fee based services and they include investment in private equity, structured equity, bridge financing and so on.

Internationally merchant bankers are known as Investment Bankers who provide various financial services to corporates such as issue management, corporate restructuring, loan syndication and advisory services with reference to mergers and acquisitions.

1.1.2 Definitions

In short, a merchant bank can be defined as a service provider who provides support, knowledge and resources to individuals and organisations for starting, improving and expanding their business and investments.

A merchant bank is an organisation that underwrites securities for corporations, advises such clients on mergers and is involved in the ownership of commercial ventures.

According to **Charles P Kinidleberger**, "*merchant banking is the development of banking commerce which frequently encountered a prolonged intermediate stage known in England originally as merchant banking.*"

According to the **Securities and Exchange Board of India** (Merchant Bankers) Rules, 1992. "*A merchant banker has been defined as any person who is engaged in the business of issue management either by making arrangements regarding selling, buying or subscribing to securities or acting as manager, consultant, advisor or rendering corporate advisory services in relation to such issue management.*"

1.1.3 Scope of Merchant Banking

The expert services and consultation from merchant bankers is required for:

- Foreign institutional investors who are allowed to invest in the primary and secondary markets in India.
- Indian companies who are allowed to directly tap foreign capital through euro issues.
- NRIs who make foreign direct investments as a result of incentives offered to them.
- Indian companies who have joint ventures abroad.
- The disinvestment process undertaken by the government of India where it has raised ₹ 2000 crores through disinvestment of equity shares of selected pubic sector undertakings in 93-94.
- Sophistication and penetration of the new issues markets whose growth is unprecedented since 1990-1991.
- Innovations in the introduction of financial instruments and acting as market makers for these instruments.
- New strategies, structures and methods of functioning adopted by the corporate sector such as corporate restructuring including mergers, acquisitions, etc.; due to liberalisation and globalisation.
- Increase in demand for technical and financial services and encouragement of small and medium industries, due to the policy of decentralisation.
- Development of debt market.

1.1.4 SEBI (Merchant Bankers) Rules and Regulations

Merchant banking activity is regulated by SEBI (Securities Exchange Board of India) and SEBI had first issued certain rules and regulations in 1992 to regulate the merchant banking activity in India. These rules get revised from time to time, to suit the changing situation. SEBI's regulations can broadly be categorised as: (a) Registration, (b) Cancellation/Suspension of registration, (c) Code of conduct and (d) Defaults and penalties

1.1.4.1 Registration

As per this regulation, no institution can act as a merchant banker unless it holds a registration certificate granted by SEBI. SEBI may grant / renew the registration certificate to a merchant banker subject to the following conditions:

- Merchant banker shall abide by the rules and regulations made under the SEBI Act 1992, with respect to the activities carried out by it as a merchant banker;
- It shall pay the amount of fee for registration / renewal, as the case may be, in the manner provided in the regulation, and
- It shall take adequate steps for the redressal of grievances of the investors within one month of the date of receipt of the complaint. The certificate of registration or its renewal is valid for three years from the date of issue.

The applicant has to be a corporate body other than non-bank finance company, as defined under RBI Act 1934.

Before issuing the registration certificate, SEBI verifies whether the applicant has necessary infrastructure, such as office space, equipment, technology and professional man-power, so as to discharge the activities effectively.

Table 1.1: Merchant bankers are classified into four categories as given below:

Type of Merchant Banker	Minimum Net Worth Requirement (₹)
Category I	50,00,0000
Category II	50,00,000
Category III	20,00,000
Category IV	Nil

Each category is required to maintain a net worth (paid–up capital plus free reserves) as shown in the above table.

- A Category I merchant banker can carry any activity of issue management which includes prospectus preparation and other information related to issue management, determining the financial structure, tie-up of financiers, final allotment and refund of subscription. It can also act as advisor, consultant, manager, underwriter or portfolio manager.
- A Category II merchant banker can act as the advisor, consultant, co-manager, underwriter or portfolio manager.
- A category III merchant banker can act as an underwriter, advisor or consultant to issue.
- A Category IV merchant banker can only act as advisor or consultant to issue.

Every merchant banker has to maintain books of accounts, records and documents which include balance sheet, profit and loss, auditor's report for the minimum period of preceding five years.

1.1.4.2 Procedure for Getting Registration

- The applicant is required to submit an application to SEBI in Form A of the SEBI (Merchant Bankers) Regulations, 1992.
- SEBI then reviews the application and if satisfied, issues a certificate of registration in Form B of the SEBI (Merchant Bankers) Regulations, 1992.
- The applicant needs to pay ₹ 5 lakhs within 15 days of date of receipt of intimation regarding grant of certificate. Validity period of certificate of registration is three years from the date of issue.
- The merchant banker needs to submit an application along with renewal fee of ₹ 2.5 lakhs, to SEBI in Form A of the SEBI (Merchant Bankers) Regulations, 1992 before three months of the expiry period.
- SEBI then reviews the application and if satisfied, renews certificate of registration for a period of another 3 years.

1.1.4.3 Suspension/Cancellation of Registration

The certification of registration issued by SEBI may be suspended if:

- The merchant banker violates the provisions of SEBI Act.
- The merchant banker fails to furnish any information relating to activities as required by SEBI or furnishes wrong or false information.
- The merchant banker fails to maintain the adequate capital as required.
- The merchant banker fails to pay the prescribed fees.

The certificate of registration may be cancelled if:

- The merchant banker indulges in deliberate manipulation or price rigging or cornering activities affecting the security market and the investors' interest.
- The merchant banker is guilty of fraud or convicted of criminal offence.
- The financial position of the merchant banker deteriorates to such an extent that its continuance as merchant banker is not in the interest of investors.

1.1.4.4 Operational Guidelines by SEBI for Merchant Bankers

SEBI has set certain guidelines for compliance by the eligible merchant bankers as mentioned below:

1. Submission of Offer Document

- Lead merchant bankers are required to file the offer documents of issue size of up to ₹ 20 crores, with the concerned regional office of the Board under whose jurisdiction, the registered office of the issuer company falls. The jurisdiction of regional offices / head office shall be as per Schedule XXII.

- According to Clause 5.6 of Chapter V of the Guidelines, the merchant banker should make the draft offer document filed with the Board public.
- The lead merchant banker is required to make 10 copies of the draft offer document available to the Board and 25 copies to the stock exchange(s) where the issue is proposed to be listed.
- The lead merchant bankers / Stock Exchange shall make copies of the draft offer document available to the public. The lead merchant banker and the Stock Exchanges(s) may charge a reasonable charge for providing a copy of the draft offer document.
- The lead merchant banker is also required to submit the draft offer document on a computer floppy, to the Board, in the format specified in Schedule XXIII.
- The lead merchant banker shall submit two printed copies of the final offer document, to dealing offices of the Board, "within three days of filing offer document with Registrar of Companies / concerned Stock Exchange(s) as the case may be."
- The lead merchant banker is required to submit one printed copy of the final offer document to the Primary Market Department, SEBI Head Office, "within three days of filing the offer document with Registrar of Companies / concerned Stock Exchange(s) as the case may be."
- The lead merchant banker shall submit a computer floppy containing the final prospectus / letter of offer to the Primary Market Department, SEBI, Head Office, as specified in Schedule XXIII, within three days of filing the final prospectus / letter of offer with the Registrar of Companies / concerned Stock Exchange(s).
- Along with the floppy, the lead manager is required to submit an undertaking to SEBI, certifying that the contents of the floppy are in HTML format, and are identical to the printed version of the prospectus / letter of offer filed with the Registrar of Companies / concerned Stock Exchange, as the case may be.

Whenever offer documents (for public / rights issues, takeovers or for any other purpose) are filed with any Department / office of the Board, the lead merchant banker needs to provide details "certified as correct" in the forwarding letters as listed below:

(a) Registration number.
(b) Date of Registration / Renewal of registration.
(c) Date of expiry of registration.
(d) If applied for renewal, date of application.
(e) Any communication from the Board prohibiting them from acting as a merchant banker.
(f) Any inquiry / investigation being conducted by the Board.

(g) Period up to which registration / renewal fees have been paid.

(h) Whether any promoter / director / group and / or associate company of the issuer company is associated with securities related business and registered with SEBI.

(i) If any one or more of these persons / entities are registered with SEBI, their respective registration numbers.

(j) If registration has expired, reasons for non renewal.

(k) Details of any enquiry / investigation conducted by SEBI at any time.

(l) Penalty imposed by SEBI (Penalty includes deficiency / warning letter, adjudication proceedings, suspension / cancellation / prohibitory orders).

(m) Outstanding fees payable to SEBI by these entities, if any.

Offer documents that do not include the information as listed above may be rejected. Lead merchant bankers shall obtain similar information from other intermediaries, to ensure that they comply with these guidelines and are eligible to be associated with the concerned issue. The intermediaries are also required to indicate in their letters that they have obtained such information from other intermediaries.

2. Dispatch of Issue Material

Lead merchant bankers need to ensure that whenever there is a reservation for NRIs, 10 copies of the prospectus together with 1000 application forms are dispatched to Advisor (NRI), Indian Investment Centre, Jeevan Vihar Building Sansad Marg, New Delhi, in advance of the issue opening date, directly along with a letter addressed in person. Twenty copies of the prospectus and application forms shall be dispatched to the various Investors Associations, in advance of the issue opening date.

3. Underwriting

While selecting underwriters and finalising underwriting arrangements, lead merchant bankers are required to make sure that the underwriters do not overexpose themselves in a way that, it becomes difficult to fulfil their underwriting commitments. The lead merchant banker should carefully assess the overall exposure of underwriter(s), belonging to the same group or management in an issue, OTC Dealers registered with the Board under SEBI (Stock Brokers and Sub-Brokers) Rules and Regulations, 1992 shall be treated at par with the brokers of other stock exchanges in respect of the underwriting arrangement.

4. Compliance Obligations

The merchant banker needs to ensure compliance with certain post-issue obligations as listed below:

(a) Association of Resource Personnel: In terms of Clause 7.1 of Chapter VII of these Guidelines, in case of over-subscription in public issues, a Board nominated public representative shall be involved in the process of finalisation of the basis of allotment. The lead merchant banker shall intimate the date, time, venue etc. regarding the process of finalisation of the basis of allotment, to the person so nominated.

The lead merchant bankers are required to bear the expenses of the public representatives associated in the allotment process of oversubscribed issues and recover them from the issuers. Honorarium at a minimum of ₹ 500/- per day, plus normal conveyance charges shall be paid to them, and the Board's Regional Managers at New Delhi, Chennai and Kolkata shall be associated with them.

(b) Redressal of Investor Grievances: The merchant bankers need to address the investor grievances on a priority basis, and take all preventive steps to minimise the number of complaints. The lead merchant banker is required to set up a proper grievance monitoring and redressal system, in coordination with the issuers and the Registrars to Issue. They shall actively associate with post-issue refund and allotment activities, and regularly monitor investor grievances arising from it.

(c) Submission of Post Issue Monitoring Reports: The concerned lead merchant banker shall submit, in duplicate, the Post Issue Monitoring Reports specified in Clause 7.2 of Chapter VII of these Guidelines, within 3 working days from the due dates, either by registered post or deliver them at the respective regional offices / head office, given in Schedule XXII. A copy of the report shall be sent to the Board's Head office, Mumbai, where the offer documents have been dealt with by any of the regional offices of the Board. Important developments about the particular issues being lead managed by the lead merchant bankers during the period intervening the reports should be informed to the Board by them.

(d) Issue of No Objection Certificate (NOC): The issuer companies shall deposit 1% of the amount of securities offered to the public and / or to the holders of the existing securities of the company, as the case may be, with the regional Stock Exchange, in accordance with the Listing Agreement of the Stock Exchanges. These securities can be released by the concerned Stock Exchange, only after obtaining an NOC from the Board. The issuer company shall submit an application for NOC to the Board, in the format specified in Schedule XXIV.

Before submitting the application for the issue of NOC, certain conditions need to be complied with, as mentioned below:

- Completion of 4 months from the date of obtaining the listing permission from the concerned Regional Stock Exchange, or the last date when the listing permission was obtained from any of the other Stock Exchanges, where the securities are proposed to be listed, whichever is later.
- Satisfactory redressal of all the complaints received by the Board against the filing company.

- Certificate from the Regional Stock Exchange to the issuer company, to the effect that underwriting / brokerage commission, as well as the Registrars / Lead merchant banker's fees have been duly paid by the company.

Applications for issue of NOC shall be filed with the concerned regional office of the Board, under whose jurisdiction, the registered office of the issuer company falls, as specified in Schedule XXII.

An NOC from the Board may not be required and the concerned regional Stock Exchange can refund the 1% security deposit, after duly verifying that the refund orders have actually been dispatched, in cases where issues (i.e. public / rights / offer of sale or any other) fail, and the investors' funds are fully refunded.

The complaints regarding the non-receipt of underwriting / brokerage commission and Registrars / Lead merchant bankers fees, may be filed with the concerned Regional Stock Exchanges. Responses to complaints forwarded by the Board to the concerned companies, shall be submitted to the Board in the proforma specified in Schedule XXV for updation of records.

(e) Registration of Merchant Bankers: The merchant bankers are required to make the application for renewal of Certificate of Registration, according to Regulation 9 of SEBI (Merchant Bankers) Rules and Regulations, 1992. The renewal application shall provide a statement highlighting the changes, that have taken place in the information, that was submitted to the Board for the earlier registration, and a declaration stating that no other changes besides those mentioned in the above statement have taken place, while filing the renewal application for the certificate of registration as merchant banker.

XXVI Merchant Bankers shall also forward the additional information as specified in Schedule, while forwarding the renewal application in Form A of the SEBI (Merchant Bankers) Rules and Regulations, 1992. Registered Merchant Bankers shall inform the Board about becoming a member or AMBI, along with the relevant details.

(f) Reporting Requirements: In terms of Regulation 28 of SEBI (Merchant Bankers Regulation) 1992, the merchant bankers need to send a half yearly report, relating to their merchant banking activities, in the format specified in Schedule XXVII. The report referred to in sub-clause (a) shall be submitted twice a year, on March 31 and September 30, and it should reach the Board within three months from the close of the period to which it relates.

(g) Impositions of Penalty Points: Penalty points may be imposed on the merchant banker for violation of any of the provisions for operational guidelines. The merchant banker with four or more penalty points, may be restrained from filing, any offer document or associating or managing any issues for a particular period. Irrespective of whether any penalty point is imposed, the Board has right to initiate action against the merchant bankers, under the SEBI (Merchant Bankers) Regulations. Imposition of penalty point is not a pre-condition for initiation of proceedings against the merchant banker under the SEBI (Merchant Bankers) Regulations.

1.1.4.5 Code of Conduct

SEBI has prescribed the following code of conduct for merchant bankers:

- A merchant banker should not associate with any business other than that of the securities market.
- A merchant banker should observe high standards of integrity and fairness in all its dealings.
- A merchant banker should, at all times, render high standards of service, exercise due diligence, ensure proper care and independent professional judgement.
- A merchant banker should not make any exaggerated statements.
- A merchant banker must maintain secrecy of client's account.
- A merchant banker should always endeavour to give best possible advice to the customer.
- A merchant banker should follow the prevailing corporate governance practices.
- A merchant banker should ensure that investors are provided true and correct information and complaints from the investor are dealt with promptly.

1.1.4.6 Defaults and Penalties

In case of violation of any of the provisions of SEBI regulations, SEBI has powers to impose suitable penalty. These penalties depend on gravity of default. The defaults are classified into four categories such as general, minor, major and serious. These defaults have penalty points as 1, 2, 3 and 4 respectively.

Unethical conduct and non-cooperation to SEBI is treated as a category four default and will attract 4 penalty points. A merchant banker that attracts 4 or more penalty points may be suspended for a certain period.

1.2 Indian Financial System and its Participants

1.2.1 Introduction

A financial system is a set of elements that are interrelated and interactive. Indian financial system mainly consists of financial institutions, financial markets and various financial instruments. The common objective of all the participants in a financial system is to mobilise the available resources and put them in productive use, so as to achieve the overall economic development of our country.

Regulators such as RBI, SEBI, FMC, IRDA and PFRDA are an integral part of the Indian Financial System.

The main functions of the Indian Financial System are listed below:
- To act as a bridge between savers and users of the funds.
- To encourage savings and investment.
- To allocate funds across all the sectors efficiently, so as to have targeted economic growth of the country.
- To provide regulated services.

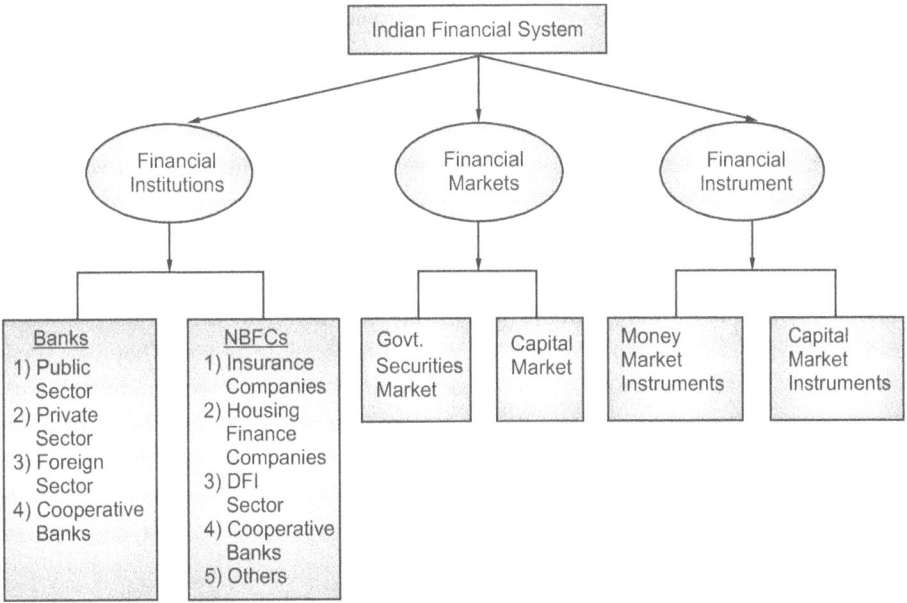

Fig. 1.1: Components of the Indian Financial System

The major participants of the Indian financial system are: commercial banks, financial institutions, encompassing term lending institutions, investment institutions, specialised financial institutions, state-level development banks, Non-bank Financial Companies (NBFCs) and other market intermediaries such as stockbrokers and money lenders. Commercial banks and certain variants of NBFCs are among the oldest of the market participants. The FIs on the other hand are relatively new entities in the financial marketplace.

1.2.2 Components of the Indian Financial System

As shown in above Fig. 1.1. The main components of the Indian financial system are: (1) Financial Institutions (2) Financial Markets (3) Financial Securities (Instruments) and (4) The Regulators.

1.2.2.1 Financial Institutions

Financial Institutions include different kinds of banks such as commercial banks, co-operative banks and NBFCs include leasing companies, housing finance companies, gold loan companies and auto finance companies.

In addition to this, NABARD (National Bank for Agricultural and Rural Development) provides various types of finance for agricultural activities and rural development. SIDBI (Small Industries Development Bank of India) provides finance for development of small and medium activities all over the country. Exim bank provides guidance and support for export and import activities.

Insurance companies provide life and non life insurance services where as merchant bankers provide corporate services. There are other financial institutions such as mutual funds, venture capital funds, hedge funds and registrar and transfer agents who provide specialised financial services.

1.2.2.2 Financial Markets

Financial markets are also a significant component of Indian financial system. They act as a conduit through which the funds are transferred form savers to users. Financial markets provide a buying and selling platform to various financial securities. They are broadly classified as government securities market, capital market, money market and forex market. These markets are further divided into primary market and secondary market. In the primary market, securities are issued for the first time from the issuer to invest directly whereas these securities are traded in secondary markets.

Capital markets are further divided into debt market, equity market and derivative market.

Various currencies are traded in forex markets.

1.2.2.3 Financial Securities

Financial Securities also known as financial instruments are broadly classified into government securities and corporate securities (capital market securities). These financial securities are financial assets, representing claims to the payment of money in future. Government securities are issued by the Government for raising public loans as notified in the Official Gazette. These securities are in the form of treasury bills and bonds. They play an important role in the Indian economy. Capital market securities are of two types viz. debt and equity. Debt instruments are fixed income securities which have specific maturity, e.g. debenture bonds, fixed deposits, loans etc. Whereas equity instruments generally represent ownership interest and are entitled dividend payment when declared, but there is no specific right to a return on capital. Another type of capital market security is derivative. Derivative securities are those securities whose values are derived from the values of underlying assets.

Each type of security has its own risk and return characteristics.

1.2.2.4 Regulators

Financial institutions such as banks, NBFCs, Housing Finance Companies, Leasing Companies and Government Securities market, Money Market, Forex market are regulated by RBI whereas insurance companies are regulated by IRDA. Pension funds are regulated by PFRDA and capital markets are regulated by SEBI.

1.3 Stock Exchanges

1.3.1 Introduction

Section 4 of Securities Contracts (Regulation) Act (SCRA), 1956 defines the term **stock exchange** as; *an association, organisation or body of individuals, whether incorporated or not, established for the purpose of assisting and controlling the business of buying, selling and dealing in securities*. A stock market can operate only if it is recognised by the government under SCRA. This recognition is granted under Section 3 of the Act by the Central Government, Ministry of Finance, Stock Exchange Division.

Business enterprises, especially corporates can directly access the savings of individuals and utilise them for productive purposes. By offering different kinds of securities, such as equity shares, preference shares, debentures, bonds etc. which possess different risk, returns and rights suitable to individual investors, provide much needed avenues of investment to them. However these efforts of corporates to mobilise these savings can be successful only with adequate marketability and liquidity of the investment made by the individuals. It is in this context that the stock exchanges play a very important role in the capital market.

1.3.2 History of Stock Exchanges

The advent of securities trading in India goes back to East India Company. Records show that trades were carried out in securities in Bombay and Calcutta in the first half of the 19th century. Brokers organised themselves into an informal association and in 1874 assembled at a place to trade, which is now known as the Dalal Street. The Bombay Stock Exchange came into formal existence in December 1887. Later on SCRA, 1956 was passed, which contains the rules and regulations for securities trading. The act gave recognition to BSE in 1957. This act has power to control the functioning of the stock exchanges. There have been changes in this act from time to time.

In 1992, the need for a separate regulatory body for stock exchanges was felt by all the participants and accordingly SEBI (Securities Exchange Board of India) came into existence under the SEBI Act, 1992. Subsequently NSE (National Stock Exchange) was set up by leading financial institutions (IDBI, LIC, UTI, ICICI and SBI) in 1992. NSE started functioning as stock exchange in April 1993.

Some of the stock exchanges in India are voluntary non-profit making associations, while some are joint stock companies and some others are companies with limited guarantee.

Our government is now moving towards demutualisation of all the stock exchanges. Demutualisation means that ownership and management of stock exchanges would be separated. It is decided that stock exchanges will now be joint stock companies. In NSE this has already been done and BSE has also been demutualised recently.

The governing body of the stock has wide range of powers and is the decision making body of the stock exchange. It has powers, subject to government approval, to make, amend and suspend the operations of the rules, bylaws and regulations of the exchange. It also has complete jurisdiction over all the members and its power of management and control is almost absolute. The governing body has powers to admit, warn, suspend, censure, fine and expel the member.

SEBI has over the years initiated various reforms in working of stock markets. Accordingly, it has initiated measures to prohibit unfair trade practices, manipulation of prices, misleading statements and any such fraudulent act which will impact the stock price and make undue profit or gain out of such practices.

Further, lock in period of three years for preferential allotment has been removed except for the promoters. IPO (Initial Public Offer) norms have been further tightened.

In terms of SCRA, 1956 there are 23 government recognised stock exchanges in India as listed below:

- Bombay Stock Exchange (BSE)
- National Stock Exchange (NSE)
- MCX-Ex
- Ahmedabad Stock Exchange
- Bangalore Stock Exchange
- Bhubaneshwar Stock Exchange
- Cochin Stock Exchange
- Coimbatore Stock Exchange
- Delhi Stock Exchange
- Guwahati Stock Exchange
- Hyderabad Stock Exchange
- Jaipur Stock Exchange
- Ludhiana Stock Exchange
- Madhya Pradesh Stock Exchange
- Madras Stock Exchange

- Magadha Stock Exchange
- Mangalore Stock Exchange
- Meerut Stock Exchange
- Pune Stock Exchange
- Saurashtra Kutch Stock Exchange
- Uttar Pradesh Stock Exchange
- Vadodra Stock Exchange

However in recent years one can see the structural changes in the Indian stock markets. There are two major stock exchanges i.e. BSE and NSE. After introduction of online trading operations, which has provided nationwide trading platform, resultantly all the above mentioned regional stock exchanges have now became defunct and are likely to get closed shortly. Even very recently started MCX-Ex could not gather the momentum.

1.3.3 Bombay Stock Exchange (BSE)

It is the oldest stock exchange in Asia. Popularly known as BSE, it was established as "The Native Share & Stock Brokers Association" way back in 1875. This is the first stock exchange to obtain permanent recognition in 1956, from the government of India under SCRA, 1956. It started as a membership-based firm and an association of persons. It is now demutualised and a corporate entity has been established in 2007. Now the list of investors includes Deutsche Boerse, Singapore Exchange (SGX) with 5% stake each. Indian corporates viz. Bajaj Auto, Mahindra & Mahindra, Bennett & Coleman has also invested in BSE.

BSE has introduced BOLT (BSE online trading) was introduced in 1995 to facilitate efficient processing of order driven system. BSE has a network all over the country.

Share Groups

The equity shares traded on BSE are classified as A, B1, B2, F, C & Z groups. Of this A, B1, B2 represent equity group whereas F represents debt market (fixed income securities) and Z group was introduced in July 1999 and it covers the companies which have failed to comply with the listing norms or failed to resolve investor complaints or have not made required arrangements with both NSDL and CDSL. The C group covers trading in odd lot securities in A < B, B2 and Z group securities and Right renunciations.

Thus BSE provides facility of online trading to the market participants across the country.

BSE INDICES

For the benefit of the investors and traders, BSE has constructed several stock indices and these are quite popular amongst the investors and traders. They are listed below:
- Sensex (BSE -30)
- Dollex (BSE-200)

- BSE-500
- BSE National Index (BSE-100)

Sensex comprises the top 30 companies of 'A' group, based on floating stock market capitalisation, liquidity, depth and industry representation. Since 1st September 2003, free float market capitalisation methodology is a globally accepted practice.

In free float methodology, only the free float market capitalisation of a company is considered for the purpose of index calculation, assigning the weight to the stock in index.

1.3.4 National Stock Exchange (NSE)

Following the recommendations of a study group on the establishment of new stock exchanges, NSE was established in November 1992 with the objectives given below:

- Establishing nationwide trading facility for equity, debt and hybrid securities.
- Ensuring equal access to investors from across the country through an appropriate communication network.
- Providing fair, efficient and transparent securities market.
- Enabling shorter settlement cycles and book entry settlements.
- Meeting the current international standards of securities markets.

NSE was promoted by leading institutions like IDBI, IFCI, LIC, SBI, Corporation Bank and ICICI Bank. This is a demutualised stock exchange where the ownership and management is completely separated from the right to trade on it. The Board of Directors comprises eminent professionals and includes a SEBI Nominee. Day-to-day management of NSE is delegated to the Managing Director who is supported by professional staff. NSE commenced its operations in November 1994 and its derivative segment in June 2000.

NSE Indices:

NSE has constructed several stock indices and these are quite popular amongst the investors and traders. They are as given below:

- S & P CNX NIFTY
- S & P CNX DEFTY
- S & P CNX 500
- S & P CNX NIFTY JUNIOR
- CNX MID-CAP
- Sectoral Indices

S & P CNX NIFTY comprises of top 50 companies based on floating stock market capitalisation, liquidity, depth and industry representation. Since 26th June 2009, NIFTY -50 is also using free float methodology for index calculation purpose. Criteria for inclusion of stock in NIFTY-50 are listed below:

- Liquidity with an average impact cost of 0.75% or less.
- Market capitalisation has to be ₹ 500 crores or more during last six months.
- Industry representation.
- Track record.

1.3.5 Over the Counter Exchange of India (OTCEI)

OTCEI was incorporated in the year 1990, as a Section 25 company under the Companies Act 1956. It started its operations in the year 1994. It is recognised as a stock exchange by the Securities Contracts Regulation Act, 1956.

The OTC Exchange of India (OTCEI) was set up with an objective to provide a suitable and cost effective platform for raising finance from the capital market. It was promoted by an association of financial institutions to bring together the investors and promoters and aid enterprising promoters in raising finance for new projects at low cost through provision of transparent and efficient mode of trading for the investors.

OTCEI is framed based on the lines of the NASDAQ market and has introduced several innovative concepts to the Indian capital markets such as market making, screen-based nationwide trading, scripless trading and sponsorship of companies. It has helped the enterprises in providing capital which have become successful brands eventually, e.g. VIP, Advanta, Sonora Tiles, Brilliant Mineral Water etc. Presently the exchange has 115 listings.

Features of OTCEI:

Given below are the underlining features of OTCEI:

1. Entry for small and medium sized companies: The Securities Contract Act, 1956 specifies a minimum issued equity capital of ₹ 3000 crores, as the listing requirement. The OTC Exchange provides an ideal opportunity to these companies to enter the capital market which were not able to enter the capital market earlier.

2. Sponsorship agreement: The companies looking for listing on the OTC Exchange, need to approach one of the members appointed by the OTC which acts as the sponsor to the issue. The sponsor appraises the project. By entering into the sponsorship agreement, the sponsor is committed to making market in that scrip, by giving buy/sell quote, for a minimum period of 1 year.

3. Nationwide listing: The OTC network is spread all over India through its members, dealers and representative office counters. Thus by listing on just one stock exchange, the company and its products get worldwide exposure and investors all over India can start trading in that scrip.

1.3.6 Trading Operations and Settlement of Transactions

Online trading means purchase and sale of stock on the internet. E-trading facility is offered by all the stock exchanges. The investor assesses a stock broker's website through internet enabled personal computer and places sale / purchase order through the broker's internet base order routing and trading engine. All the players in the security market viz. stockbroker, stock exchanges, clearing corporations, depositories, DPs, clearing banks etc. are electronically linked. The information flow among them is on real time basis and in matter of seconds.

1.3.6.1 Procedure for Online Trading

- The investor has to register with the online trading portals listed on the site.
- He has to open a bank account with one of the Internet trading portals and depository services partners.
- He must be a registered iConnect user.
- On placing an order for buying / selling of securities through the listed online trading portal, he has to click on 'pay through' bank option listed on the online portal which will direct to a login screen of the investor's account.
- Once the details of login ID and password are entered, the investor has to verify the transaction details and confirm the transaction by entering his transaction ID and password.
- Once his order is executed, an email confirmation regarding the status of his transaction is sent.
- Investor's account status is updated on a real time basis. Securities status can be viewed online after the day of settlement

1.3.6.2 Day Trading

Real day trading means holding the stocks positions within the current trading day. In other words, it means not holding any stock overnight. This is really the safest way to do day trading because the trader is not exposed to the potential losses that can occur overnight when the stock market is closed, due to news that can affect the prices of the particular stock. Any news received after the closure of the stock exchange, regarding a particular company or any macro-economic factor, may affect the opening price of the stock on the next day. Thus, day trading involves taking a position in the market with a view of squaring that position before the end of that day.

- A day trader typically trades several times a day looking for fractions of a point to a few points per trade, but closes out all his positions by end of the day.
- The goal of day trader is to capitalise on price movement within one trading day.

- Unlike investors, a day trader may hold positions for only a few seconds or minutes and never overnight.

1.3.6.3 Types of Orders

The types of orders are as follows:

1. **Limit Order:** In the limit order, buy or sell order is placed with a price limit. For example, if the investor places a buy order of Ranbaxy shares with the limit price of ₹ 450, he puts a cap on the purchase price. In case the current price is higher than the limit price, the order will be kept pending. It will be executed only when the price hits ₹ 450 or below. If the actual price in the market is ₹ 447, the order will be immediately executed. Thus, the buyer may get an execution below hit limit price but in no case the execution price will exceed the limit buy price. Likewise, a limit sell order places a limit on the floor price, below which the securities cannot be sold.

2. **Market Order:** In the market order, the buy and sell orders are executed at the best price offered in the exchange. For example, the last quote of Infosys was ₹ 1494 (15 January 2008) and the buyer placed a market buy order. Then the execution was at the best offer price on exchange, which could be above or below ₹ 1494.

3. **Stop Loss Order:** These orders are given to limit the loss due to unfavourable price movement in the market. A particular limit is given for waiting. If the price falls below the limit, the broker is authorised to sell the shares to prevent loss. The limit price is also known as trigger price. The trigger price is marked by the investor. For example, if the investor has a stop loss buy order in Infosys booked at ₹ 1500, the stock will be purchased at ₹ 1500 or less.

1.3.6.4 Margin Trading

Trading with borrowed funds or securities is called as margin trading. It helps the investor to trade over and above their owned funds. It is a leveraging mechanism. Margin trading is regulated by SEBI. It prescribes the eligibility conditions and procedures to be followed in the margin trading. The scrip-wise gross outstanding in margin accounts with all the brokers is disclosed by the stock exchanges. Disclosures regarding any day are made available after the trading hours on the following day.

According to SEBI norms:

- The client has to avail the facility from only one broker at a time.
- Margin trading facility is provided by brokers with a net worth of ₹ 3 crore.
- A format is specified by SEBI for entering into an agreement with a client before providing the margin trading facility.

- Margin trading facility is provided for group one securities and the securities that are offered in the initial public offer and satisfies the requirements to be traded in the derivative segment.
- If the broker wants to borrow funds for offering margin trading facility, he can borrow only form scheduled commercial banks or NBFCs regulated by RBI and not from any other source.
- If the broker uses borrowed funds, he has to disclose the name of the lender and the amount borrowed.
- The broker's total exposure in margin trading should not exceed the borrowed funds. Further, is should not exceed 50 per cent of the broker's net worth.
- Single client level exposure should not exceed 10 per cent of the total exposure of the broker. Initial margin is fixed as 50 per cent and the maintenance margin has been prescribed as 40 per cent. These margins are subject to changes.
- The broker has to disclose details on the gross exposure including name of the client to the stock exchange.
- Margin trading leads to levered portfolio. The higher the leverage, the higher is the magnification effect. A client is likely to lose more money or gain more money when he transacts on margin, depending on the movement of the market. Margin trading becomes more risky, if his portfolio constitutes a few stocks, which are volatile. An investor faces the risks as mentioned below when he carries margin trading.
- He is exposed to a loss of more money that he has invested.
- Fall in the value of securities leads to the payment of additional funds to avoid forced sale of the securities.
- The investor / client will have to deposit additional cash on short notice to cover market loss.

1.3.6.5 Settlement

In the early period, trades were settled on account period settlement which was combined with 'badla' system of carrying forward the positions. It distorted the price discovery process. The carry forward system encouraged:

- Leveraged trading by postponement of settlement
- Generated trading by postponement of settlement
- A large number of brokers defaults

A rolling settlement is one in which trades outstanding at the end of the day have to be settled at the end of T + X time framework. T is the trade date and X is the number of days as specified by SEBI. In this settlement, payments are made quicker than in the weekly settlements. Thus, investors benefit from increased liquidity.

T + 5 settlement was introduced in NSE's major stocks on 2nd July 2001. In a rolling settlement of a T + 5 period, trades are settled within five days from the date of transaction. This means that all the open positions on trading day are settled on the fifth working day after the trading day.

With a view to derive benefits of increased efficiency of rolling settlement and to ensure speedier settlement, SEBI decided to shorten the rolling settlement cycle from T + 5 to T + 3. The compulsory rolling settlement on T + 3 basis, commenced on 1st April 2002.

In the light of the experience gained from the working of T + 5 and T + 3 settlements, it was considered desirable to shorten the settlement period to T + 2. Therefore, the NSE further shifted to a T + 2 settlement cycle from 1st April 2003. Under the new trading cycle, all the transactions are closed in two trading days after the deal is struck.

Pay-in day: broker makes payment of delivery of securities to the exchange

Pay-out day: the exchange makes payment or delivery of securities to the broker.

T + 2 Trading settlement cycle:

Activity	Days
Rolling settlement trading	T
Custodial confirmation	T + 1 working days
Delivery generation	T + 1 working days
Securities and funds Pay-in	T + 2 working days
Securities and funds Pay-out	T + 2 working days
Valuation debit	T + 2 working days
Auction	T + 3 working days
Bad delivery reporting	T + 4 working days
Auction settlement	T + 5 working days
Rectified bad delivery pay-in and pay-out	T + 6 working days
Re-bad delivery reporting pickup	T + 8 working days
Close out of re-bad delivery and funds pay-in and pay-out	T + 9 working days

1.3.7 Regulations of Stock Exchanges

The Indian stock market is regulated according to the guidelines laid down by the Securities and Exchange Board of India (SEBI). Securities and Exchange Board of India (SEBI) was established in 1992, as a regulatory body, to protect the interest of investors. It stipulates the regulations with the aim to to ensure organised growth and smooth functioning of the Indian capital market.

The most important function of SEBI is to regulate the Indian stock market and the related regulations are listed below:

1. **Performance assessment of Various Stock Exchanges:** SEBI is responsible for auditing the performance of various stock exchanges and ensuring transparency in their functioning.
2. **Stipulating Rules and Regulations:** SEBI has the authority to stipulate the rules and regulations to control the functioning of stock exchanges. For example, the opening (9.15 am) and closing (3.30 pm) time of the market has been determined by SEBI, and it has the right to change the timing if deemed necessary.
3. **Eliminating Unfair Trade Practices in the Market:** At times, companies undertake unfair / unhealthy activities despite specific guidelines by SEBI that promote fair trade practices. SEBI has the power to stop such activities and take action against the parties involved in such a trade.
4. **Issuing Licenses to Dealers and Brokers:** No dealer or broker can start distributing securities to investors in the absence of a prior approval and license from SEBI. It also has the right to withhold or cancel the license of brokers and dealers not adhering to the specified guidelines.
5. **Controlling Mergers, Acquisitions and Take-overs of the Companies:** Some companies try to manipulate stocks and buy a majority stake in other companies with an intention of a take-over. SEBI controls and prohibits such movements if it is not in the interest of the company.

SEBI has many other responsibilities in addition to the above mentioned, which it exercises to regulate the Indian stock market.

1.4 Money Market

1.4.1 Introduction

Money market is a market for short term financial assets that are close substitutes of money. Short term means that the duration is less than one year. A money market instrument is liquid and can be converted into money at low cost. It provides a platform for parking of short term surpluses and meeting short term requirements.

Functions of Money market:
- Provide platform to even out short demand and supply of funds.
- To assist central bank to maintain liquidity and to decide interest rates in the economy.
- To provide an easy access for raising short term funds.

1.4.2 Requirements of Money Market

- Well developed and organised commercial banking system.
- Strong central bank to influence and regulate the money market.
- Suitable money market instruments.
- Active secondary market for trading of money market instruments.
- More and more market participants.
- Suitable technology and efficient communication system.

1.4.3 Structure of Money Market

The entire money market in India can be divided into two parts. They are: organised money market and the unorganised money market. The unorganised money market can also be known as an unauthorised money market. Both of these components comprise several constituents. The chart given below will help you in understanding the organisational structure of the Indian money market.

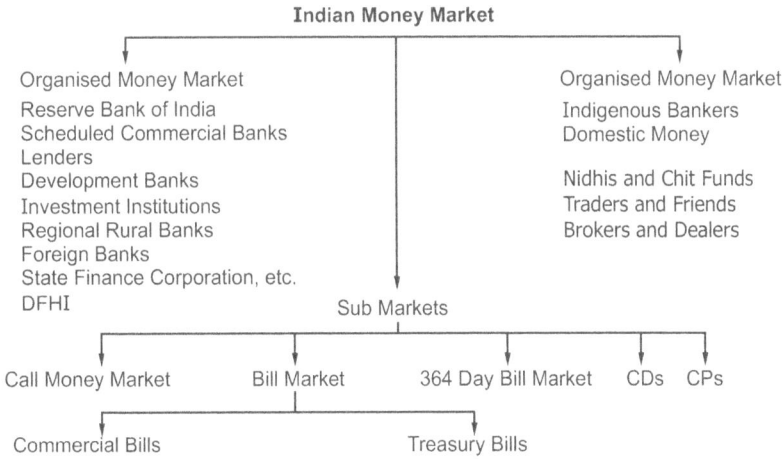

Chart 1.1: Structure of Indian Money Market

Components or Sub-markets of Indian Money Market:

After studying the structure of the Indian money market let's understand various components or sub-markets within it.

1. **Treasury Bill Market:** In this market, sale and purchase of short term government securities take place. These securities are called Treasury Bills, which are promissory notes or financial bills issued by the RBI on behalf of the Government of India. There are two types of treasury bills viz. Ordinary or Regular Treasury Bills and Ad Hoc Treasury Bills. The maturity period of these securities range from a minimum of 14 days to a maximum of 364 days. They have become very popular recently, due to high level of safety involved in them.

2. **Call Money Market:** It an important sub-market of the Indian money market and is also known as money at call and money at short notice. It is also called as inter bank loan market. The duration of transactions is extremely short ranging from few hours to 14 days. These transactions help stock brokers and dealers to fulfil their financial requirements. The rate at which money is made available is called as a call rate since the rate is fixed by the market forces such as the demand for and supply of money. It is basically located in the industrial and commercial locations such as Mumbai, Delhi, Kolkata, etc.

3. **Commercial Bill Market:** It deals in the short term, self liquidating and negotiable money market instruments. Commercial bills are used to finance the movement and storage of agriculture and industrial goods in domestic and foreign markets. This market in India is still underdeveloped.

4. **Market for Commercial Papers (CPs):** This was introduced by the government in 1990. Commercial Paper (CP) is an investment instrument, which can be issued by a listed company, having working capital of more than or equal to ₹ 5 crores. The CPs can be issued in multiples of ₹ 25 lakhs however the minimum subscription should be at least ₹ 1 crore. The maturity period for the CP is of minimum 3 months and maximum 6 months.

5. **Market for Certificate of Deposits (CDs):** It is an important segment of the Indian money market. The government initiated a market of CDs with an objective to widen the range of instruments in the money market and to provide a higher flexibility to investors for investing their short term money. The certificate of deposits is issued by the commercial banks which has the value of ₹ 25 lakhs and in multiple of ₹ 25 lakhs however the minimum subscription of CD should have a value of ₹ 1 Crore. The maturity period of CD ranges between 3 months to 1 year. These are the transferable investment instruments in a money market.

6. **Short Term Loan Market:** In this market, short term loan requirements of corporates are met by the Commercial banks. Banks provide short term loans to corporates in the form of cash credit or overdraft. Cash credit is given to industrialists and overdraft is given to businessmen.

1.4.4 Developments in Indian Money Market

Indian money market has shown significant progress since the last 20-25 years. Suitable changes have been made in our money market instruments from time to time. These timely changes and upgradation has provided desired depth and liquidity to the Indian money market. Money market reforms that have taken place between the years 1999 to 2005 are given below:

- LAF (Liquidity Adjustment Facility) was introduced on 5th June 2000.
- Setting up of CCIL (Clearing Corporation of India Ltd.) This has helped lowering risk and expanding the volume in money market.
- Introduction of CBLO (Collateral Borrowing and Lending Obligation) through CCIL.
- Issuance of CP & CD in D-Mat form.
- Introduction of NDS (Negotiated Dealing System), RTGS (Real Time Gross Settlement) and CFMS (Centralised Funds Management System)
- Reduction in minimum maturity period of CP and CD.

1.4.4.1 Features of Indian Money Market

Though the Indian money market is not a developed money market, it is a leading money market among the developing countries. The main features of the Indian Money Market, which could also be termed as its drawbacks, are listed below:

1. **Concurrent Structure:** It has a simultaneous existence of both the organised money market as well as unorganised money markets. The organised money market consists of RBI, all scheduled commercial banks and other recognised financial institutions. However, the unorganised part of the money market comprises domestic money lenders, indigenous bankers, trader etc. The organised money market is in full control of the RBI. However, the unorganised money market remains outside the RBI control. Thus both the organised and unorganised money market exist simultaneously and there is lack of integration between the two.

2. **Seasonality:** The demand for money in the Indian money market is seasonal in nature. India being an agriculture predominant economy, the demand for money is generated from agricultural operations. During the busy season i.e. between October and April more agricultural activities take place, leading to a higher demand for money.

3. **Multiplicity of Interest Rates:** There are many levels of interest rates in the Indian money market. They differ from bank to bank, from period to period and even from borrower to borrower. Again in both organised and unorganised segments, the interest rates differ. Thus there is an existence of many rates of interest in the Indian money market.

4. **Lack of Organised Bill Market:** In the Indian money market, the organised bill market is not prevalent. Though the RBI tried to introduce the Bill Market Scheme (1952) and then the New Bill Market Scheme (1970), still there is no properly organised bill market in India.

5. **Absence of Integration:** This is a very important feature of the Indian money market. It is divided among several segments or sections at the same time, which are loosely connected with each other. There is a lack of coordination among these different components of the money market. RBI has full control over the components in the organised segment but it cannot control the components in the unorganised segment.

6. **High Volatility in Call Money Market:** The call money market is a market for very short term money. Here money is demanded at the call rate. Basically the demand for call money comes from the commercial banks. Institutions such as the GIC, LIC, and so on suffer huge fluctuations and thus it has remained highly volatile.

7. **Limited Instruments:** It is in fact a defect of the Indian money market. The supply of various instruments such as the Treasury Bills, Commercial Bills, Certificate of Deposits, Commercial Papers etc. is very limited. In order to meet the varied requirements of borrowers and lenders, it is necessary to develop numerous instruments.

8. **Insufficient Funds or Resources:** The Indian economy with its seasonal structure faces frequent shortage of financial recourse. Lower income, lower savings, and lack of banking habits among people are some of the reasons for it.

9. **Lack of Organised Banking System:** In India, even through we have a big network of commercial banks, still the banking system suffers from major weaknesses such as the NPA, huge losses, poor efficiency. etc. The absence of an organised banking system is a major problem for the Indian money market.

10. **Less number of Dealers:** The number of dealers in the short-term assets, who can act as mediators between the government and the banking system, is very low. Less number of dealers leads to the slow contact between the end lender and end borrowers.

1.4.4.2 Players in Indian Money Market

The players in money market include:

1. Government: Government intervenes in the money market to increase the constancy of financial institutions and markets. It intervenes in the interest rates and money supply in the money market. This is done by implementing two policies: Fiscal Policy and Monetary Policy.

Under the fiscal and monetary policies government intervenes in the forex market, in order to regulate the exchange rate and affect the supply of money. When currency falls, government buys foreign currency and this leads to reduced money supply. Similarly when currency rises, it sells foreign currency leading to increased money supply. For doing this the government may issue or buy securities to decrease or increase the money supply and thus protect the currency which is done in money market. The government also intervenes in money market to adjust its budget deficit. It borrows money by issuing short-term securities and adjusts its deficits.

2. Central Bank: Central Bank acts as an mediator between government and money market. It issues securities on behalf of the government. It also regulates the money markets by issuing guidelines from time to time. Central Bank regulates money supply in the money market by issuing guidelines to banks, regarding cash reserve ratio, manipulating the interest ratio and involving in open market operations.

3. Banks: They act as borrowers and issuers in the money market. They take debt when they fall short of statutory reserve requirements, due to change in rates or when they fall short of reserves to meet the withdrawal requirements of customers.

When Banks provide debt when they have surplus funds, they may also require short-term funds. If they have some attractive loan proposal at their disposal but do not have funds, they may at that time borrow funds from the money market.

4. Discount and Acceptance Houses: They act as Market Makers and participate in the Bill Market. Discount houses perform the function of discounting / rediscounting the T-Bills or commercial bills. Acceptance houses accept the bills of exchange on behalf of their clients, in lieu of commission, which increases the liquidity of the bill.

5. Financial institutions act as Borrowers and Lenders of short-term funds.

6. Corporate houses act as Issuers of securities for meeting their working capital requirements.

7. Mutual Funds and Foreign Institutional Investments (FIIs) etc. act as investors in the money market and FIIs contribute a small share in total participation as per the limitations to investment laid down on them.

8. Various Dealers / Satellite Dealers also participate as intermediaries in the Money Market.

1.4.4.3 Reforms in Indian Money Market

Indian Government appointed a committee under the chairmanship of **Mr. Sukhamoy Chakravarty** in 1984, to review the Indian monetary system. Later, **Mr. Narayanan Vaghul** working group and **Narasimham** Committee was also set up. As per the recommendations of these study groups and with the financial sector reforms initiated in the early 1990s, the government has adopted major reforms in the Indian money market as discussed below:

1. **Deregulation of the Interest Rate:** In recent period, the government has adopted an interest rate policy of a liberal nature. It lifted the ceiling rates of the call money market, short-term deposits, bills rediscounting etc. Commercial banks are advised to see the interest rate change that takes place within the limit. There was a further deregulation of interest rates during the economic reforms. Currently interest rates are determined by the working of market forces except for a few regulations.

2. **Money Market Mutual Fund (MMMFs):** In order to provide additional short-term investment revenue, the RBI encouraged and established the Money Market Mutual Funds (MMMFs) in April 1992. MMMFs are allowed to sell units to corporate and individuals. The upper limit of ₹ 50 crores of investments has also been lifted. Financial institutions such as the IDBI and the UTI have set up such funds.

3. **Establishment of the DFI:** The Discount and Finance House of India (DFHI) was set up in April 1988, to impart liquidity in the money market. It was set up jointly by the RBI, Public Sector Banks and Financial Institutions. DFHI has played an important role in stabilising the Indian money market.

4. **Liquidity Adjustment Facility (LAF):** Through the LAF, the RBI remains in the money market on a continued basis through the repo transaction. LAF adjusts liquidity in the market, through absorption and or injection of financial resources.

5. **Electronic Transactions:** In order to impart transparency and efficiency in the money market transactions, the electronic dealing system has been started. It covers all deals in the money market. Similarly, it is useful for the RBI to keep a watch on the money market.

6. **Establishment of the CCIL:** The Clearing Corporation of India limited (CCIL), was set up in April 2001. The CCIL clears all transactions in government securities and repose reported on the Negotiated Dealing System.

7. **Development of New Market Instruments:** The government has consistently tried to introduce new short-term investment instruments. For example, Treasury Bills of various duration, Commercial Papers, Certificates of Deposits, MMMFs, etc.

These are the major reforms undertaken in the money market in India. Apart from these, the stamp duty reforms, floating rate bonds etc. are some other prominent reforms in the money market in India. Thus, at the end we can conclude that the Indian money market is developing at a good speed.

1.4.5 Money Market Instruments

The commonly used money market instruments are listed below:

(1) Call / Notice Money

(2) Treasury Bills

(3) Commercial Paper (CP)

(4) Certificates of Deposits (CoD)

(5) Money Market Mutual Funds

(6) Repos and Reverse Repos

1.4.5.1 Call / Notice Money

Borrowing or lending in the call money market is for a short duration, usually overnight to fortnight to meet transient defaults. The surplus funds of banks and financial institutions are traded in the call market. These short term loans are payable on demand at the option of lender as well as borrower. The money borrowed for one day and repaid on the next day is called call money whereas money repaid within a fortnight is called as notice money.

All commercial banks, co-operative banks, DHFI, financial institutions, primary dealers are the major participants in the call / notice money market.

Banks those are short of their SLR / CRR obligations borrow from this market to meet the obligations. Also banks with short term surplus funds lend in this market.

1.4.5.2 Treasury Bills

Treasury bills are short-term (up to one year) borrowing instruments of the government. In other words, these are short-term rupee-denominated government securities i.e. the promissory notes issued by the government. Since the government guarantees the payment of the treasury bills, they are more liquid than the trade bills. They are like zero-coupon bonds. They do not pay interest prior to maturity; instead they are sold at a discount on par value to create a positive yield to maturity. Treasury bills are considered to be the most risk-free investments. The Bank of England first issued treasury bills in 1877. In India, these were first issued with an aim at mobilising resources for the First World War and mop excess liquidity in the economy due to the heavy war expenditure.

Issuing Authority

Originally, the government used to issue treasury bills directly. They were sold through the tender method and the periods of maturity were three months, six months, nine months and twelve months. In 1935, the Reserve Bank of India took over their issue. Till 1950, state governments occasionally issued treasury bills.

Characteristics of Treasury bills

These are as follows:
- Treasury bills have a short-term maturity period.
- They are highly liquid in nature.
- Their default risk is absent.
- Their transaction cost is very low.
- They are regularly available (The RBI auctions them on a weekly and fortnightly basis).
- Their yield is assured.
- They are eligible for inclusion in securities for Statutory Liquidity Ratio (SLR) purposes.
- Their capital depreciation is negligible.

Types of Treasury bills
- The 14-day treasury bill.
- The 91-day treasury bill.
- The 182-day treasury bill.
- The 364-day treasury bill.
- Ad hoc treasury bills.

Sise of the Treasury Bills

The minimum denomination of 91-day treasury bills is ₹ 25000 i.e. the minimum amounts of bids for the 91-day treasury bill are to be made for a minimum amount of ₹ 25000 and in multiples thereafter. The notified amount for 91-day treasury bills was ₹ 250 crores but the amount has been increased to ₹ 1000 crore from December 2002.

The minimum amount of the 365-day treasury bills is ₹ 10,00,00. The bidding of treasury bills normally takes place in multiples of ₹ 1 crore.

Auctions

Treasury bills are issued through Auctions and accordingly 91-day T-bills are auctioned every week on Wednesdays, 182-day and 364-day T-bills are auctioned every alternate week on Wednesdays. The Reserve Bank of India issues a quarterly calendar of T-bill auctions, which is available at its website (www.rbi.org.in). It also announces the exact dates of auction, the amount to be auctioned and payment dates by issuing press release prior to each auction.

Payment

Payment by the allottees at the auction is required to be made by making debit to their custodian's current account.

Purchase Method

T-bills auctions are held on the NDS and the members electronically submit their bids on the system. Non-competitive bids are routed through the respective custodians or any bank or Primary Dealer (PD), which is an NDS member.

Participants

All entities registered in India like banks, financial institutions, primary dealers, firms, companies, corporate bodies, partnership firms, institutions, mutual funds, foreign institutional investors, state governments, provident funds, trusts, research organisations, Nepal Rashtra Bank and even individual treasury bills are the participants.

1.4.5.3 Commercial Paper (CP)

After accepting Vaghul Committee recommendations, RBI allowed the issuance of CPs from 1989.

CPs are short-term negotiable instruments issued by large firm having high credit ratio. CP is in the form of usance primary notes with fix maturity, indicating the short-term obligation of an issuer. Companies issue it as a means of raising short-term debt. It is issued on a discount to face value basis, but can also be issued in interest bearing form. The issuer promises the buyer, a fixed amount at a future date but pledges no assets.

A CP, as a short-term financial instrument, has several advantages to the issuer. It involves very little documentation. It is flexible in terms of maturity. It is unsecured. There are no limitations on the end use of the funds used in this manner. They are negotiable and transferable instruments and are highly liquid. Nowaday's CP can be issued in D-Mat form.

Denomination

They can be issued in denominations of ₹ 5 lakhs or its multiples thereof however; the minimum lot or investment is ₹ 25 lakhs (face value) per investor. The secondary market transactions can be for ₹ 5 lakhs or its multiples thereof.

Maturity

Originally a commercial paper was for a minimum period of three months and maximum of one year. At present, it can be issued for maturities between a minimum of seven days and a maximum of up to one year from the date of issue. The maturity date of the CP should not go beyond the date up to which the credit rating of the issuer is valid. There shall be no grace period for the CP on maturity. If the date of Maturity happens to be a holiday, the company is liable to pay on the previous working day.

Parties Involved

The parties involved in the CP are the:
- Issuing company
- Issuing and paying agent
- Credit rating agency
- Investor

Eligibility Criteria for Issuing Company

A company shall be eligible to issue CP provided that:
a) The tangible net worth of the company is not less than ₹ 4 crores as per the latest audited balance sheet.
b) The working capital (fund-based) limit of the company from the banking system is not less than ₹ 4 crores.
c) The borrowal account of the company is classified as a standard asset by the financing banks.
d) The minimum credit of CP issuing company has to be CRISIL or equivalent to ICIRA and CARE.

The participants in this market are the corporate bodies, banks, mutual funds, UTI, LIC, GIC and others who have surplus funds and are on a lookout for opportunities for short-term investments. The DFHI also operates both in the primary and secondary markets for CPs by quoting its bid and offering prices.

The CP market is fairly popular these days; however a secondary market in these is yet to develop.

Every CP issue has to be reported to the Chief General Manager, Industrial and Export Credit Department (IECD), Reserve Bank of India, Central Office, Mumbai; through the Issuing and Paying Agent (IPA), within three days from the date of complication of the issue, incorporating details as per schedule II.

1.4.5.4 Certificate of Deposits (CODs)

This is another money market instrument introduced by RBI in 1989. COD is a marketable document of title to time deposit of a bank and can be distinguished by conventional deposit in respect of negotiability and hence marketability.

CODs are marketable receipts of funds deposited in a bank for an affixed period, at a specified rate of interest; they are bearer instruments and are negotiable.

Features of COD:
- These are securities in the form of usance promissory notes and they attract stamp duty.
- They are governed by the Negotiable Instruments Act and transferable by endorsement.
- Bank cannot sanction loan against COD and cannot buy back before maturity.
- Rate of interest is deregulated and market determined.
- Now CODs are issued only in dematerialised form.
- Minimum size of COD is ₹ 1 lakh and additional investment can be in multiples of ₹ 1 lakh and are issued at a discount to face value.

- Minimum maturity period is 7 days and maximum up to 1 year (same has now been extended up to 3 years).
- They are freely transferable for endorsement and delivery after 45 days from the date of issuance.

COD can be issued by the scheduled commercial bank (excluding RRBs) and specified all India financial institutions. Issuing bank or FI has to report the issue size of COD to RBI in the fortnightly return.

An individual, trust, HNI (High Net Worth Individual) association and NRI (Non-Resident Indian) can invest in COD. Primary dealers also buy and sell CODs.

1.4.5.5 Money Market Mutual Funds (MMMF)

To enable the small investors to participate in the money market, MMMF is the conduit through which they can earn market related returns.

MMMFs invest the funds collected from the investors in instruments like:

(a) Treasury bills and government securities

(b) Call / Notice money

(c) Commercial bills

(d) Commercial papers and COD

They are free to determine the extent of their investment in each of the above instruments, in accordance with RBI guidelines.

1.4.5.6 Repos and Reverse Repos

The repurchase agreement is called Repos. Repos are buy back transactions, in which two parties agree to sell and repurchase the same securities. Repo is a collateralised lending and borrowing mechanism between two market participants. Repos are hybrid transactions that combine the feature of secured loan and outright purchase and sale transaction but it cannot be construed as either secured or unsecured transaction. Reverse Repo is exactly opposite of Repo. Both Repo and Reverse Repo is essentially a short term loan to the seller with security issued as collateral. Similarly the buyer purchases securities with an agreement to sell the same to the seller, on the agreed date in future, at a prefixed prize.

1.5 Capital Market

1.5.1 Introduction

Capital Market is one of the significant components of every financial market and should be studied carefully. The capital market is basically a market for financial assets which have a long or indefinite maturity. Unlike money market instruments, the capital market instruments become mature for the period more than one year. It is an institutional arrangement to borrow and lend money for a longer period of time. It consists of financial institutions like

IDBI, ICICI, UTI, LIC, etc. which play the role of lenders in the capital market. Business units and corporate are the borrowers in the capital market.

Capital market involves various instruments which can be used for financial transactions. Capital market provides long term debt and equity finance for the government and the corporate sector. Capital market can be classified into primary and secondary markets. The primary market is a market for new shares, whereas the existing securities are traded in the secondary market. Capital market institutions provide rupee loans, foreign exchange loans, consultancy services and underwriting.

1.5.2 Importance of Capital Market

Capital market is also very important like the money market and it plays a significant role in the national economy. A developed, dynamic and vibrant capital market can immensely contribute to speedy economic growth and development.

Mentioned below are the important functions and role of the capital market.

1. **Mobilisation of Savings:** Capital market is an important source for mobilising idle savings from the economy. It mobilises funds from people for further investments in the productive channels of an economy. In that sense it activates the ideal monetary resources and puts them in proper investments.

2. **Capital Formation:** Capital market helps in capital formation. Capital formation is net addition to the existing stock of capital in the economy. Through mobilisation of ideal resources, it generates savings. The mobilised savings are made available to various segments such as agriculture, industry, etc. This helps in increasing capital formation.

3. **Provision of Investment Avenue:** Capital market raises resources for longer duration thereby providing an investment avenue for people who wish to invest resources for a long period of time. It also provides suitable interest rate returns to investors. Instruments such as bonds, equities, units of mutual funds, insurance policies, etc. definitely provide diverse investment avenues for the public.

4. **Speed up Economic Growth and Development:** Capital markets make funds available for a long period of time and the financial requirements of businesses are met. It in turn helps in research and development and increasing production and productivity in economy, by generation of employment and development of infrastructure. Capital markets enhance production and productivity in the national economy.

5. **Proper Regulation of Funds:** Capital markets not only help in fund mobilisation, but also in proper allocation of these resources. Capital market can have regulation over the resources so that it can direct funds in a qualitative manner.

6. **Service Provision:** As a significant financial set up, capital markets provide various types of services. It includes long term and medium term loans to industry, underwriting services, consultancy services, export finance, etc. These services facilitate the manufacturing sector in a large spectrum.
7. **Continuous Availability of Funds:** Capital market is a place where the investment opportunity is continuously available for long term investment. This is a liquid market as it makes funds available on a continuous basis. Both buyers and sellers can easily buy and sell securities as they are continuously available. Basically capital market transactions are related to the stock exchanges. Thus marketability in the capital market becomes easy.

1.5.3 Capital Market Instruments

Capital Market Instruments are vehicles through which investments are made and hence these are investment vehicles. The investing public normally look for new capital market instruments to satisfy their evolving financial needs. Investors always try to maximise the returns with the minimum risk. This does not mean that the investors do not accept risky products. They do accept risky products provided, there is a return commensurate with the risk and make tradeoff between risk and returns.

Following are the major Capital Market Instruments.
- Preference Shares
- Equity Shares
- Non-voting Shares
- Debentures
- Bonds
- ADR / GDR
- Global Debt Instruments

1.5.3.1 Preference Shares

Preference shares possess the characteristics of equity as well as debt. Like a debt security holder, a Preference Shareholder receives dividend at a fixed percentage from the company. Unpaid dividend on the Preference Shares may cumulate and be paid to a Preference Shareholder before any dividend is paid to Equity Shareholders. Such Preference Shares are known as a Cumulative Preference Share. The preference shareholder gets the preference over the Equity shareholder at the time of payment of dividend, but the Preference Shareholder cannot participate in the profits of the company beyond specified percentage of dividend. Dividend is not taxable for investors and preference shares are redeemable.

1.5.3.2 Equity Shares

Most popular method for raising the long term capital of a company has been Equity Shares. Equity shares are issued by a company to raise long term funds, while holder of a Debt Security becomes creditor and holder of a Equity Security becomes owner of the company. Thus Equity Share holding represents ownership of the company with certain rights and responsibilities. Company that issues shares may not buy these shares from the shareholders, except in special circumstances (Buy Back issue). But Shareholders can sell the equity shares in the secondary market, to those who want to buy these shares, and hence investor can buy the equity share either directly from the company (in primary market) or from the existing shareholder (in secondary market) of the company.

As an owner of the company, the equity shareholders share company's success and failure. If the company performs well, equity shareholder can receive high rates of returns and vice versa. On liquidation, the company sells its assets and pays of all its creditors first. The equity shareholders may receive, what is left after the creditors, including preference shareholders and others are paid off. The success or failure of the company is the success or failure of the investment by an equity shareholder and hence investment in equity share is considered relatively risky as compared to the investment in debt instruments.

However equity shareholders have certain rights, which other investors such as Creditors and Preference shareholders do not have. As an owner of the company, Equity shareholders are the highest authorities in the organisation and decide all the key matters concerning the company. They have voting rights, which they may exercise during the election of Board of Directors. Further, liability of Equity shareholders is limited to the extent of their holding. Investors prefer equity investment as they out perform other investments i.e. Debentures, Bonds, FDs etc.

Equity shares are of two types: Voting rights shares and non-voting rights shares.

1.5.3.3 Non-voting Rights Shares

Non-voting Rights Shareholders are entitled for higher dividend than the Voting Right shareholders, if the dividend is declared by the company. But they do not have the voting right to participate in corporate decision making. Company can issue Non-voting Shares up to maximum 25% of the total capital of the company. The Non-voting Rights Shareholders are entitled for rights and bonus issue as and when declared. But if a company is not able to declare the dividend for successive two years, non-voting shares automatically get converted into voting shares. By issuing non-voting shares, a company can raise equity capital without diluting the control of the company.

1.5.3.4 Debentures

A debenture is a debt security issued by the company, acknowledging its obligation to repay sum as well as interest, at the specified rate of interest as per the contract. The contract is made between the issuing company and investor (Debenture Holder) and it contains rights of debenture holders and issuer's legal requirements. Nowaday's, usually unsecured debentures are issued and they do not have lien on specific assets of the company as a security obligation. Debenture holders have rights to receive interest at the rate specified in the debenture certificate, before any dividend is paid to the shareholders. Even if the company incurs loss, it has to pay interest on Debentures. If a company fails in business, the debenture holders will be preferential creditors and they will be entitled to repayment of the principle and interest before the shareholders are paid anything.

As per Section 117 B of the Companies Act 1956, any company making public or right issue of debentures, should appoint one or more debenture trustees before issuing prospectus or letter of offers. Debentures are classified as Convertible and Non-convertible debentures.

Convertible debentures are unsecured debt instruments, which can be converted into equity shares of the issuing company, at the option of their holders. There are many advantages of convertible debentures:

(a) Investors get opportunity to convert their investments partly or fully into the shares of issuing company, at a much lower price than the market price.

(b) This gives them chance to sell the shares at a profit soon after the conversion.

(c) The main advantage for the company issuing the convertible debentures is that, debentures get converted into shares at a substantial premium in most cases.

1.5.3.5 Bonds

A Bond is a promissory note i.e. issued by the borrower for the repayment of the principal amount, with interest to the lender. Specifically, issue of the bond agrees to pay a fixed amount of interest periodically and repays the principal amount on maturity.

Features of Bonds:

(a) **Face value:** It is the principal amount involved in the bond which may be different from the market value of the bond.

(b) **Coupon:** This is the rate of interest paid by the issuer to the lender.

(c) **Tenure:** This is the period for which the bond is issued.

(d) **Market value:** This is the price at which the bond is available in the market.

(e) **Period to maturity:** This is the period left till maturity.

(f) **YTM (Yield till maturity):** YTM is the actual return from the purchase of bond at market value, till maturity.

Bonds are broadly classified as Zero coupon bonds (Deep Discount Bonds), Tax Free Bonds and Junk Bonds.

Zero coupon bonds are the fixed income securities that pay interest at maturity instead of periodically, during the life of the bond.

Tax Free bonds are debt securities, whose interest income is totally exempted from Income Tax. In certain cases amount invested in these bonds may also be exempted from the wealth tax.

Junk Bonds are high yield bonds with the speculative grade or below investment grade.

1.5.3.6 Global Depository Receipts (GDR)/ American Depository Receipts (ADR)

American Depository Receipts (ADR) and Global Depository Receipts (GDR) are negotiable financial instruments, representing foreign company shares. They are traded on local exchanges. ADR / GDR are certificates that allow investors to hold shares of a foreign listed company. ADR / GDR trade freely in the overseas financial markets, like any other foreign currency denominated security. Depository receipts are known as GDR, when they are marketed globally rather that in the specific country or market. Whereas when depository receipts are denominated in the US Dollars and are marketed in the USA, only then they are known as American Depository Receipts. The DR denominated in Indian rupees is known as IDR.

The process of issuing DR:
- A depository buys certain number of shares of a foreign listed company through its foreign branch.
- Based on the shares purchased, the Depository issues DR in the predetermined ratio. In short each DR represents fixed number of shares underlying.
- Then these DRs are sold to the investors and listed on the local stock exchange for trading. DRs are traded freely like any other local currency denominated security.

An Indian company can issue ADR / GDR, in accordance with FCCB, ordinary shares scheme 1993 and guidelines issued by SEBI from time to time. As per existing guidelines, an Indian company can issue GDR / ADR if it is eligible to issue shares to a foreigner, including an NRI under the FDI scheme. The proceeds raised through GDR / ADR have to be kept abroad till actually required in India. Pending repatriation or utilisation of the proceeds, the Indian company can invest only in specified securities. There is no end use restriction, except for the ban on deployment of such a fund in the real estate or stock market. Voting rights of underlying shares shall be as per the provision of Companies Act 1956.

1.5.3.7 Convertible Cumulative Debentures (CCD)

CCD is an odd instrument, as it is a mix of debt and equity features – it is debt now, but equity in future. A CCD is a debt instrument mandatorily and automatically convertible into equity at a specified time, or on happening of specified events. In that sense, it is difficult to call it "debt", as debt implies a commitment to pay. In view of its mandatory conversion feature, a CCD is a deferred equity instrument. There may be several reasons for issuance of a CCD. One of the reasons is that, while it provides several of the advantages of equity, it defers the issuance of equity.

This may provide tax advantages to the issuer, at potentially better equity pricing based on future value. It is a decent way of ensuring a fixed rate of return with an upside on conversion for an investor, whereas straight equity cannot promise any fixed rate of return. As a device of offering fixed returns with a possible upside, a CCD is far preferable to a preference share which has higher servicing costs (as dividends are not tax-deductible).

1.5.3.8 Fixed Deposits

Fixed deposits are an attractive source of short-term capital, both for companies and investors as well. Corporates are in favour of fixed deposits as an ideal form of working capital mobilisation without going through the process of mortgaging assets and the associated procedures of documentation, etc. Investors find fixed deposits a simple avenue for investment, in popular companies at attractively reasonable and safe interest rates. Moreover, investors are relieved of the problem of the hassles of market value fluctuation to which instruments such as shares and debentures are exposed. There are no transfer formalities either. In addition, it is quite possible for investors to have the option of premature repayment after 6 months, although such an option entails some interest loss.

Since these instruments are unsecured, there is a lot of uncertainty about the repayment of deposits and regular payment of interest. The issue of fixed deposits is subject to the provisions of the Companies Act and the Companies (Acceptance of Deposits) Rules introduced in February 1975.

1.5.3.9 Warrants

A 'warrant' is an option issued by a company, whereby the buyer is granted the right to purchase a number of shares (usually one) of its equity share capital, at a given exercise price, during a given period. Although trading in warrants are in vogue in the U.S. Stock markets for more than 6 to 7 decades, they are being issued to meet a range of financial requirements by the Indian corporates.

Warrants may be issued with either debentures or equity shares. They clearly specify the number of shares entitled, the expiration date, along with the stated / exercise price. Warrants have a secondary market. The exchange value between the share at its current price and the shares to be purchased at the exercise price represents the minimum value of a warrant. They have no floatation costs and when they are exercised, the firm receives additional funds at a price lower than the current market, yet higher than those existing at the time of issue. Warrants are issued by new or growing firms and venture capitalists. They are also issued during mergers and acquisitions. Warrants in the Indian context are called 'sweeteners' and were issued by a few Indian companies since 1993.

Both warrants and rights, entitle a buyer to acquire equity shares of the issuing company. However, they are different in the sense that warrants have a life span of three to five years whereas, rights have a life span of only four to twelve weeks (duration between the opening and closing date of subscription list). Moreover, rights are normally issued to effect current financing, and warrants are sold to facilitate future financing. Similarly, the exercise price of warrant, i.e. the price at which it can be exchanged for share, is usually above the market price of the share so as to encourage existing shareholders to purchase it. On the other hand, one warrant buys one equity share generally, whereas more than one rights may be needed to buy one share. The detachable warrant attached to each share provides a right to the warrant holder to apply for additional equity share against each warrant.

1.5.3.10 Global Debt Instruments

Some of the debt instruments that are popular in the international financial markets are described below:

Income Bonds: These are similar to cumulative preference shares in respect of which fixed dividend is paid only if there is profit earned in a year otherwise is carried forward and paid in the following year. Interest income on such bonds is paid only where the corporate has adequate cash flows. There is no default on income bonds if interest is not paid. Unlike the dividend on cumulative preference shares, the interest on income bond is tax deductible. These bonds are issued by corporates that undergo financial restructuring.

Asset Backed Securities: These are a category of marketable securities, that come with a collateral of financial assets such as installment loan contracts. This type of financing involves a dis-intermediating process called securitisation, whereby credit from financial intermediaries, in the form of debentures, are sold to third parties, to finance the pool. Repos are the oldest asset backed security in our country.

Junk Bonds: Junk bond is a high risk, high yield bond which finances either a Leveraged Buyout (LBO) or a merger of a company in financial distress. These are popular in the USA and are used primarily for financing takeovers. The rates range from 16 to 25 percent.

Indexed Bonds: Interest payment and redemption value of these bonds are indexed with movements in prices. These bonds protect the investor from the eroding purchasing power of money due to inflation. For example, an inflation-indexed bond implies that the payment of the coupon and / or the redemption value increases or decreases according to movements in prices. The bonds are likely to hedge the principal amount against inflation. Such bonds are designed to provide investors an effective edge against inflation so as to enhance the credibility of the anti-inflationary policies of the Government. The yields of an inflation-indexed hand provide vital information on the expected rate of inflation.

Zero Coupon Bonds (ZCBs) / Zero Coupon Convertible Debentures: These were first introduced in the U.S. securities market. Initially, such bonds were issued for high denomination and were purchased by large security brokers in large chunks, who resold them to individual investors, at a slightly higher price in affordable lots. Such bonds were called 'Treasury Investment Growth Receipts' (TIGRs) or 'Certificate of Accruals on Treasury Securities' (CATSs) or ZEROs as their coupon rate is Zero. Moreover, these certificates were sold to investors at a hefty discount and the difference between the face value of the certificate and the acquisition cost was the gain. The holders are not entitled for any interest except the principal sum on maturity.

Advantages:
   (a) No botheration of periodical interest payment for the issuers.
   (b) The attraction of conversion of bonds into equity shares at a premium or at par.
   (c) The investors usually being rewarded by way of a low premium on conversion.
   (d) There is only capital gains tax on the price differential and there is no tax on accrued income.
   (e) Possibility of efficient servicing of equity, as there is no obligation to pay interest till maturity and its eventual conversion.

Mahindra & Mahindra came out with the scheme of Zero Coupon Bonds for the first time in India along with 115 percent convertible bonds, for part financing of its modernisation and diversification scheme. Similarly, Deep Discount Bonds were issued by IDBI at ₹ 2,000 for a maturity of ₹ 1 lakh after 25 years. These are negotiable instruments transferable by endorsement and delivery by the transferor. IDBI also offered Option Bonds which may be either cumulative or non-cumulative bonds where interest is payable either on maturity or periodically. Redemption is also offered to attract investors.

Floating Rate Bonds (FROs): Bonds that carry the provision for payment of interest at different rates for different time periods are known as 'Floating Rate Bonds'. The first such bond was issued by the SBI, in the Indian capital market. The SBI, while issuing such bonds, adopted a reference rate of highest rate of interest on fixed deposit of the Bank, provided a minimum floor rate payable at 12 percent p.a. and attached a call option to the Bank after 5 years to redeem the bonds earlier than the maturity period of 10 years at a certain premium. A major highlight of these bonds was the provision to reduce interest risk and assurance of minimum interest on the investment provided by the Bank.

Secured Premium Notes (SPNs): Secured debentures that are redeemable at a premium over the issue price or face value are called as secured premium notes. Such bonds have a lock-in period during which period no interest will be paid. It entitles the holder to sell back the bonds to the issuing company at par after the lock-in period.

A case in point was the issue made by the TISCO in the year 1992, where the company wanted to raise money for its modernisation programme, without expanding its equity excessively in the next few years. The company made the issue to the existing shareholders, on a rights basis, along with the rights issue. The salient features of the TISCO issue were as given below:

- Face value of each SPN was ₹ 300.
- No interest was payable during the first three years after allotment.
- The redemption started at the end of the fourth year of issue.
- Each of the SPN of ₹ 300 was repaid in four equal annual installments of ₹ 75, which comprised the principal, the interest and the relevant premium. (Low interest and high premium or high interest and low premium, at the option to be exercised by the SPN holder at the end of the third year).
- Warrant attached to each SPN entitled the holder the right, to apply for or seek allotment of one equity share for cash payment of ₹ 80 per share. Such a right was exercisable between first year and one-hand-a-half year after allotment by which time the SPN would be fully paid up.

This instrument tremendously benefited TISCO, as there was no interest outgo. This helped TISCO to meet the difficulties associated with the cash generation. In addition, the company was able to borrow at a cheap rate of 13.65 percent as against 17 to 18 percent offered by most companies. This enabled the company to start redemption earlier, through the generation of cash flow by the company's projects. The investors had the flexibility of tax planning while investing in SPNs. The company was also equally benefited as it gave more flexibility.

Euro Convertible Bonds: These bonds give the holders of euro bonds to have the instruments converted into a wide variety of options such as the call option for the issuer and the put option for the investor, which makes redemption easy. A euro-convertible bond essentially resembles the Indian convertible debenture, but comes with numerous options attached. Similarly, a euro-convertible bond is an easier instrument to market than equity. This is because it gives the investor an option to retain his investment as a pure debt instrument, in the event of the price of the equity share filling below the conversion price or where the investor is not too sure about the prospects of the company.

Points To Remember

- Merchant bank is any organisation that undertakes issue management and corporate advisory services.
- Within the domain of corporate advisory services, fall the capital restructuring, portfolio management, project advisory services, financial engineering, issue management and loan syndication including venture capital.

- Issue management consists of all the activities related to public issue of securities (both debt and equity). It starts from structuring the financial instruments to post issue management.
- Merchant banking activities are well regulated by SEBI.
- Merchant banks are classified into four categories and the respective category merchant banker has to maintain the prescribed net worth.
- Indian financial systems are broadly categorised as a) Financial Institutions, b) Financial Markets, c) Financial securities and 4) Regulators.
- Financial Markets act as conduits through which the funds are transferred from savers to users.
- The role of regulatory authorities is to ensure that participants in the financial system conduct their activities according to the guidelines and directives of the government, in efficient and transparent manner.
- Stock exchanges provide platform for the sale and purchase of already issued and listed securities.
- Online trading facility has made trading very easy.
- NSE and BSE are the only major stock exchanges in India.
- Regional stock Exchanges have became defunct.
- T+2 settlement cycle has reduced trading time considerably.
- Risk management systems are now in place.
- Money market is a market of short term financial assets and liabilities.
- Money market consists of many sub markets such as Inter Bank Call Money market, CP and COD market, Repo and Reverse Repo market and Treasury Bill market.
- RBI regulates the money market.
- Banks, Financial Institutions, Corporate and Primary Dealers are participants in the money market.
- Equity share holding represents the ownership in the company, with certain rights and responsibilities.
- Preference shares are hybrid instruments having characters of both equity and debt.
- Bonds are instruments of long term nature having strong secondary market.
- Depositories are negotiable financial instruments, representing foreign companies shares but are traded on local exchanges.

Questions for Discussion

1. Explain the nature and meaning of merchant banking.
2. Describe the various services of merchant banking.
3. Critically evaluate the SEBI guidelines for merchant banking.
4. Explain the categories of merchant banking and their capital requirements.
5. Explain the Indian Financial System and its participants.
6. What is the role of financial markets in Indian economy?
7. Explain the role of regulators in the financial system.
8. What is a stock exchange? Explain the role of a stock exchange in the secondary market.
9. Explain different types of orders.
10. Explain the settlement system.
11. How are stock exchanges regulated?
12. Describe the structure of NSE and BSE.
13. What are the criteria for selecting the index stock?
14. Explain the free float methodology of index calculation.
15. What is money market and explain the instruments of Money Market?
16. What is a Commercial Paper and explain the features of a Commercial Paper?
17. What is a Call Money Market and state the participants in a Call Money Market?
18. What is a Certificate of Deposit and how it is issued?
19. Explain the various capital market instruments.
20. What is a debenture and differentiate between convertible and non-convertible debentures?
21. Explain the features of bonds and what are the types of bonds?
22. What are non-voting shares and why does a company issue non-voting shares?
23. What are preference shares and how does it differ from equity shares and debentures?

Chapter **2**...

Public Issue Management and Regulations

Contents ...

2.1 Public Issue Management

    2.1.1 Functions of Public Issue Management

    2.1.2 Mechanism of Public Issue Management

    2.1.3 Role of Issue Manager

    2.1.4 Activities Involved in Public Issue

    2.1.5 SEBI Guidelines and Regulations for Public Issue

2.2 Various Methods of Marketing of New Issues

2.3 Prospectus

2.4 Underwriting

    2.4.1 Types of Underwriting

    2.4.2 Variants of Underwriting

2.5 Post-issue Activities

2.6 Pricing of Issues

- Points to Remember
- Questions for Discussion

Learning Objectives

- To be aware of Public Issue Management, its functions, its mechanism and related matters
- To examine various methods of Marketing of New Issues
- To learn about Prospectus, its various types and the importance of prospectus
- To be able to discuss underwriting
- To study post-issue activities and Pricing Models

2.1 Public Issue Management

Issue management refers to the management of various kinds of issues of securities, which includes public and rights issues and offers for sale. *A public issue is an invitation by a company to the public to subscribe to the securities offered through prospectus.*

There are two components of capital market viz. primary market and secondary market, and the primary market is the market for public issues where new securities are issued directly by the issuing company to investors.

Types of Issues:

(1) Public issue

(2) Preferential issue

(3) Right issue

Further public issues are of three types which are as following:

- Initial Public offer(IPO)
- Follow-on Public Issue(FPO)
- Fast Track Issue

2.1.1 Functions of Public Issue Management

The general functions that form part of the capital issues management functions of merchant bankers are as follows:

1. Obtaining approval for the issue from SEBI.
2. Arranging for underwriting the proposed issue.
3. Preparation of draft and finalisation of the prospectus and obtaining its clearance from the various agencies concerned.
4. Preparation of draft and finalisation of other documents, such as application forms, newspaper advertisements and other statutory requirements.
5. Making a choice regarding registrar to the issue, printing press, advertising agencies, brokers and bankers to the issue and finalisation of the fees to be paid to them.
6. Arranging for press conferences and the investors' conferences.
7. Coordinating printing, publicity and other work in order to get everything ready at the time of the public issue.
8. Complying with SEBI guidelines after the issue is over by sending various reports as required by the authorities.

2.1.2 Mechanism of Public Issue Management

Mechanism of Public Issue Management : Book building method is an ideal mechanism of public issue management.

Meaning of Book Building : When any company in India comes out with a new issue, it decides the issue price of the shares. However, a new concept called book building has been evolved recently. Under this scheme, the issuer does not decide the selling price of the new issue but it is decided by the demand for the new issue.

Definition of Book Building : "Book-Building" refers to collecting orders from the investment banker / investor based on an indicative price range and fixing the final price at the end of an offering period/a closing date which can last from a couple of days to a couple of weeks.

Book Building Process : The book building process is divided into two parts : (a) Private placement, and (b) Public offer.

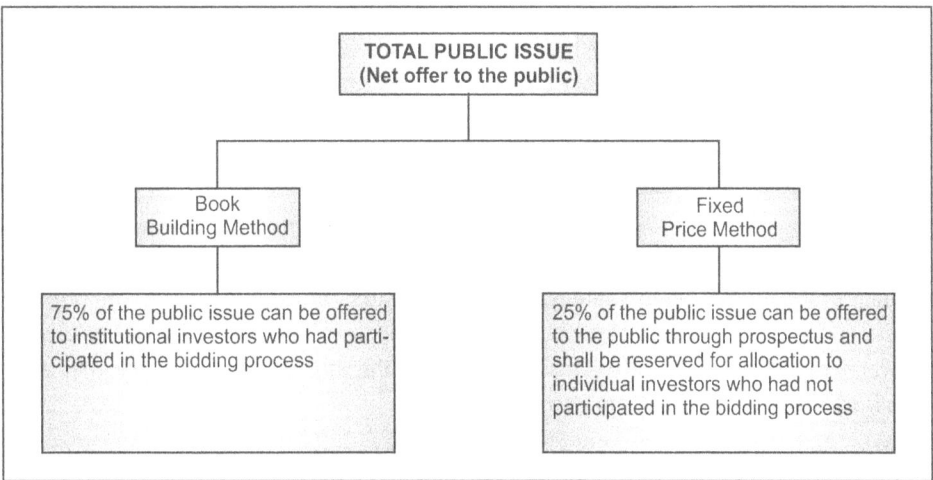

Fig. 2.1 : Book Building Process

2.1.3 Role of Issue Manager

The merchant banker as an issue manager is helpful in the following ways:

1. **Easy floatation:** An issue manager acts as an indispensable pilot facilitating a public/rights issue. This is made possible with the help of a repository of special skills possessed by him to execute the management of issues.

2. **Financial consultant:** An issue manager essentially acts as a financial architect, by providing advice relating to capital structuring, capital gearing and financial planning for the company.

3. **Underwriting:** An issue manager allows for underwriting the issues of securities made by corporate enterprises. This ensures due subscription of the issue.

4. **Market makers:** Merchant bankers, as issue managers often act as the market makers for the issues lead-managed by them. They invest, continue to hold and provide, buy and sell quotes for the listed scrips of the company.
5. **Due diligence:** The issue manager has to comply with SEBI guidelines. The merchant banker will carry out activities with due diligence and furnish a Due Diligence Certificate to SEBI. The detailed diligence guidelines that are prescribed by the Association of Merchant Bankers of India (AMBI) have to be strictly observed. SEBI has also prescribed a code of conduct for merchant bankers.
6. **Coordination:** The issue manager is required to coordinate with a large number of institutions and agencies while managing an issue in order to make it successful.
7. **Liaison with SEBI:** The issue manager, as a part of merchant banking activities, should register with SEBI. While managing issues, constant interaction with the SEBI is required by way of filing of offer documents, etc. In addition, they should file a number of reports relating to the issues being managed.

2.1.4 Activities Involved in Public Issue

There are several activities that have to be performed by the issue manager in order to raise money from the capital market. Adequate planning needs to be done while chalking out an appropriate marketing strategy. An analytical study of various sources, the quantum, the appropriate time, the cost of raising capital and the possible impact of such resources on the overall capital structure will greatly help this task. The various activities involved in raising funds from the capital markets are described below:

Pre-Issue Activities

1. **Signing of MoU:** Signing of MoU between the client company and the merchant banker-issue management activities, marks the award of the contract, the role and responsibility of the merchant banker as against the issuing company are clearly spelt out in the MoU.
2. **Obtaining appraisal note:** An appraisal note containing the details of the proposed capital outlay of the project and the sources of funding is either prepared in-house or is obtained from external appraising agencies. viz., financial institutions/banks etc. A project may be funded either by borrowing money from outside agencies or by injecting capital.
3. **Optimum capital structure:** The level of capital that would maximise the shareholders value and minimise the overall cost of capital has to be determined. This has to be done considering the nature and size of the project. Equity funding is preferable especially when the project is capital intensive.

4. **Convening meeting:** A meeting of the Board of Directors of the issuing company is convened. This is followed by an EGM of its members. The purpose of these meetings is to decide the various aspects related to the issue of securities. An application to RBI, seeking its permission is made, where capital issue of shares is to be offered to NRIs/OCBs or FIIs.

5. **Appointment of financial intermediary:** Financial intermediaries such as Underwriters, Registrars etc. have to be appointed. Necessary contracts need to be made with the underwriter to ensure due subscription to the offer. Similar contracts, when entered into with the Registrars to an issue, will help in share allotment related work, appointment of bankers to an issue for handling the collection of applications at various centres, printers for bulk printing of issue related stationery, legal advisors, and advertising agency. Simultaneously, consents from various experts such as auditors, solicitors, legal advisors, etc. has to be obtained under Section 58 of the Companies Act, 1956.

6. **Preparing documents:** As part of the issue management procedure, the documents to be prepared are initial applications of submission to those stock exchanges where the issuing company intends to get its securities listed, MoU with the Registrar, with bankers to the issue, with advisors to the issue and co-managers to the issue, agreement for purchase of properties, etc. This will have to be sent for inclusion in the prospectus.

7. **Due diligence certificate:** The lead manager issues a 'due diligence certificate' which certifies that the company has scrupulously followed all logical requirements, has exercised utmost care while preparing the offer document and has made a true, fair and adequate disclosure in the draft offer document.

8. **Submission of offer document:** The draft offer document along with the due diligence certificate is filed with SEBI. The SEBI in turn, makes necessary corrections in the offer document and returns the same with relevant observations, if any, within 21 days from the receipt of the offer document.

9. **Finalisation of collection centres:** In order to collect the issue-application forms from the prospective investors, the lead manager finalises tile collection centers.

10. **Filing with RoC:** The offer document, completed in all respects, after incorporating SEBI observations, is filed with Registrar of Companies (RoC) to obtain acknowledgement.

11. **Launching the Issue:** The process of marketing the issue starts once the legal formalities are completed and statutory permission for issue of capital is obtained. The lead manager has to arrange for the distribution of public issue stationery to

various collecting banks, brokers, investors etc. The issue is opened for public immediately after obtaining the observation letter from SEBI, which is valid for a period of 365 days from the date of issue.

Conducting press conferences, brokers' meets, issuing advertisements in various newspapers and mobilising brokers and sub-brokers marks the launching of a public issue. The announcement regarding opening of issue is also required to be made through advertising in newspapers, 10 days before the opening of the public issue.

12. **Promoter's contribution:** A certificate to the effect that the required contribution of the promoters has been raised before opening of the issue, has to be obtained form a Chartered Accountant and duly filed with SEBI.

13. **Issue closure:** An announcement regarding the closure of the issue should be made in the newspapers.

2.1.5 SEBI Guidelines and Regulations for Public Issue

Any company coming to capital market with issue such as IPO, FPO or Fast Track Issue has to fulfill the conditions laid down by SEBI. Accordingly any unlisted company with IPO (i.e. issuing the shares to the public for the first time) has to fulfill the following conditions:

1. **Issue by Unlisted Company**

According to SEBI Disclosure and Investor Protection Guidelines, an unlisted company may make an initial public offering, only if it meets the following conditions:

- The company has net tangible assets of at least ₹ 3 crore in each of the preceding three full years (of twelve months each)o of which not more than 50 per cent is held in monetary assets.
- If more than 50 per cent of the net tangible assets are held in monetary assets, the company has to make firm commitments to deploy such excess monetary assets in its business/project.
- The company has a track record of distributable profits in terms of Section 205 of the Companies Act, 1956, for at least three out of immediately preceding five years.
- In case the company has changed its name within the last one year, at least 50 per cent of the revenue for the preceding one full year is earned by the company from the activity suggested by the new name; and the aggregate of the proposed issue and all the previous issues made in the same financial year in terms of size (offer through offer document plus firm allotment and promoters' contribution through the offer document), does not exceed five times its pre-issue net worth as per the audited balance sheet of the last financial year.

2. Issue by Listed Company

There are certain conditions to be fulfilled by a listed company if it wants to make public issue of equity shares or any other security which may be converted into equity at a later date, the same are as given below:

A listed company is eligible to make a public issue of equity shares or any other security which may be converted into or exchanged with equity shares at a later date, if it satisfies the following conditions:

- The aggregate of the proposed issue and all the previous issues made in the same financial year in terms of size (offer through offer document + firm allotment + promoters` contribution through the offer document), issue size, does not exceed five times its pre-issue net worth as per the audited balance sheet of the last financial year.
- In case there is a change in the name of the issuer company within the last one year (reckoned from the date of filing of the offer document), the revenue accounted for by the activity suggested by the new name is not less than 50 per cent of its total revenue in the preceding one full-year period.

Exemption from Eligibility Norms

Exemptions are provided to the following companies subject to certain conditions:

- Banking companies
- Infrastructure companies
- Listed companies

2.2 Various Methods of Marketing of New Issues

1. Pure Prospectus Method

The method whereby a corporate enterprise mops up capital funds from the general public by means of an issue of a prospectus is called 'Pure Prospectus Method'. It is the most popular method of making public issue of securities by corporate enterprises.

Features :

(a) **Exclusive Subscription:** Under this method, the new issues of a company are offered for exclusive subscription of the general public. According to the SEBI norms, a minimum of 49 per cent of the total issue at a time is to be offered to the public.

(b) **Issue Price:** Direct offer is made by the issuing company to the general public to subscribe to the securities at a stated price. The securities may be issued either at par, of at a discount or at a premium.

(c) **Underwriting:** Public issue through the 'pure prospectus method' is usually underwritten. This is to safeguard the interest of the issuer in the event of an unsatisfactory response from the public.

Advantages:

The pure prospectus method offers the following advantages to the issuer and the investors alike:

(a) **Benefits to Investors:** The pure prospectus method of marketing the securities serves as an excellent mode of disclosure of all the information pertaining to the issue. Besides, it also facilitates satisfactory compliance with the legal requirements of transparency, etc. It also allows for good publicity for the issue. The method promotes confidence of investors through transparency and non-discriminatory basis of allotment. It prevents artificial jacking up of prices as the issue is made public.

(b) **Benefits to Issuers:** The pure prospectus method is the most popular method among the large issuers. In addition, it provides for wide diffusion of ownership of securities contributing to reduction in the concentration of economic and social power.

Drawbacks

The raising of capital through the pure prospectus method is fraught with a number of drawbacks as specified below:

(a) **High Issue Costs:** A major drawback of this method is that it is an expensive mode of raising funds from the capital market. Costs of various hues are incurred in mobilising capital. Such costs as underwriting expenses, brokerage, administrative costs, publicity costs, legal costs and other costs are incurred for raising funds. Due to the high cost structure, this type of marketing of securities is followed only for large issues.

(b) **Time Consuming:** The issue of securities through prospectus takes more time, as it requires due compliance with various formalities before an issue could take place. For instance, a lot of work such as underwriting, etc. should be formalised before the printing and the issue of a prospectus.

2. Offer for Sale Method

Where the marketing of securities takes place through intermediaries, such as issue houses, stockbrokers and others, it is a case of 'Offer for Sale Method'.

Features:

Under this method, the sale of securities takes place in two stages. Accordingly, in the first stage, the issuer company makes an en-bloc sale of securities to intermediaries such as the issue houses and share brokers at an agreed price. Under the second stage, the securities are re-sold to ultimate investors at a market-related price. The difference between the purchase price and the issue price constitutes 'profit' for the intermediaries. The intermediaries are responsible for meeting various expenses such as underwriting commission, prospectus cost, advertisement expenses, etc.

The issue is also underwritten to ensure total subscription of the issue. The biggest advantage of this method is that it saves the issuing company the hassles involved in selling the shares to the public directly through prospectus. This method is, however, expensive for the investor as it involves the offer of securities by issue houses at very high prices.

3. Private Placement/QIP

As per SEBI guidelines dated May 8, 2006, an additional mode has been introduced for listed companies to raise funds from the domestic market in the form of "Qualified Institutions Placement" (QIP).

Issuer: A company whose equity shares are listed on a stock exchange having nation wide trading terminals and which is complying with the prescribed requirements of minimum public shareholding of the listing agreement will be eligible to raise funds in domestic market by placing securities with Qualified Institutional Buyers (QIBs).

Securities: Securities which can be issued through QIP are equity shares or any securities other than warrants, which are convertible into or exchangeable with equity shares (hereinafter referred to as "specified securities"). A security which is convertible into or exchangeable with equity shares at a later date, may be converted or exchanged into equity shares at any time after allotment of security but not later than sixty months from the date of allotment. The specified securities shall be made fully paid up at the time of allotment.

Investors/Allottees: The specified securities can be issued only to Qualified Institutional Buyers (QIBs), as defined under sub-clause (v) of clause 2.2.2B of the SEBI (DIP) Guidelines. Such QIBs shall not be promoters or related to promoters of the issuer, either directly or indirectly. Each placement of the specified securities issued through QIP shall be on private placement basis, in compliance with the requirements of first proviso to clause (a) of sub-section (3) of Section 67 of the Companies Act, 1956. A minimum of 10% of the securities in each placement shall be allotted to Mutual Funds. For each placement, there shall be at least two allottees for an issue of size up to ₹ 250 crores and at least five allottees for an issue size in excess of ₹ 250 crores. Further, no single allottee shall be allotted in excess of 50 per cent of the issue size. Investors shall not be allowed to withdraw their bids / applications after closure of the issue.

Issue Size: The aggregate funds that can be raised through QIPs in one financial year shall not exceed five times of the net worth of the issuer at the end of its previous financial year.

Placement Document: Issuer shall prepare a placement document containing all the relevant and material disclosures. There will be no pre-issue filing of the placement document with SEBI. The placement document will be placed on the websites of the Stock Exchanges and the issuer, with appropriate disclaimer to the effect that the placement is meant only for QIBs on private placement basis and is not an offer to the public.

Pricing: The floor price of the specified securities shall be determined on a basis similar to that for GDR / FCCB issues and shall be subject to adjustment in case of corporate actions such as stock splits, rights issue, bonus issue etc.

Other procedural requirements: The resolution approving QIP, passed under sub-section (1A) of Section 81 of the Companies Act, 1956 or any other applicable provision, will remain valid for a period of twelve months from the date of passing of the resolution. There shall be a gap of at least six months between each placement in case of multiple placements of specified securities pursuant to authority of the same shareholders' resolution. Issuer and Merchant Banker shall submit documents / undertakings, if any, specified in this regard in the listing agreement, for the purpose of seeking in-principle approval and final permission from Stock Exchanges for listing of the specified securities.

Involvement of Merchant Banker: QIP shall be managed by a SEBI registered merchant banker who shall exercise due diligence and furnish a due diligence certificate to Stock Exchanges stating that the issue complies with all the relevant requirements. The merchant banker shall file a copy of the placement document and post issue details with SEBI within thirty days of the allotment, for record purpose.

The purpose behind the Qualified Institutions Placement (QIP) is to encourage Indian companies to raise the funds domestically. QIP should not exceed 5 times pre-issue network as per the audited balance sheet of the company for the previous financial years.

Allotment under QIP shall be made subject to the following conditions:

(a) Minimum 10% eligible securities shall be allotted to Mutual Funds. If mutual funds do not subscribe to the extent of 10% the remaining portion may be allotted to other Qualified Institutions buyer.

(b) No allotment shall be made either directly or indirectly to any qualified institution buyers who is promoters or to any person related to promoters of Issuer Company.

Features:

Under this method, securities are offered directly to large buyers with the help of share brokers. This method works in a manner similar to the 'Offer for Sale Method' whereby securities are first sold to intermediaries such as issues houses, etc. They are in turn placed at higher prices to individuals and institutions. Institutional investors play a significant role in the realm of private placing. The expenses relating to placement are borne by such investors.

Advantages:

Private placement of securities offers the following advantages:

(a) Less expensive as various types of costs associated with the issue are borne by the issue houses and other intermediaries.

(b) Less troublesome for the issuer as there is not much of stock exchange requirements concerning contents of prospectus and its publicity etc. to be complied with.

(c) Placement of securities suits the requirements of small companies.

(d) The method is also resorted to when the stock market is dull and the public response to the issue is doubtful.

Disadvantages:

The major weaknesses of the private placement of securities are as follows:

(a) Concentration of securities in a few hands.

(b) Creating artificial scarcity for the securities thus jacking up the prices temporarily and misleading general public.

(c) Depriving the common investors of an opportunity to subscribe to the issue, thus affecting their confidence levels.

4. **Initial Public Offer (IPO)**

When the company is coming for the first time in the capital market to raise capital such an issue is called as IPO. The shares issued in IPO are listed and traded on one or more stock exchanges as specified in the offer document.

Advantages of Initial Public Offer:

(a) **Access to capital to fund growth:** Public placement of shares on a stock exchange allows the company to attract capital to fund both organic growth (modernisation and upgrade of production facilities, implementation of capital-intensive projects) and acquisitive expansion. If retained earnings and debt funding are insufficient, IPO becomes one of the most realistic and convenient ways to secure the continuing growth of the business. It provides access to a massive, timeless pool of capital and boosts the investment credibility of the business.

(b) **Creation of liquidity and potential exit for the current owners:** Formation of a public market for the company's shares at fair price creates liquidity and provides an opportunity to sell the shares promptly with minimal transactional costs. The private owners of the company can dispose of their stakes in the business both during an IPO (this route is often taken by the minority financial investors such as venture or private capital funds) and at a later stage (this is often preferred by the majority shareholders).

(c) **Maximum value of the company:** Normally, an IPO is an offer to a large number of institutional and retail investors to become shareholders of the company. The very multitude of large investors and their confidence in the liquidity of their investment in a public entity assure the current owners of a private company about achieving the maximum possible valuation of the business at the time of an IPO or afterwards.

(d) Enhancement of the company's public profile: Listing on a recognised stock exchange means that the business will receive wide media coverage, usually a very favourable one, thus increasing the company's visibility and recognition of its products and services. The company's activities will also be reflected in the reports by professional financial analysts. Such public profile supports liquidity of the shares and contributes to the expansion of the business contacts. It also helps to increase confidence among the company's business partners.

(e) Improvement in debt finance terms: For domestic financial institutions – used to working with the low-transparency businesses and often inadequate financial reporting – a company listed on a recognised stock exchange becomes a desirable and reliable partner. Banks are often ready to extend loans to public companies in larger amounts, under smaller collateral, for longer maturities and with lower interest rates. Even the largest and most prestigious banking institutions are keen to work with public companies – whose transparency and corporate governance serve as additional factors of confidence for banks and other suppliers of credit.

(f) Extra assurances for partners, suppliers and clients: Partners and contractors of a public company feel more confident about its financial state and organisational capabilities as compared to those of a non-transparent private business. Partners take additional comfort in the fact that the public company has gone through rigorous legal, financial and corporate due diligences – all of which are required for a successful completion of an IPO. Confidence among partners and contractors is a sound foundation for stable and predictable business relations with the public company, and allows the latter to obtain additional leverage in negotiating better terms for doing business.

(g) Enhanced loyalty of key personnel: Publicly available information about the share price of a public company allows development of employee motivation schemes based on partial remuneration of staff in the form of participation in the equity capital (for example, share options). Equity-based incentive schemes stimulate the key personnel to become more efficient in their work in order to support the company's growth rates and profitable development – which in turn increase the operational and financial efficiency of the company and its market value.

(h) Superior efficiency of the business: Conduct of various due diligences during the IPO process requires a thorough and comprehensive analysis of the company's business model. During the IPO implementation process, certain internal changes take place, including modification of the organisational structure; selection of the key personnel and delegation of responsibilities; improvement of internal reporting and controls; as well as critical evaluation of the efficiency of the entire business.

Normally, such extensive internal efforts result in significant improvements of the communication system, management and controls; they also help eliminate any previously hidden shortcomings in the internal functioning of the business.

Disadvantages of Initial Public Offer

(a) **Share price of a public company is exposed to the stock market fluctuations:** Regardless of how well the company is managed, in certain circumstances imposed by the external market, price and liquidity of the shares may drop. For example, smaller companies may discover that their shares are not sufficiently liquid, while the medium-sized and large companies may experience share price movements based on unfounded market expectations, general economic trends, or even unrelated events in the industry, sector or country. In order to minimise the influence of such unfavourable events on a public company's share price, the management should retain constant communication with the market and investors, keeping them informed about the company's current developments and prospects.

(b) **The interests and expectations of the minority public investors must be taken into consideration:** Sale of an equity stake during the IPO inevitably transfers a certain degree of influence to the new public shareholders; their interests and opinions must be considered going forward. This means that the owners of a formerly private business are no longer allowed the same autonomy in making strategic decisions. In order to satisfy current expectations of the public investors, the company might need to achieve the short-term operational goals at the expense of the longer-term strategic prospects.

(c) **Wide-ranging disclosure requirements and financial reporting:** The IPO implementation process and a listing on a reputed stock market are only possible when the company discloses the necessary financial information and provides periodic financial reporting of scope and quality substantially in excess of those required from a private company. For example, a public company must disclose the names of its ultimate beneficiaries, provide detailed information about the financial position and development plans, disclose remuneration of the directors, and other relevant information.

(d) **Substantial investment in the IPO process:** Aggregate investment in the IPO process on a leading stock exchange (such as the London Stock Exchange) may be quite significant. Even though most of these expenses will be reimbursed from the funds raised during the IPO and therefore will not impact the operating results of the company, a part of the preparation expenses will have to be funded by the company's own resources before the IPO takes place. Thus it is necessary to plan the investments into the IPO process carefully.

(e) **New responsibilities and restrictions for the management:** The IPO process, as well as the ongoing responsibilities that arise from the new public status, require substantial amounts of the executives' time that otherwise might have been spent on the operational business. The directors and executives of a public company also face certain restrictions, for example related to dealings with the company shares and disclosures of the market-sensitive information. Hence the activities of the directors and top management of public companies are more regulated and require additional attention.

5. Rights Issue (RI)

Under Section 81(1) of Companies Act 1956 right issue means capital issue where shares are offered to existing shareholders of the company through letter of offer. A listed company issues fresh shares to its existing shareholders only. Rights are offered in a specific ratio of existing share holding prior to the rights issue. Ratio and offer price is decided considering requirement of capital. The stake of shareholders does not get diluted in rights issue since everybody gets the shares in the same proportion. E.g. if rights are given in 1:5 ratio that means for every 5 shares an existing shareholder will get the right to purchase 1 share at offered price, but shareholder has option to purchase fully, partly , or renounce fully or partly or not to respond to the offer.

Right issue is taken as a reward to existing shareholders as the right shares are offered at lower price than the market price.

Advantages:

Rights issue offers the following advantages:

(a) **Economy:** Rights issue constitutes the most economical method of raising fresh capital, as it involves no underwriting and brokerage costs. Further, the expenses by way of advertisement and administration, etc. are less.

(b) **Easy:** The issue management procedures connected with the rights issue are easier as only a limited number of applications are to be handled.

(c) **Advantage to shareholders:** Issue of rights shares does not involve any dilution of ownership of existing shareholders. Further, it offers freedom to shareholders to subscribe or not to subscribe the issue.

Drawbacks:

The method suffers from the following limitations:

(a) **Restrictive:** The facility of rights issue is available only to existing companies and not to new companies.

(b) **Against society:** The issue of rights shares runs counter to the overall societal considerations of diffusion of share ownership for promoting dispersal of wealth and economic power.

6. Bonus Issue

Like IPO/FPO bonus issue is not for raising capital and new funds are added to companies capital since the shares are given free of cost to the existing shareholders only. Company allots the share to the existing shareholders in proportion to their existing shareholders. The proportion (ratio) is decided by the company. E.g. if the ratio is 1:2 in that case a shareholder having 100 shares will get 50 shares as bonus from the company. Hence total share holding of an individual shareholder remains unchanged after the bonus issue i.e. no dilution of holding.

Bonus shares are issued from free reserves of the company as such it is just transfer entry where free reserves are transferred to paid up capital and hence there is no change in company's net worth. As the free reserves are built up ploughing back the profits in the company over the years and bonus shares are issued out of free reserves it means bonus shares are nothing but distribution of accumulated profit. There no real gain to the investor or loss to the company with bonus shares issue. But due to increased number of shares the liquidity of the shares increases in the stock market to some extent after the bonus issue.

Advantages of issue of bonus issues:

(a) **Conservation of Cash:** Issue of bonus shares does not involve cash outflow. The company can retain earnings as well as satisfy the desire of the shareholders to receive dividend.

(b) **Keeps the EPS at a reasonable level:** A company with high EPS may face problems both from employees and consumers. Employees may feel that they are underpaid. Consumers may feel that they are being charged too high for the company's products. Issue of bonus shares increases the number of shares and reduces the earning per share.

(c) **Increases the marketability of company's shares:** Issue of bonus shares reduces the market price per share. The price of the share may come within the reach of ordinary investors. This increases the marketability of shares.

(d) **Enhances prestige of the company:** By issuing bonus shares, the company increases its credit standing and its borrowing capacity. It reflects financial strength of the company.

(e) **It helps in financing its projects:** By issuing bonus shares, the expansion and modernisation programmes of a company can be easily financed. The company need not depend on outside agencies for finances.

(f) **Retention of managerial control:** Any new issue of shares has a danger of dilution of managerial control over the company. Since bonus shares are issued to the existing shareholders in proportion to their current holdings, there is no threat of dilution of managerial control over the company.

Disadvantages of Bonus Issues:

(a) Issue of bonus shares leads to an increase in the capitalisation of the company. The increased capitalisation can be justified only if there is increase in the earning capacity of the company.

(b) After the issue of the bonus shares the shareholders expect the existing rate of dividend per share to continue. It is really a challenging task for the company to retain the existing rate of dividend per share.

(c) Issue of bonus shares prevents new investors from becoming the shareholders of the company (no doubt they can buy the shares in the secondary market).

7. Bought-out Deals

A company can raise capital through a Bought-out Deal. Bought-out Deal is a deal in which the entire equity or any security issue is bought in full or in lot by an institution with an intention of offloading it later in the market. A company that chooses the bought-out deal route first approaches an institution or institutions (i.e. Bank or Financial Institutions). The concerned institute appraises the proposal and negotiate. A deal is reached between the company and the institution for price and volume. Once the agreement is signed the Institution passes the consideration money to the Company and in turn gets the security duly transferred to it. Depending upon the market situation these securities will be disinvested to the public to an offer and security may also be listed to stock exchanges.

Features:

(a) **Parties:** There are three parties involved in bought-out deals. They are promoters of the company, sponsors and co-sponsors who are generally merchant bankers and investors.

(b) **Outright sale:** Under this arrangement, there is an outright sale of a chunk of equity shares to a single sponsor or the lead sponsor.

(c) **Syndicate:** Sponsor forms a syndicate with other merchant bankers for meeting the resource requirements and for distributing the risk.

(d) **Sale price:** The sale price is finalised through negotiations between the issuing company and the purchaser, the sale being influenced by such factors as project evaluation, promoters image and reputation, current market sentiments, prospects of off-loading these shares at a future date, etc.

(e) **Fund-based:** Bought-out deals are in the nature of fund-based activity where the funds of the merchant bankers get locked in for at least the prescribed minimum period.

(f) **Listing:** The investor-sponsors make a profit, when at a future date, the shares get listed and higher prices prevail. Listing generally takes place at a time when the company is performing well in terms of higher profits and larger cash generations from projects.

(g) **OTCEI:** Sale of these shares at Over-the-Counter Exchange of India (OTCEI) or at recognised stock exchanges, at the time of listing these securities and off-loading them simultaneously are being generally decided in advance.

Bought-out Deals Vs. Private Placements

Sr. No.	Feature	Private Placement	Bought-out Deal
1.	Trading Scrips	Limited securities	Unlisted securities
2.	Creating Securities	Results in the creation of additional securities for the buying institutions	Securities are simply transferred from promoters to sponsors who in turn off-load them to the public
3.	Lock-in Period	Five years	18 months

Benefits:

Bought-out deals provide the following benefits :

(a) **Speedy sale:** Bought-out deals offer a mechanism for a speedier sale of securities at lower costs relating issue.

(b) **Freedom:** Bought-out deals offer freedom for promoters to set a realistic price and convince the sponsor about the same.

(c) **Investor protection:** Bought-out deals facilitate better investor protection as sponsors are rigorously evaluated and appraised by the promoters before off-loading the issue.

(d) **Quality offer:** Bought-out deals help enhance the quality of capital floatation and primary market offerings.

Limitations:

Bought-out deals pose the following difficulties for the promoters, sponsors and investors:

(a) **Loss of control:** The apprehensions in the minds of promoters, particularly of the private or the closely held companies that the sponsors may usurp control of the company as they own large chunk of the shares of it company.

(b) **Loss of sales:** Bought-out deals pose considerable difficulties in off-loading the shares in times of unfavourable market conditions. This results in locking up of investments and entailing losses to sponsors.

(c) **Wrong appraisal:** Bought-out deals cause loss to sponsors on account of wrong appraisal of the project and overestimation of the potential price of the share.

(d) Manipulation: Bought-out deals give great scope for manipulation at the hands of the sponsor through insider trading and rigging.

(e) No accountability: Bought-out deals pose difficulty of penalising the sponsor as there are no SEBI guidelines to regulate offerings by sponsors.

(f) Windfall profits: Bought-out deals offer the advantage of windfall profits by sponsors at the cost of small investors.

(g) Loss to investors: Where the shares taken up by issue brokers and a coterie of select clients are being bought back by the promoters at a pre-fixed higher price after allotment causing loss to investment of the company.

8. Follow-on Public Offer (FPO)

A company whose shares are already listed on the stock exchange and comes to the market for raising additional capital through public offer such public offer is known as FPO.There is no need to list the newly issued shares since the company's shares are already listed.

9. Fast track Issue (FTI)

Fast track system was introduced by SEBI in November 2007, as suggested by the primary market committee of SEBI. In FTI well established and complaint listed companies need to make only rationalised disclosures, rather than comprehensive ones, for FPO and rights issue. This facility is available for companies listed on NSE & BSE for at least three years. Also market capitalisation of such a company has to be ₹ 10,000 crore or more for more than one year. Trading volume has to be at least 2% of the total number of shares. No prosecution proceedings or show cause notice issued by SEBI should be pending against the company or its promoters and whole time directors.

10. Preferential Issue

Preferential issue entails allotment of securities to a select group of people on priority placement basis. The main advantage of raising funds through Preferential Issue is that it reduces the cost and time compared to public issue. In case of temporary trouble a company finds it difficult to go in for a public issue and some institutions understand the temporary nature of the trouble and infuse the capital to take the company out of trouble. The shares issued in preferential issue have a lock in period of 3 years from the date of allotment. However not more than the 20% of the total capital shall be locked in for 3 years from the date of allotment. The locking of the shares does not permit the trading for the 3 years from the date of allotment.

11. Book Building

SEBI guidelines define book building as a process adopted in pubic issue for efficient price discovery. During the issue period (which is normally between 3 to 4 days) the investors bid either at floor price or cap price or in between floor and cap price and in book building method bids are collected at different prices and the offer price is decided only after the issue is closed.

According to SEBI (Disclosure and Investor Protection) guidelines, 2000 an issuer company may make an issue of security to the public through prospectus in a manner of 100% of the net offer to the public through the book building process or 75% of the net offer to the public through the book building process or 25% at the price determined through the book building process, but as per the latest regulations issued by SEBI in August 2009, the division of 75% book building and 25% fixed price issue is done away with. An issuer can offer specified securities at different prices subject to certain conditions but the book building process is the main highlight of the new regulations issued by SEBI.

In order to allow investors to decide the price rather than the issuer SEBI announced on November 2009 a pure action method. In pure action method of book building the issuer mentions a floor price and cap price. Investors are free to bid at any price between the floor and cap price.

Process of Book Building
- Issuing company appoints a merchant banker usually a lead manger as a book runner.
- The book runner keeps his book open for minimum 5 days.
- Investors bid in lot size and he is allowed to alter his bid both in price and size before the issue.
- All these bids are forwarded to the book runner.
- The book runner decides the issue price (known as cut-off price) as a weighted average of the offers received.
- Shares are allotted to the successful bidders.

Benefits:
(a) The price of an instrument is set in a much more realistic fashion.
(b) The primary aim of the book building process is to fix the highest market price for shares and securities.
(c) As investors have a voice in the pricing of the issue, they have a greater certainty of being allotted what they demand.
(d) The issue price is determined by the market. As there is a distant possibility of the market price of shares falling lower than the issue price, an investor is less likely to suffer from erosion of his investment on listing.
(e) Well organised capital raising with enhanced issue procedures, which leads to a reduction in (a) issue costs (b) paper work and (c) lead times.

(f) Flexibility to increase/decrease price and/or size of offering the issues is possible.

(g) There is transparency of allocations to investors.

(h) Instant allotment and listing of placement portion of securities.

Limitations:

(a) Book building is suitable only for mega issues.

(b) The issuer firm must be fundamentally strong and well known to the investors.

(c) The book building system functions very well in matured market conditions. So, the investors are knowledgeable of the various parameters influencing the market price of the securities. But, such conditions are generally not seen in practice.

(d) There is a chance of price rigging on the listing as promoters shall try to bail out associate members.

12. Stock Option

Stock options are Employee Stock Option Plans under which employees receive the right to purchase a certain number of shares in the company at a predetermined price, as a reward for their performance and also as motivation for employees to keep increasing their performance. Employees typically have to wait for a certain duration known as vesting period before they can exercise the right to purchase the shares.

The main aim of giving such a plan to its employees is to give shares of the company to its employees at a discounted price of the market price at the time of the exercise. Many companies (especially in the startup phase) have now started giving Employee Stock Options as this is beneficial to both the employer as well as the employee.

Benefits of ESOPs:

The major benefits of awarding Employee Stock Options are mentioned below:

(a) **Lock-in Period:** ESOP's come with a lock-in period known as vesting period and employees can exercise the options only after this period. If the employee leaves the organisation before completing the specified period – these ESOP's get lapsed and the employee will not get any benefit.

(b) **A 'Sense of Ownership' for the employees:** When the employees are given shares of the same company in which they are working, it gives them a sense of feeling that now they are not employees of this organisation but are the owners. As they are now the owners, they also have a share in the profits of the company. In fact, since employees directly benefit from the increase in the share price, they focus on overall value creation for the company.

(c) **Kind instead of Cash:** ESOPs are a way of awarding the employees in kind instead of cash. In the initial days of ESOPs in India, small organisations who were cash strapped used to give ESOPs to their employees to increase the overall pay package.

In this manner, they were able to compensate the employees in kind without affecting their cash reserves (if a organisation issues ESOPs- its cash reserves are not affected).

13. Sweat Equity

A company may issue shares to its employee and promoters on very favourable terms in recognition of their services to the company. Such equity shares are known as Sweat Equity. As per the Companies Act 1956 Sweat Equity shares are equity shares issued by a company to its employees or directors at a discount or for consideration other than cash for providing know how or making available rights in the nature of Intellectual Property Rights (ITR) or value addition, by whatever name it is called. In order to avoid the misuse of the provision of the Companies Act 1956 and to protect the interest of the stake holders of the company SEBI had issued certain regulations in this regards.

2.3 Prospectus

After getting the company incorporated, promoters have to raise finances. The public is invited to purchase shares and debentures of the company through an advertisement. A document containing detailed information about the company and an invitation to the public subscribing to the share capital and debentures is issued. This document is called 'prospectuses.

Private companies cannot issue a prospectus because they are strictly prohibited from inviting the public to subscribe to their shares. Only public companies can issue a prospectus. Section 2 (36) of the Companies Act defines prospectus as, "A prospectus means any document described or issued as prospectus and includes any notice, circular, advertisement or other documents invent deposits from public or inviting offers from the public for the subscription or purchase of any shares in or debentures of a body corporate."

The prospectus is not an offer in the contractual sense but only an invitation to offer. A document constructed to be a prospectus should be issued to the public. A prospectus should have the following essentials.

- There must be an invitation offering to the public.
- The invitation must be made on behalf of the company or intended company.
- The invitation must to be subscribed or purchase.
- The invitation must relate to shares or debentures.

A prospectus must be filed with the Registrar of companies before it is issued to the public. The issue of prospectus is essential when the company wishes the public to purchase its shares or debentures.

If the promoters are confident of obtaining the required capital through private contacts, even a public company may not issue a prospectus. The promoters prepare a draft prospectus containing required information and this document is known as 'a statement is lieu of prospectus.' A prospectus duly dated and signed by all the directors should be field with Register of Company before it is issued to the public.

A prospectus brings to the notice of the public that a new company has been formed. The company tries to convince the public that it offers best opportunity for their investment. A prospectus outlines a detail the terms and conditions on which the shares or debentures have been offered to the public. Every prospectus contains an application from on which an intending investor can apply for the purchase of shares or debentures. A company must get minimum subscription within 120 days from the issue of prospectus. If it fails to obtain minimum subscription from the members of the public within the specified period, then the amount already received from public is returned. The company cannot get a certificate of commencement of business because the public is not interested in that company.

The following matters are to be disclosed in a prospectus:

- Name and full address of the company.
- Full particulars about the signatories to the memorandum of association and the number of shares taken up by them.
- The number and classes of shares. The interest of shareholders in the property and profits of the company.
- Name, address and occupations of members of the Board of Directors or proposed Directors.
- The minimum subscription fixed by promoters after taking into account all financial requirements at the beginning.
- If the company acquires any property from vendors, their full particulars are to be given.
- The full address of underwriters, if any, and the opinion of directors that the underwriters have sufficient resources to meet their obligations.
- The time of opening of the subscription list.
- The nature and extent of interest of every promoter in the promotion of the company.
- The amount payable on application, allotment and calls.
- The particulars of preferential treatment given to any person for subscribing shares or debentures.
- Particulars about reserves and surpluses.
- The amount of preliminary expenses.
- The name and address of the auditor.
- Particulars regarding voting rights at the meeting of the company.

- A report by the auditors regarding the profits and losses of the company.
- These are some of the contents which every prospectus must include. The prospectus is an advertisement of the company, so the company may give any information which promotes its interest. Any information given in the prospectus must be true, otherwise the subscribe can beheld guilty for misrepresentation.

Importance of Prospectus:

Importance of Prospectus can be discussed in the following points:

1. It helps companies in raising capital by inviting deposits or offers for shares and debentures from the public.
2. Prospectus provides information about promoters and objectives of the company. Prospective shareholders analyse the contents and take decisions whether to apply for shares or not.
3. Prospectus is a reliable document, as promoters, generally, do not enter wrong facts in the prospectus due to the seven penalties imposed for mis-statements found in the prospectus.
4. As the prospectus discloses all relevant facts and information it acts as a substantial proof to settle disputes which may arise between the company and shareholders.

Abridged Prospectus

- Prospectus is a bulky document and it is not economically feasible to supply a full-fledged prospectus to the prospective investors. Therefore, as a cost saving measure, a provision has been made to issue prospectus in an abridged form.
- The dictionary meaning of 'Abridged Prospectus' is a condensed prospectus, reduced prospectus, abbreviated prospectus or shortened prospectus. Thus, it means a prospectus in brief where the company need not provide information in the prospectus in detail under several sub-headings as required by the Schedule II, but, the information is given in a condensed form.
- Under Section 2(1), 'Abridged Prospectus' means a memorandum containing such salient features of a prospectus as may be prescribed.
- In the Companies Amendment Act, 1988, the word 'prospectus' has been substituted by "memorandum containing such salient features of prospectus as may be presented". Such memorandum is the abridged form of a prospectus. After this amendment, companies are not required to issue a full/detailed prospectus along with an application form, which may be issued only on the request of the applicant.
- New rule 4cc has been inserted in the Companies (Central Government) Rules and Forms 1956 and as per this rule, the salient features should be given in Form 2A which requires information to be given under nine heads:

1. General information
2. Capital Structure
3. Terms of Present Issue
4. Particulars of the Issue
5. Company Management and Project
6. Financial Performance during 5 years
7. Payments/Refunds
8. Companies under same Management
9. Risk Factors

The Department of Company Affairs (now Ministry of Corporate Affairs) circular no 1/92 dated 9th January, 1992 provides that

(i) Share application form should be a part of the abridged prospectus.
(ii) Abridged prospectus and application form (attached with) are allowed to be the same printed numbers.
(iii) SEBI requirements in respect of abridged prospectus will also have to be fulfilled.

Disclosures in Prospectus

Consequent to the acceptance of the recommendations of the Malegam Committee, the following disclosures are made mandatory by the SEBI to be made by issuing companies with effect from November 1995. This is in addition to the requirements of Schedule II of the Companies Act.

1. **An index** to the contents of the prospectus.
2. **Project cost:** Details of actual expenditure incurred on the project within a period of 2 months of filing the prospectus with the SEBI or Registrar Of Companies (ROC), whichever is later, means and source of financing such expenditure and the year-wise break-up of the expenditure proposed to be incurred on the said project. Details of bridge loan or other financial arrangement, if any, for financing the project together with the sources from which to service the loans.
3. **Turnover:** Turnover details such as the turnover disclosed in the profit or loss statement should be bifurcated into turnover of products manufactured by the company and turnover of products traded in by the company.
4. **Assets and liabilities:** The statement of assets and liabilities as reduced by the amount of revaluation reserve from both fixed assets, and reserves and the net worth arrived at after such deduction.
5. **Major expansion:** Companies undertaking major expansions or new projects shall disclose such details as technology, market, competition, managerial competence, and capacity build-up.

6. **Future projections:** Future projections about profitability of the company is to be furnished where such projections are based solely on an appraisal by a financial institution or a scheduled commercial bank, the appraising agency has financed the whole or a part of the project or is committed to finance the project or a part of it, the projections are for a period up to two years from the date of expected commencement of commercial production or three years from the date of the closure of the issue, whichever is later and where the major assumptions on which the projections based are specified. Further, projections of future profits should be made only by a new company or by an existing company only if such company is undertaking a new project or is proposing to substantially expand its activities beyond 100 per cent of the existing capacity.

7. **Director's statement:** A statement of the directors on the expected financial and profitability position of the company indicating the ability of the company to pay its liabilities within the next twelve months.

8. **Promoter definition:** The term 'promoter' in relation to securities offered to the public for subscription means and includes the following:
   (a) The person or persons who are in overall control of the company.
   (b) The person or persons who are instrumental in the formulation of a plan on the basis of which securities are offered to the public.
   (c) The person or persons named in the prospectus as promoters, a director/officer of the issuer company or person merely acting in their professional capacity should not be included as promoters.

9. **Promoter group definition:** The term 'promoter group' in relation to securities offered to the public for subscription includes the following:
   (a) The 'promoter'.
   (b) An immediate relative of the promoter, (i.e. any spouse of that person, or any parent, brother, sister or child of the person or of the spouse).
   (c) Where the 'promoter' is a corporate body, promoter group includes a subsidiary or holding company of that body; any company in which the 'promoter' holds 10 per cent or more of the equity capital or which holds 10 per cent or more of the equity capital of the promoter, any corporate body in which a group of individuals or corporate bodies or their combinations who hold 20 per cent or more of the equity capital in that company also hold 20 per cent or more of the equity capital of the issuer company.
   (d) Where the 'promoter' is an individual, the promoter group includes any company in which 10 per cent or more of the share capital is held by the 'promoter' or an immediate relative of the 'promoter' or a firm of Hindu Undivided Family (HUF) in

which the 'promoter' or any one or more of his immediate relatives is a member; any company in which a above-specified company holds 10 per cent or more of the share capital and any HUF or firm in which the aggregate share of the promoter and his immediate relatives is equal to or more than 10 per cent of the total.

(e) All persons whose shareholding is aggregated for the purposes of disclosing in the prospectus as "shareholding of the promoter group."

(f) Financial institutions and the mutual funds would be exempted from this definition, if they get included merely on account of the fact that they hold 10 per cent or more of the equity of the concerned company. This exemption would not apply to the subsidiaries or companies promoted by the financial institutions or to the companies which sponsor the mutual fund.

10. **Promoters shareholdings:** Details of promoters' shareholdings relating to the following are to be disclosed:

   (a) Aggregate shareholding of the promoter group and of the directors of the promoter, where the promoter is a body corporate.

   (b) Aggregate number of securities purchased or sold by the promoter group and the directors of the promoter during a period of six months preceding the date on which the draft prospectus is filed with the SEBI (updating must continue up to such time the prospectus is filed with the RoC).

   (c) The maximum and minimum price at which purchases and sales indulged in by any relative of the promoter were made along with the relevant dates.

11. **Share prices:** Details of share prices as noted below must be disclosed in the prospectus:

   (a) High, low and average market prices of the shares and the number of shares traded of the company during the preceding three years.

   (b) Monthly high and low prices, and the number of shares traded for the six months preceding the date of filing the draft prospectus with the SEBI, which should be updated till the time of filing the prospectus with the RoC/stock exchange concerned.

   (c) The stock market data referred to above, should be shown separately for periods marked by a change in capital structure with such period commencing from the date the concerned stock exchange recognises the change in the capital structure (e.g. when the shares have becomes ex-rights or ex-bonus).

   (d) The market price immediately after the date on which the resolution of the Board of Directors approving the issue was approved.

(e) The volume of securities traded in each month during the six months preceding the date on which the issue opens for subscription.

(f) Management perception of the internal and external risk factors which should be given immediately after each of the risk factors and not as a separate heading under management perception.

12. **Agreements:** Details of persons with whom technical and financial agreements have been entered into, place of registration and year of incorporation, issued share capital, turnover of the last financial year of operation, and general information regarding such persons relevant to the issuer.

13. **Management discussion and analysis:** Details of discussion and the analysis made by the management of the company based on the financial statements as regards the financial condition and results of the operations as regards the following shall be disclosed:

    (a) A comparison of the significant items of income and expenditure between the last period for which financial statements have been prepared and the immediately preceding period and the period preceding that period detailing unusual or infrequent events or transactions.

    (b) Significant economic changes that is materially affected or are likely to affect income from continuing operations.

    (c) Known trends or uncertainties that have had or are expected to have a material adverse impact on sales, revenue or income from continuing operations.

    (d) Future changes in relationship between costs and revenues, in case events such as future increase in labour or material costs or prices that will cause a material change are known.

    (e) The extent to which material increases in net sales or revenue are due to increased sales volume, introduction of new products or services or increased sales prices.

    (f) Total turnover of each major industry segment in which the company operates.

    (g) Status of any publicly announced new products or business segment.

    (h) The extent to which business is seasonal.

    (i) Any significant dependence on a single or few suppliers or customers, and

    (j) Competitive conditions.

14. **Buy-back:** Details of all "buy-back" and "stand-by", and similar arrangements made for purchase of securities by promoters, directors and lead merchant bankers subject to the provisions that no buy-back or stand-by or similar arrangement would be allowed with the persons for whom securities are reserved for allotment on a firm basis.

15. **Major shareholders:**
    (a) Such details regarding major shareholders, 10 days and 2 years prior to the date of filing of prospectus with the RoC, as the names of the ten largest shareholders as on the date of filing of the prospectus with the RoC, number of shares held (or to be held by them on account of conversion option) by them.
    (b) Where the company has made a public issue for the first time, within the two preceding years, the above information should be given separately indicating the names of persons who acquired shares by subscriptions to the public issue and those who acquired the shares by allotment on a firm basis or by private placement.

16. **No responsibility statement:** A statement that the issuer company accepts no responsibility in respect of statements made in the offer document or in the advertisement or any other material issued and that people who respond to such a statement will be doing so only at their risk.

17. **Qualified notes:** In respect of qualified information by the auditor on the statement of assets and liabilities, the following quantifiable adjustments and rectifications shall be made in such statements in order to arrive at profits:
    (a) All incorrect accounting practices or failures to make provisions or other adjustments resulting in audit qualifications.
    (b) Material amounts relating to adjustments for previous years aimed at arriving at the profits of the years to which they relate, irrespective of the year in which the event triggering the profit or loss occurred.
    (c) Profit and loss account figures shall be reworked to account for the difference between figures as per the change in accounting policy and the uniform accounting policy and recomputation of financial statements shall be done in accordance with the correct accounting policies where incorrect accounting policy is being followed.
    (d) Statement of profit or loss should disclose both the profit and loss arrived at before considering extraordinary items and after considering the profit or loss from extraordinary items.
    (e) Changes that will have a material effect on the statement of profit/loss for five years.
    (f) All significant accounting policies followed in the preparation of the financial statements.
    (g) All financial information given in the offer document including accounting ratios should be audited.

18. **Information about ventures promoted:** Following information about the ventures/ companies promoted by the same promoters shall be disclosed: date of incorporation, nature of activities, equity capital, reserves (excluding revaluation reserve), sales, Profit After Tax (PAT), Earnings Per Share (EPS), Net Asset Value (NAV), the highest and lowest market price of shares during the preceding six months with suitable disclosures for changes in capital structure during the period and the market value on the date of filing the offer document with the RoC, the current market price and particulars of changes in the capital structure if any, in respect of issue made in the preceding three years together with a statement regarding the cost and progress of implementation of the project.

19. **Risk factors:** Information regarding adverse factors, if any, as relating to whether the company has become a sick company within the meaning of the Sick Industrial Companies (Special Provisions) Act, 1985 or a Board for Industrial and Financial Reconstruction (BIFR) company having a negative net worth or is under winding up and whether the company has made a loss in the immediately preceding year and if so, the profit or loss for the immediately preceding three years.

20. **Tax benefits:** Various tax benefits in the form of tax shelters, tax holidays, etc. that are availed by the company shall be disclosed so as to help determine the extent of tax incidence.

21. **Basis for issue price:** Such information regarding the basis of determining the issue price as EPS pre-issue for the last three years, P/E ratio pre-issue and its comparison with industry P/E ratio, average return on net worth in the last three years, minimum return on increased net worth required, maintaining pre-issue EPS, NAV based on the last balance sheet, NAV after issue and its comparison with the issue price, etc. be disclosed.

22. **Ratios:** Information about such accounting ratios as earnings per share, return on net worth and net asset value share shall be disclosed.

23. **Other disclosures:** In addition to the above, the following also need to be disclosed:
    (a) Sale or purchase between companies in the promoter group where such sales or purchases exceed 10 per cent of the total sales or purchases of the issuer.
    (b) Material items of income or expenditure arising out of transactions in the promoter group.
    (c) A forecast of the estimated profits of the financial year ending immediately before the date of the offer document (if such information is not already given in the other document).
    (d) A capitalisation statement showing total debt and net worth, and the debt/equity ratios before and after the issue is made.

Disclosures in Abridged Prospectus and Letter of Offer

In addition to the above disclosures as required for a regular prospectus, the following disclosures as specified in Part I & II of Schedule II of the Companies Act are required for an abridged prospectus and a letter of offer:

Part I:

1. **Clause 1 (d):** Punishment for fictitious applications as per the provisions of sub-section (1) of Section 68-A.
2. **Clause 1 (f):** Declaration about the issue of allotment letters/refunds within a period of 10 weeks and interest in case of delay in refund at the prescribed rate under Section 73(2)/(2A).
3. **Clause V (d):** Names, addresses and occupation of non-wholetime directors, giving their directorship in other companies.
4. **Clause VII (a):** Outstanding litigation.
5. **Clause VII (c):** Any material development after the date of the latest balance sheet, and its impact on performance and prospects of the company.

Part II:

1. **Clause A.2:** Expert opinion obtained, if any.
2. **Clause A.3:** Change, if any, in directors and auditors during the last three years and reasons thereof.
3. **Clause C.9:** Option to subscribe.
4. **Clause C.15:** Material contracts, and time and place of inspection.

Other items are required under SEBI norms, 1995, such as details of expenditure on project, stock market data, management discussion and analysis, buy-back and stand-by arrangements, details of shareholders, basis of issue price and accounting ratios.

Types of Prospectus:

1. **Red Herring Prospectus:** It is a preliminary registration statement that must be filed with the Securities and Exchange Commission, usually in connection with the company's initial public offering. It describes the issue (IPO) and the prospects of the company. In this type of prospectus particulars about pricing and size of issue is not given. It needs to be announced only a day before the issue opening through a separate advertisement.
2. **Information Memorandum:** According to Section 2 (19B) of the Companies Amendment Act of 2000, 'Information Memorandum' is defined as 'a process undertaken prior to the filing of a prospectus by which a demand for the securities proposed to be issued by a company is elicited, and the price and the terms of issue for such securities is assessed by means of a notice, circular, advertisement or document.'

Features:

The features of 'information memorandum' are as follows:

(a) **Circulation:** It must be circulated before filing the prospectus with the RoC. It can be circulated as a notice, circular, advertisement or document to ascertain the probable demand for the issue of securities and the price at which such securities could be issued.

(b) **Prospectus:** Any company issuing an information memorandum is required to file a prospectus prior to the opening of the subscription list and offer as a red-herring prospectus three days before the opening of the offer.

(c) **Obligations:** It carries the same obligations and liabilities as are applicable to an ordinary prospectus (Section 62 and 63).

(d) **Price:** It does not contain information about the price of the security being offered, but contains all other relevant details necessary to make investment decisions as per Section 56.

(e) **Issue:** It can be issued only by a company, which is either already listed or which intends to be listed after the issue. It shall be issued to the public prior to the filing of the prospectus before the opening of the subscription list, and its issue is to be followed by the issue of prospectus.

(f) **Norms:** It shall conform to the norms as prescribed in Schedule II of the Companies Act and signed by all the directors.

3. **Shelf Prospectus (Section 60 A):** Information about issue of shares contained in a file lying on a shelf is called 'Shelf Prospectus'. Financial institutions and banks issue this type of prospectus. A company filing such a prospectus is also required to file an information memorandum on all material facts relating to new charges created, changes occurring in the financial position in the period from the first offer, previous offer, and the succeeding offer of securities within such time as may be prescribed by the Central Government prior to the making of a second or subsequent offer of securities under the shelf prospectus.

The information memorandum has to be issued to the public along with the 'shelf prospectus' at the stage of first offer of securities. The prospectus remains valid for one year from the date of opening of the first issue of securities. Where an update of the information is filed every time an offer of securities is made, such information memorandum together with the shelf prospectus shall constitute the prospectus.

2.4 Underwriting

Definition: *Underwriting is an agreement with or without condition to subscribe to the unsubscribed portion of the capital issue.*

Underwriting per say is not mandatory for public issue, however a public issue is said to be successful when the subscription is at least 90% of the issue size. Lesser known companies are not sure about the success of the issue, in order to avoid this embarrassment such companies opt for underwriting. Underwriting is an agreement between the company and the underwriter accordingly in the event of non-subscription by the investors to the desired extent (i.e. issue is undersubscribed) then the underwriter subscribes this unsubscribed portion. Thus the assurance giving party is known as an underwriter to the issue. Underwriting is permissible upto 25% of the issue size. Normally no single party underwrites the entire amount of 25% of issue size and depending upon the issue size underwriters are arranged by the lead manager. In the event of issue being unsubscribed each underwriter purchases the shares proportionate to his share in underwriting.

2.4.1 Types of Underwriting

1. **Firm Underwriting:** It is an underwriting agreement whereby, the underwriter agrees to take up a specified number of securities, irrespective of the securities being offered to the public. It is an agreement for outright purchase of securities, the underwriter being given a preference in allotment over the general public in respect of the commitment given by the company issuing the securities. This is in addition to the shares not taken up by the public. Such an agreement is designed to create confidence in the minds of the investing public.

2. **Sub Underwriting:** Underwriters can reduce their commitment by getting a capital issue sub underwritten by others. That is an underwriter can arrange for sub underwriting of his underwriting obligation on his own account with any person or persons on the terms to be agreed upon between them. However an underwriter shall be primarily responsible for sub underwriting and any failure or default on part of sub underwriter to discharge their respective underwriting obligations shall not or discharge the underwriter of its underwriting obligations under this agreement.

3. **Joint Underwriting:** When an issue of securities by a company is underwritten by two or more underwriting intermediaries jointly, it is called 'joint underwriting'. The objective is to minimise the risk and share the benefits arising from the capital issue. Besides, this also helps underwriters with limited resources to pool them and successfully take up the issue.

4. **Syndicate Underwriting:** In Syndicate Underwriting one or more underwriter come together and takes the responsibility of entire underwriting requirement on the sharing basis. In the event of under subscription the unsubscribe portion is shared on proportionate basis.

Benefits/Functions of Underwriting

The financial service of 'underwriting' is found advantageous for the issuers and the public alike. The function and the role of underwriting firms is given below:

1. **Adequate Funds:** Underwriting, being a kind of a guarantee for subscription of a public issue of securities, enables a company to raise the necessary capital funds. By

undertaking to take up the whole issue, or the remaining shares not subscribed by the public, it helps a company to undertake project investments with the assurance of adequate capital funds. An underwriting agreement assures the company of the required funds within a reasonable or agreed time.

2. Expert Advice: Underwriters of repute often help the company by providing advice on matters pertaining to the soundness of the proposed plan etc. thus enabling the company to avoid certain pitfalls. It is therefore, possible for an issuing company to obtain the benefit of expert advice through underwriting before entering into an agreement. Further, underwriters supply important information to the issuing company with regard to investor's attitude, market conditions etc. and suggest changes in their financial plans too, wherever necessary.

3. Enhanced Goodwill: The fact that the issues of securities of a firm are underwritten, would help the firm achieve a successful subscription of securities by the public. This is because, intermediaries, of financial integrity and established reputation usually do the underwriting. Such an activity, therefore, helps enhance the goodwill of the issuing company. By purchasing securities, either directly from the company or from the market, they vouchsafe the financial soundness of the company.

4. Assurance to Investors: Underwriters, before underwriting the issue, satisfy themselves with the financial integrity of the issuer-company and viability of the plan. The underwriting firms assure this way, the soundness of the company. The investors are, therefore, assured of having low risk when they buy shares or debentures which have been underwritten by them. Their firm commitment towards fulfilling their underwriting obligations helps create confidence in the minds of the investing public about the company.

5. Better Marketing: Underwriters ensure efficient and successful marketing of the securities of a firm through their network arrangements with other underwriters and brokers at the national and global level. This promotes a wide geographical dispersion of securities and facilitates tapping of financial resources for the company.

6. Benefits to Buyers: Underwriters are very useful to the buyers of securities due to their ability to give expert advice regarding the safety of the investment and the soundness of companies. The information and the expert opinion published by them in various newspapers and journals are also helpful.

7. Price Stability: Underwriters provide stability to the price of securities by purchasing and selling various securities. This ultimately benefits the stock market.

2.4.2 Variants of Underwriting

There are variants of the underwriting business, which have evolved owing to the series of changes that have taken place in the control and regulatory ambience of the capital market in India.

1. Offer for Sale

Offer for sale takes place when a company arranges to obtain money from private sources, by making the issue of securities fully to them. The private sources include issue houses and merchant bankers. Issue is generally made below the par value, which is then sold to the public. In such an eventuality, the company issues a 'statement in lieu of prospectus' instead of a regular prospectus. A statement in lieu of prospectus with information to be disclosed according to Schedule III of the Companies Act (Sec. 70(1)) should be filed with ROC three days before the allotment of shares or debentures.

2. Bought-out Deals (BODs)

Meaning: An arrangement, whereby the entire equity or related security is bought in full or in lots, with the intention of off-loading it later in the market is called a 'bought-out deal'.

Features

(a) **Arrangement:** The arrangement takes place between the merchant banker/sponsor and the company, the shares being held by the sponsor until they are ready for public participation.

(b) **No retailing:** BODs eliminate retailing, thereby saving time and cost. They are the cheapest and quickest source of finance for small and medium companies.

(c) **Fund-based activity:** BODs convert a fee-based activity into a fund-based activity for merchant bankers.

(d) **Wholesale activity:** The capital raised from public, which is a retail activity, is rendered into a wholesale activity by the guidelines issued by SEBI in 1994, for reservation of issues without lock-in periods.

(e) **Reserved portions:** From the reserved category for institutional investors, lead managers can take a stake upto 5 per cent of the post-issue equity. The reserved portion of the issue need not be underwritten. The public offer is 25 per cent of the issue and underwriting is optional.

Advantages:

(a) Efficient appraisal of the project by the merchant bankers before the funds are invested.

(b) Appropriate avenue to price the securities of companies.

(c) Helpful in raising funds upfront and thus saving the cost of raising funds through a public issue.

(d) Helpful to entrepreneurs who are not confident enough of tapping the capital market directly.

(e) Measure of assurance and safety to the investor since the project is appraised by a merchant banker.

(f) Benefits of larger participation of FIs, merchant bankers and FIIs and consequent higher credibility.

(g) Handsome gains for the merchant banker if proper issue and prices are selected.

Private Placement

Definition: *The direct sale of securities by a company to institutional investors is called private placement.* It is another variant of underwriting. Private placement assumes that the offerees are limited and few, and have sufficient knowledge and experience to evaluate the merits and risk of investment.

Private placement facility is available for both listed and unlisted companies with a good track record of sales and profit. In the case of listed companies, private placements take into account their trading volumes, the level of floating stock and the purpose for which additional funds are being raised.

Features:

(a) **No prospectus:** In private placement no prospectus is issued.

(b) **Instrument covered:** Private placement covers shares, preference shares and debentures.

(c) **Issuers:** The issuers could be public limited companies or private limited companies.

(d) **Investors:** Investors include Unit Trust of India, Life Insurance Corporation, General Insurance Corporation, State Finance Corporations, and Pension and Insurance Funds. Investors have sufficient knowledge and experience to be capable of evaluating the merits and risks of the investment.

(e) **Intermediaries:** The intermediaries are credit rating agencies, trustees (e.g. ICICI) and financial advisors such as merchant banks. The financial intermediary plays a vital role in preparing an offer memorandum, and negotiating with investors.

(f) **Negotiation:** By dealing with a limited number of institutional investors, the credit rating agents or trustees like ICICI can negotiate a loan directly tailored to suit the issuer's needs.

(g) **Popular instrument:** The most widely used instrument in private placement is non-convertible debenture, which is preferred by institutional investors because it gives stable and assured yield. The debentures are generally held until maturity.

(h) **Market size:** The private placement market is as big as the market for public issue through prospectus and rights combined.

Rationale: Many factors contributed to the need for the development of opportunities for privately placing the securities. Some of these factors are as follows:

(a) **Capital market conditions:** The conditions that were prevailing in the Indian capital market with regard to pricing, listing and trading conditions made it difficult for corporates to raise capital for new projects. The cost of raising capital in terms of publicity and brokerage, which has always been prohibitive, along with uncertainties, has prompted companies to look for private placement opportunities for public subscription. Activity in the institutionalised private placement market has been quite intense, with most public sector enterprises, financial institutions and corporations meeting their requirements through private equity funding.

(b) **FIs resources:** A huge pool of savings with Financial Institutions (FIs) such as banks, including rural banks, insurance companies, provident funds, trusts and foreign private equity funds, made it possible for the growth of private placements.

(c) **Preferences:** The preferences of institutional investors, details of the company, promoters, management, project to be undertaken, pricing norms, and projections also played an important part in the development of the private placement market

Advantages:

(a) **Popular mode:** Private placement has obvious advantages of speed, low cost, confidentiality, and accommodates smaller debt financing than is possible in a public issue.

(b) **Quick access:** Private placement offers access to capital more quickly than the public issue.

(c) **Secrecy:** Confidentiality is ensured in private placement, especially for private limited companies and closely held public limited companies, which do not want to make public issues for fear of takeover, wealth tax hassles and institutional interference.

(d) **Influence:** Private placement is not influenced by the, prevailing bull or bear phases in the stock markets.

2.5 Post-issue Activities

These activities are undertaken immediately after the closure of the issue. The lead manager has to manage the post-issue activities. Certificates such as Certificate of 90% subscription from the Registrar, and Final Collection Certificate from bankers are to be obtained. The major activities covered are:

1. Finalisation of basis of allotment: If the public issue is over-subscribed to the extent of greater than five times, a SEBI-nominated public representative is required to participate in the finalisation of Basis of Allotment (BoA), in case of rights issue that is over-subscribed greater than two times, a SEBI-nominated public representative is required to participate in the finalisation of BoA. If it is under-subscribed, information regarding accepted applications is formalised, and Regional Stock Exchanges are approached for finalisation of BoA.

2. Despatch of share certificates: Immediately after finalising the BoA, share certificates are despatched to the eligible allotees, and refund orders made to unsuccessful applicants. In addition, a 78 days report is to be filed with SEBI. Permission for listing of securities is also obtained from the stock exchange.

3. Advertisement: An announcement in the newspaper has to be made regarding the basis of allotment, the number of applications received and the date of despatch of share certificates and refund orders, etc.

2.6 Pricing of Issues

While fixing an appropriate price, the relevant guidelines for capital issues given by SEBI from time to time must be considered. Companies, themselves in consultation with the merchant bankers, do the pricing of issues. While fixing a price for the security issue, the following factors should be considered:

1. Qualitative factors, which include the prospects of the industry, track record of the promoters, the competitive advantage the company has in making the best use of the business opportunities, and growth of the company as compared to the industry, etc.

2. Quantitative factors, which include the earnings per share, book value, the average market price for 2 or 3 years, dividend payment record, the profit margins, the composite industry price earnings ratio and the future prospects of the company, etc.

With the abolition of the office of the Controller of Capital Issues, companies can adopt free pricing.

The CCI Model

Although the CCI was abolished long ago, it would be interesting to discuss the mode of fixing the price for the issues. The fair value of the share is calculated on the basis of the NAV of the share, Profit Earning Capacity Value and "Average Market Price".

(A) Net Asset Value

NAV = Total Net Worth ÷ Total number of shares outstanding

where,

Total Net Worth = [Equity Capital + Free Reserves – Contingent Liability] + Fresh capital

(B) Profit Earning Capacity Value (PECV)

$$\text{Share price} = \frac{\text{EPS} \times 100}{\text{Capitalisation rate}}$$

where, EPS = [Average Profit before tax – Provision for taxation + Contribution to profits by fresh issue] – Total number of shares outstanding

(C) Average Market Price

In this method, the fair price of the share is determined as an average of the NAV and PECV. The average market price is kept in the background, as a relevant factor while settling the fair value.

Safety Net Scheme

This is the most popular method of pricing public issue used by a number of companies in India. The method aims at affording a measure of protection while fixing the price. Some companies, while making public issues at a premium, use this scheme. Under this scheme, the merchant bankers provide a buy-back facility to the individual investor, in case the price of the shake goes below the issue price after listing. This arrangement is of great help to the investors as it reduces losses. In this connection, SEBI has laid down guidelines for the safety net scheme.

Points to Remember

Public Issue Management

(1) Public issue

(2) Preferential issue

(3) Right issue

Role of Issue Management

1. Easy floatation
2. Financial consultant
3. Underwriting
4. Market makers
5. Due diligence
6. Coordination
7. Liaison with SEBI

Activities involved in Pubic Issue

1. Signing of MoU
2. Obtaining appraisal note

3. Optimum capital structure

4. Convening meeting

5. Appointment of financial intermediary

6. Preparing document

7. Due diligence certificate

8. Submission of offer document

9. Finalisation of collection centres

10. Filing with RoC

11. Launching the Issue

Types of Underwriting

1. Firm Underwriting:

2. Sub Underwriting:

3. Joint Underwriting:

4. Syndicate Underwriting:

Benefits/Functions of Underwriting

1. Adequate Funds:

2. Expert Advice:

3. Enhanced Goodwill:

4. Assurance to Investors:

5. Better Marketing:

6. Benefits to Buyers:

7. Price Stability:

Questions for Discussion

1. State the functions of public issue management.

2. State the various activities involved in Public Issue.

3. Discuss the various methods of marketing new issue.

4. What is Underwriting ? Explain the types and advantages of underwriting.

5. Explain : Pricing of Issue.

6. Explain : Post-issue Management

7. Write short notes on :

   (a) Abridged Prospectus.

   (b) Disclosure in Prospectus.

   (c) Initial Public Offer.

   (d) Pricing Models.

   (e) Types of Prospectus.

Chapter 3...

Services Offered by Merchant Bankers

Contents ...

3.1 Mergers and Acquisition Services
    3.1.1 Types of Mergers
    3.1.2 Financial Evaluation of Mergers
    3.1.3 Economics of Mergers
3.2 Buy Back of Shares
3.3 Delisting of Shares
3.4 Issue of Debentures
    3.4.1 SEBI Guidelines for Debentures
3.5 Portfolio Management Services (PMS)
3.6 Loan Syndication
    3.6.1 Types of Loan Syndications
    3.6.2 Parties to Syndicated Loan
    3.6.3 Documentation for Syndicated Loan
3.7 Project Appraisal
• Points to Remember
• Questions for Discussion

Learning Objectives

- To be aware of the procedure for a registration of merchant banking
- To learn the operation of guidelines by SEBI for merchant banking
- To be able to discuss the structure of money market
- To be able to explain shares and debentures

Introduction

Mergers and acquisitions are part of corporate restructuring. The corporate restructuring are the activities related to expansion/contraction of a firms operations or changes in assets and liabilities or ownership of the company.

Profit maximisation is one of the prime objectives of any business organisation. This can be achieved either internally or externally. Internally it can be done by introducing or developing new product, by expanding the existing capacity. Whereas externally it can be done by acquiring existing business firm. This may be in the form of merger, acquisition, amalgamation or takeover.

There are strength and weaknesses of both internal and external approach. An internal approach enables to retain control over the firm and also gives choice of location and technology whereas its limitations are that it requires longer implementation period and hence the uncertainty. So a company may find it difficult to raise the required fund for expansion.

Whereas in acquisitions financial problem to some extent are taken care by transfer of shares of the acquired company. However evaluation of mergers are relatively complex due to a) all benefits of mergers are not quantifiable, b) buying of company is much complicated than buying a new machine. Although the terms mergers, amalgamations & acquisitions are different, their economic impact is same as far as business firms involved are concerned.

With liberalisation of economy in our country mergers and acquisitions are likely to play an important role in the years to come.

3.1 Mergers and Acquisition Services

1. Merger

A merger refers to a combination of two or more companies, usually of not greatly disparate size, into one company. A merger involves the mutual decision of two companies to combine and to become one entity. It can be seen as decisions of two equals. Merger is a marriage between two companies of roughly the same size. It is thus the combination of two or more companies in which one company survives in its own name and other ceases to exist as legal entity.

2. Amalgamation

Amalgamation signifies the transfers of all the assets and liabilities of one or more than one existing company into a new company. According to Halsubry's law of England, amalgamation is blending of two or mare existing companies into one undertaking and share holders of both the companies become the substantial share holders of the new entity.

3. Acquisition (Takeover)

Acquisition refers to the acquiring of ownership right in the property and assets without any combination of companies. Thus, in acquisition two or more companies may remain separate, independent legal entity. But there may be change of management control of the company. Acquisition results when one company purchases the controlling interest in the share capital of another company in any of the following way,

(a) Controlling interest in the company by entering into an agreement with person or persons holding.
(b) By subscribing new shares being issued by the other company.
(c) By purchasing the shares of the other company at stock exchange.
(d) By making offer to buy the shares to the existing share holders of the company.

3.1.1 Types of Mergers

The mergers are broadly categorised as following:

1. Horizontal Merger: Horizontal merger takes place when two or more corporate firms dealing in the similar lines of activity combine together. This helps to eliminate competition, puts an end to price cutting, improves the scale of economies of operations such as R&D, marketing, administration and management.

2. Vertical Merger: Vertical merger takes place when a firm acquires firm upstream or downstream from it. In case of an upstream merger it extends to the firm supplying raw material and in downstream merger it extends to the firm who eventually sell to the consumer. Thus the combination involves two or more stages of production or distribution that are usually separate.

3. Conglomerate Merger: Conglomerate Merger is a combination in which a firm established in one industry combines with the firm from an unrelated industry. Diversification of risk is the main purpose of this type of merger.

4. Diagonal merger: A company is said to be adopting a diagonal integration strategy where it pursues an acquisition that involves both horizontal and vertical elements. Under this merger strategy, content and intellectual property ownership is combined with distribution technology and infrastructure, resulting in an entirely new media industry.

5. Forward merger: In a forward merger, the shareholders of the target company exchange their shares for the shares of the acquiring company and all of the assets and liabilities of the target company are automatically transferred to the acquirer. An immediate advantage of a forward merger is that it qualifies for tax-free treatment if the shareholders of the target company receive at least 50 percent of their compensation in the form of stock of the acquiring company.

6. Reverse merger: In a reverse merger, the shareholders of the acquiring company exchange their shares for shares of the target company. It is a case of the acquiring company merging into the target company. Where a prosperous and profit making company acquires a loss-making sick company with substantial erosion in its net worth, it is a case of 'reverse merger'.

7. Forward triangular merger: In a forward triangular merger, a subsidiary company is formed by the parent company for the purpose of engaging in the merger deal. A parent company funds a subsidiary formed for this purpose. The stock of the parent company is transferred to the target company by the subsidiary. Upon completion of the merger, the target company is merged into the subsidiary. The subsidiary is the surviving entity and the shareholders of the target company are now shareholders of the parent company.

8. Reverse triangular merger: In a reverse-triangular merger, the parent company funds a subsidiary company with stock of the parent. The shareholders of the target company exchange their stock for the stock of the parent company, which is held by the subsidiary company. The subsidiary company then merges into the target company and the target company survives as the subsidiary company of the parent company. Since the target company is the surviving entity, its favorable intangible rights are preserved.

9. Conglomerate merger: A company is said to be adopting a conglomerate merger strategy where it makes acquisitions across different industries. Where several firms engaged in unrelated lines of business activity combine together to form a new company, it takes the form of 'conglomerate merger'. In this case, merging of different businesses like manufacturing of cement products, fertilisers products, electronic products, insurance investment and advertising agencies, etc. would happen. The basic advantage of this type of merger is that it results in portfolio of lines of business thus maximising the total economic activities of the firm.

A conglomerate takeover or merger involves the coming together of two companies in different industries i.e. the businesses of the two companies are not related to each other horizontally (in the sense of producing the same or competing products), or vertically (in the sense of standing towards each other in the relationship of supplier and buyer, or potential supplier and buyer).

Conglomerate mergers are of different types. In the case of a pure conglomerate merger the activities of two firms being merged are totally unrelated. Merger of an automobile company with Textile Company is an example of a pure conglomerate merger. Further, in a "pure conglomerate", there are no important common factors between the companies as regards production, marketing, research and development or technology. In practice, there is a wide range of situations falling short of "pure conglomerate" in which there is some degree of overlap in one or more of these common factors.

10. Congeneric Merger: A congeneric merger is said to take place where-the-companies that are getting merged are engaged in complementary activities and not in direct competitive activities, amalgamate to form a new company. The coming together of a car manufacturer with a scooter manufacturer is an example of a congeneric merger. The purpose of congeneric merger is not to reduce the number of competitors in an industry but to reap the benefits of operating and financial economies of scale.

Conglomerate takeovers or mergers may in turn be classified according to the purpose. of the dominant party. The dominant party may itself be a `fully-fledged conglomerate' company, i.e. a holding company staffed by professional managers exercising management control over a substantial number of subsidiaries in a wide range of industries. The common factor here is simply the belief by the holding company that it can, by centralised allocations of financial resources and selection of key personnel, and by centralised management controls - in effect the provision of management consultancy services to its subsidiaries—build up and maintain a healthy and profitable group.

The dominant party may be a "financial conglomerate", i.e. the group may have been put together largely on the basis of financial engineering by the holding company, usually by exchanging its highly-priced quoted securities (frequently in the form of convertible securities) for shares of companies in a wide range of industries.

In this category, the holding company often does not profess to exercise management control over its subsidiaries, although control of finance will usually be centralised. Financial conglomerates have been the subject of a great deal of controversial discussion in the last few years, culminating recently in many cases in a marked fall in market rating.

11. Negotiated merger: Where merger of two or more companies takes place after protracted negotiations, it is a case of 'negotiated merger'. Under this type of merger, the acquiring firm negotiates directly with the management of the target firm. The merging companies willingly reach an agreement for the merger proposal. Accordingly, if the parties to the agreement fail to reach an agreement, the merger proposal will be terminated and dropped out. The merger of ITC Classic Ltd. with ICICI Ltd., is an example of a negotiated merger.

12. Arranged merger: Where merger of a financially sick company takes place with another sound company as part of package of financial rehabilitation under the initiative of a financial body, it is a case of an 'arranged merger'. Merger schemes are crafted in consultation with the lead bank, the target firm and the acquiring firm. These are motivated-mergers and the lead bank takes the initiative and decides the terms and conditions of the merger.

In India, arranged mergers take place under the auspices of the Board for Industrial and Financial Reconstruction (BIFR). The takeover of Modi Cements Ltd. by Gujarat Ambuja Cement Ltd. is an example of an arranged takeover after the financial reconstruction of Modi Cements Ltd.

13. Agreed merger: Where the directors of target firm agree to the takeover or merger, accept the offer in respect of their own shareholdings (which might range from nil or negligible to controlling shareholdings) and recommend other shareholders to accept the offer, it is a case of 'agreed takeover or merger'. The directors may agree right from the start or after early negotiations or even after public opposition to the bid (which may or may not have resulted in an improvement in the terms of the proposed offer). The directors of the target firm may have actually approached the acquiring firm to suggest the acquisition.

14. Unopposed merger: Where the directors of the target firm, while making a deal with the acquiring firm, do not oppose the offer or recommend rejection, it is a case of 'unopposed merger'.

15. Defended merger: Where the directors of a target firm decide to oppose the bid, recommending shareholders to reject the offer and perhaps taking further defensive action, it takes the form of a 'defended merger'. The decision to defend may be with the intention of stopping the take-over (which in turn may be prompted either by the genuine belief of the directors that it is in the interests of the company to remain independent or by a desire of the directors to protect their own personal positions) or persuading the bidder to improve its terms.

16. Competitive merger: Where a second bidder (and perhaps even a third bidder) comes into the scene with a rival bid, it is a case of a 'competitive merger'. This may be an independent action on the part of the rival bidder or it may be at the invitation of the directors of the target firm, who, deciding that a takeover is inevitable, feel that the company comes under the control of a bidder selected by them rather than the original bidder.

17. Tender offer: Where a bid is made by an acquiring firm to acquire controlling interest in a target firm by purchasing the shares of the target firm at a fixed price, it is a case of 'tender offer'. Under this type of merger, the acquiring firm directly approaches the shareholders of the target firm and makes them sell their shareholdings at a fixed price. The offer price is generally fixed at a level higher than the current market price in order to induce the shareholders to divest their holding in favor of the acquiring firm. Under this arrangement, the acquiring firm stipulates in the tender offer the number of shares that it is willing to buy. The acquiring firm does not need the prior approval of the management of the target firm. The offer is kept open for a specific period within which the shares must be tendered for sale by the shareholders of the target firm. The takeover of Consolidated Coffee Ltd., by Tata Tea Ltd., is an example of a tender offer.

18. Diversification: Diversification is a case of 'conglomerate merger'. Diversification consists of a company deriving all or the greater part of its revenue from a particular industry, acquiring subsidiaries operating in other industries for one or more of the following reasons:

(a) To obtain greater stability of earnings through spreading activities in different industries with different business cycles or to diversify out of a static or dying industry.

(b) To employ spare resources, whether of capital or management.

(c) To obtain benefit of economies of scale, particularly in regard to "staff" functions (such as personnel, advertising, accounting and financial) where there are some common factors.

(d) To make the company too large to be likely to be the object of a takeover or perhaps to make it a less attractive object in the case of defensive diversification.

(e) To provide an outlet for the ambitions of management, where anti-monopoly laws make further acquisitions (or perhaps even growth) in the company's own field impracticable.

Conglomerate takeovers and mergers do not usually raise anti-monopoly questions, but may do so where it is feared that the firm may abuse its market power, such as by exerting pressure on firms from which some companies in the group purchase supplies to place business with other companies in the group, and it is also argued that a decision by a company to enter a new field by acquisition reduces by one the number of potential competitors in that field in so far as the acquiring company might otherwise have entered the field direct.

Apart from categorising mergers, takeovers and mergers may also be classified according to the degree of cooperation between the boards of directors of the two companies concerned.

3.1.2 Financial Evaluation of Mergers

In order to make sure that the acquiring firm makes a best deal out of the M&A proposal, various possible financial consequences of the deal are to be worked out. The acquiring firm aims at maximising shareholder value through better and ensured supply of raw materials, better access to capital market, better and intensive distribution network, more efficient and professional management, greater market share, tax benefits; etc.

The evaluation of financial consequences of a merger deal is done by considering the following aspects:

Purchase Price

The first and the foremost aspect to be considered while evaluating the financial consequences of a merger deal is the value of the target firm to be paid by the acquiring firm. This is called 'purchase price' or purchase consideration. Several factors are considered for this purpose. The most important of these are tangible and intangible assets of the target firm, net market/realisable value of the assets, earnings of the firm, etc. A comprehensive and analytical study of the combined effects of these factors. is to be done to determine the value of the firm.

Several approaches are used for determining the value of the target firm. They are as follows:

1. Assets approach: According to the 'assets approach', the value of the target firm is determined on the basis of the value of tangible and intangible assets of the firm. Where the value is ascertained using the book values, the values of various assets given in the latest balance sheet of the target firm form the basis for valuation. The net worth of the firm is ascertained by subtracting the amount of external liabilities from the total of the book values of all the assets. The value per share of the target firm is then arrived at by dividing the net worth by the number of equity shares. A shortcoming of this approach however is that the book values of the assets represent historical value which do not reflect the current costs.

The value of the target firm may also be arrived at by considering the net realisable market value of tangible and intangible assets of the target firm. The net worth of the firm is ascertained by subtracting the amount of external liabilities from the total of the net realisable market value of all the assets. The value per share of the target firm is then arrived at by dividing the net worth by the number of equity shares. This type of valuation is considered more realistic and therefore, acceptable to both the parties to a merger deal.

2. Earnings approach: Under the earnings approach, the value of the target firm is determined on the basis of its earnings capacity. For this purpose, the expected future profits of the target firm are considered. These profits are to be adjusted for non-cash items and present values. The total of such present value of profits is divided by the number of shares to arrive at the value per share at which the acquiring firm pays to the shareholders of the target firm.

3. Cash flow approach: Under this approach, the maximum purchase price payable by the acquiring firm is arrived at using the expected future cash flows of the target firm. For this purpose, NPV method is used. Accordingly, the value of the target firm is equal to sum of the present value of all cash inflows arising from synergistic effect and the present value of liabilities that are taken over by the acquiring firm. The drawback of this method is that it is difficult to estimate the future cash flows and to determine the appropriate discount rate.

3.1.3 Economics of Mergers

The major economic advantages of merger are (1) economies of scale, (2) synergy, (3) fast growth, (4) tax benefits, and (5) diversification

1. **Economies of scale:** In operational terms the real economies may arise from (i) production activities of the firm, (ii) R&D and technological activities, (iii) synergy effects, (iv) marketing and distribution activities, (v) transport, storage and inventories and (vi) managerial economies.
2. **Synergy:** Synergy results from the complimentary activities, for example one of the firms has manufacturing expertise while other will have marketing expertise.

3. **Fast Growth:** Merger increases the growth rate due availability of more resources and expertise.
4. **Tax Benefits:** Many a time tax benefit is one of motives of merger decision. Because our tax laws allows set off and carry forward losses and hence a firm saddled with large carry forward losses prefers to merge with a firm having sufficient current earnings. In operational term, losses of the target firm are getting set off against the profit of the acquiring firm.

Step wise procedure for merger/ amalgamation:

The merger involves following steps:
1. Determine the firm's value
2. Financial technique in merger.
3. Analysis of the merger as a capital budgeting decision.

1. Determination of Firm's Value:

Firm's value is decided on the basis of several quantitative variables such as value of assets, earnings of the firm. This includes book value, appraisal value, market value and earnings per share. A book value is the value of owner's equity determined by dividing net worth by the outstanding equity shares. Whereas appraisal value is the value acquired from an independent appraisal agency. Market value is reflected in stock market quotation. Earnings per share focuses whether acquisition will have positive impact on EPS (Earning Per share) after the merger or it will have effect of diluting the EPS, since future EPS will affect the firms' share price.

2. Financial Technique:

Once the value of the firm is decided, the next step is a choice of method of payment of acquired firm. The choice of financial instruments and techniques of acquiring a firm usually have an effect on purchasing agreement. Payment may take the form of either cash or security i.e. ordinary shares, convertible security, deferred payment plan and tender offers.

3. Merger as a Capital Budgeting Decision:

A merger should be evaluated as a capital budgeting decision. The target firm should be valued in terms of potential to generate incremental future cash flows plus non cash expenses such as depreciation and amortisation less additional investment expected to be made in long term assets and working capital of the acquired firm. These cash flows are to be discounted at an appropriate rate that reflects riskiness of a target firm's business. This involves (1) determining incremental projected free cash flows (2) determination of terminal value (3) determination of appropriate discounted / cost of capital (4) determination of NPV (Net present value) of projected free cash flows (5) determination of cost of acquisition.

Hostile Merger:

A merger transaction not supported by the target firm's management, forcing the acquiring company to try to gain control of the firm by buying shares in the marketplace.

Strategies adopted for Hostile Takeover:

The acquirer company may use any of the following strategies for takeover of the target company.

Aggressive Strategies to be adopted by the acquirer Company:

1. **Street sweep:** This technique requires that the acquirer should accumulate large amount of stock in a company before making an open offer. The advantage of this strategy is that the target firm is left with no alternative but to give in.
2. **Bear Hug:** In this strategy, the acquirer puts pressure on the management of target Company by threatening to make an open offer forcing the target Company to agree for the settlement with acquirer for a change of control.
3. **Strategic alliance:** This strategy involves disarming in the target company by offering a partnership rather than buyer.
4. **Brand power:** This implies entering into an alliance with power full brand to displace the partner's branch and as a result buy out weakened company.

Defensive Strategies to be adopted by the Target Company:

1. **Divestiture:** Strategy whereby target company arranges to divest or spin off some of its businesses in the form of an independent, subsidiary company thus reducing the attractiveness of the existing business to the predator.
2. **Crown jewels:** Strategy whereby the target company arranges to sell its crown jewels (highly profitable arm) in order to dissuade the predator.
3. **Golden parachutes:** Strategy adopted by the target company by offering hefty compensations to its managers if they manage to get ousted due to takeover, this is pursued to reduce their resistance to takeover.
4. Poison pill: This strategy involves issue of low price preference shares to existing share holders to enlarge the capital base. This would make hostile takeover more expensive.
5. **Poison put:** In this strategy target company can issue bond that encourage holders to cash in high price. The resultant cash drainage would make the target unattractive.
6. **Greenmail:** In this strategy target company should repurchase the shares corner by the raider. The profit made by the raider is after all akin to blackmail and this will keep the raider at a distance from target Company.
7. **Pac-man Decision:** This strategy aims as the target Company making a counter bid for the raider company.

8. **White knight:** In order to repel the move of raider, the target Company can make an appeal to friendly company to buy the whole or part of the Company with the understanding that the friendly company promises not to dislodge the management of the target Company.

9. **White squire:** This strategy is similar to that of White knight and involve to sale the share to a company which is not interested in take over consequently the management of target Company remains intact.

SEBI Substantial Acquisition of Shares and Takeover Code (SEBI Takeover Code)
SEBI (Substantial Acquisition of Shares and Takeovers) Regulations, 2011

The "SEBI" had been mulling over reviewing and amending the existing SEBI (Substantial Acquisition of Shares and Takeovers) Regulations, 1997 ("Takeover Code of 1997") for quite some time now. A Takeover Regulations Advisory Committee was constituted under the chairmanship of Mr. C. Achuthan ("Achuthan Committee") in September 2009 to review the Takeover Code of 1997 and give its suggestions. Based on Achuthan Committee report the SEBI finally notified the SEBI (Substantial Acquisition of Shares and Takeovers) Regulations, 2011 ("Takeover Code of 2011") on 23 September 2011. The Takeover Code of 2011 will be effective from 22 October, 2011.

The Takeover Code of 2011 adheres to the framework and principles of the Takeover Code of 1997 but the changes it brings about are significant. Some of the most important amendments are discussed below:

1. **Initial threshold limit for triggering of an open offer:**

   Under the Takeover Code of 1997, an acquirer was mandated to make an open offer if he, alone or through persons acting in concert, were acquiring 15% or more of voting right in the target company. This threshold of 15% has been increased to 25% under the Takeover Code of 2011.

   Therefore, now the strategic investors, including private equity funds and minority foreign investors, will be able to increase their shareholding in listed companies up to 24.99% and will have greater say in the management of the company. An acquirer holding 24.99% shares will have a better chance to block any decision of the company which requires a special resolution to be passed. The promoters of listed companies with low shareholding will undoubtedly be concerned about any acquirer misutilising it.

   However, at the same time, this will help the listed companies to get more investments without triggering the open offer requirement as early as 15%, therefore making the process more attractive and cost effective.

2. Creeping acquisition:

The Takeover Code of 1997 recognised creeping acquisition at two levels – from 15% to 55% and from 55% to the maximum permissible limit of 75%. Acquirers holding from 15% to 55% shares were allowed to purchase additional shares or voting rights of up to 5% per financial year without making a public announcement of an open offer. Acquirers holding from 55% to 75% shares were required to make such public announcement for any additional purchase of shares. However, in the latter case, up to 5% additional shares could be purchased without making a public announcement if the acquisition was made through open market purchase on stock exchanges or due to buyback of shares by the listed company.

The Takeover Code of 2011 makes the position simpler. Now, any acquirer, holding more 25% or more but less than the maximum permissible limit, can purchase additional shares or voting rights of up to 5% every financial year, without requiring to make a public announcement for open offer. The Takeover Code of 2011 also lays down the manner of determination of the quantum of acquisition of such additional voting rights.

This would be beneficial for the investors as well as the promoters, and more so for the latter, who can increase their shareholding in the company without necessarily purchasing shares from the stock market.

3. Indirect Acquisition

The Takeover Code of 2011 clearly lays down a structure to deal with indirect acquisition, an issue which was not adequately dealt with in the earlier version of the Takeover Code. Simplistically put, it states that any acquisition of share or control over a company that would enable a person and persons acting in concert with him to exercise such percentage of voting rights or control over the company which would have otherwise necessitated a public announcement for open offer, shall be considered an indirect acquisition of voting rights or control of the company.

It also states that wherever,

(a) The proportionate net asset value of the target company as a percentage of the consolidated net asset value of the entity or business being acquired;

(b) The proportionate sales turnover of the target company as a percentage of the consolidated sales turnover of the entity or business being acquired; or

(c) The proportionate market capitalisation of the target company as a percentage of the enterprise value for the entity or business being acquired;

is more than 80% on the basis of the latest audited annual financial statements, such indirect acquisition shall be regarded as a direct acquisition of the target company and all the obligations relating to timing, pricing and other compliance requirements for the open offer would be same as that of a direct acquisition.

4. Voluntary offer:

A concept of voluntary offer has been introduced in the Takeover Code of 2011, by which an acquirer who holds more than 25% but less than the maximum permissible limit, shall be entitled to voluntarily make a public announcement of an open offer for acquiring additional shares subject to their aggregate shareholding after completion of the open offer not exceeding the maximum permissible non-public shareholding. Such voluntary offer would be for acquisition of at least such number of shares as would entitle the acquirer to exercise an additional 10% of the total shares of the target company.

This would facilitate the substantial shareholders and promoters to consolidate their shareholding in a company.

5. Size of the open offer:

The Takeover Code of 1997 required an acquirer, obligated to make an open offer, to offer for a minimum of 20% of the 'voting capital of the target company' as on 'expiration of 15 days after the closure of the public offer'. The Takeover Code of 2011 now mandates an acquirer to place an offer for at least 26% of the 'total shares of the target company', as on the '10th working day from the closure of the tendering period'.

The increase in the size of the open offer from 20% to 26%, along with increase in the initial threshold from 15% to 25%, creates a unique situation under the Takeover Code of 2011. An acquirer with 15% shareholding and increasing it by another 20% through an open offer would have only got a 35% shareholding in the target company under the Takeover Code of 1997. However, now an acquirer with a 25% shareholding and increasing it by another 26% through the open offer under the Takeover Code of 2011, can accrue 51% shareholding and thereby attain simple majority in the target company.

These well thought out figures clearly shows the intention of the regulator to incentivise investors acquiring stakes in a company by giving them an opportunity of attaining simple majority in a company.

6. Important exemptions from the requirement of open offer

Inter-se transfer: The Takeover Code of 1997 used to recognise inter-se transfer of shares amongst the following groups:

(a) group coming within the definition of group as defined in the Monopolies and Restrictive Trade Practices Act, 1969

(b) relatives within the meaning of section 6 of the Companies Act, 1956.

(c) Qualifying Indian promoters and foreign collaborators who are shareholders, etc.

The catagorisation of such groups have been amended in the Takeover Code of 2011 and transfer between the following qualifying persons has been termed as inter-se transfer:

(a) Immediate relatives

(b) Promoters, as evidenced by the shareholding pattern filed by the target company not less than 3 years prior to the proposed acquisition;

(c) a company, its subsidiaries, its holding company, other subsidiaries of such holding company, persons holding not less than 50% of the equity shares of such company, etc.

(d) persons acting in concert for not less than 3 years prior to the proposed acquisition, and disclosed as such pursuant to filings under the listing agreement.

To avail exemption from the requirements of open offer under the Takeover Code of 2011, the following conditions will have to be fulfilled with respect to an inter-se transfer:

- If the shares of the target company are frequently traded – the acquisition price per share shall not be higher by more than 25% of the volume-weighted average market price for a period of 60 trading days preceding the date of issuance of notice for such inter-se transfer.
- If the shares of the target company are infrequently traded, the acquisition price shall not be higher by more than 25% of the price determined by taking into account valuation parameters including, book value, comparable trading multiples, etc.

7. **Rights issue:**

The Takeover Code of 2011 continues to provide exemption from the requirement of open offer to increase in shareholding due to rights issue, but subject to fulfillment of two conditions:

(a) The acquirer cannot renounce its entitlements under such rights issue; and

(b) The price at which rights issue is made cannot be higher than the price of the target company prior to such rights issue.

Scheme of arrangement: The Takeover Code of 1997 had a blanket exemption on the requirement of making an open offer during acquisition of shares or control through a scheme of arrangement or reconstruction. However, the Takeover Code of 2011 makes a distinction between where the target company itself is a transferor or a transferee company in such a scheme and where the target company itself is not a party to the scheme but is getting affected nevertheless due to involvement of the parent shareholders of the target company. In the latter case, exemption from the requirement of making an open offer would only be provided if

(a) the cash component is 25% or less of the total consideration paid under the scheme, and

(b) post restructuring, the persons holding the entire voting rights before the scheme will have to continue to hold 33% or more voting rights of the combined entity.

8. Buyback of shares:

The Takeover Code of 1997 did not provide for any exemption for increase in voting rights of a shareholder due to buybacks. The Takeover Code of 2011 however provides for exemption for such increase.

In a situation where the acquirer's initial shareholding was less than 25% and exceeded the 25% threshold, thereby necessitating an open offer, as a consequence of the buyback, The Takeover Code of 2011 provides a period of 90 days during which the acquirer may dilute his stake below 25% without requiring an open offer.

Whereas, an acquirer's initial shareholding was more than 25% and the increase in shareholding due to buyback is beyond the permissible creeping acquisition limit of 5% per financial year, the acquirer can still get an exemption from making an open offer, subject to the following:

(a) such an acquirer had not voted in favour of the resolution authorising the buy-back of securities under section 77A of the Companies Act, 1956;

(b) in the case of a shareholder resolution, voting was by way of postal ballot;

(c) the increase in voting rights did not result in an acquisition of control by such acquirer over the target company

In case the above conditions are not fulfilled, the acquirer may, within 90 days from the date of increase, dilute his stake so that his voting rights fall below the threshold which would require an open offer.

9. Other important changes:

Following are few other important amendments that have been brought about in the Takeover Code of 2011:

(a) Definition of 'share': The Takeover Code of 1997 excluded 'preference shares' from the definition of 'shares' vide an amendment of 2002. However, this exclusion has been removed in the Takeover Code of 2011 and therefore now 'shares' would include, without any restriction, any security which entitles the holder to voting rights.

(b) Non-compete fees: As per the Takeover Code of 1997, any payment made to the promoters of a target company up to a maximum limit of 25% of the offer price was exempted from being taken into account while calculating the offer price. However, as per the Takeover Code of 2011, price paid for shares of a company shall include any price for the shares / voting rights / control over the company, whether stated in the agreement or any incidental agreement, and includes 'control premium', 'non-compete fees', etc.

(c) Responsibility of the board of directors and independent directors: The general obligations of the board of directors of a target company under the Takeover Code of 1997 had given a discretionary option to the board to send their recommendations on the open offer to the shareholders and for the purpose the board could seek the opinion of an independent merchant banker or a committee of independent directors.

The Takeover Code of 2011, however, makes it mandatory for the board of directors of the target company to constitute a committee of independent directors (who are entitled to seek external professional advice on the same) to provide written reasoned recommendations on such open offer, which the target company is required to publish.

Conclusion:

The Takeover Code of 2011 is a timely and progressive regulation that would facilitate investments and attract investors. Even though SEBI has not implemented all the suggestions of the Achuthan Committee, it has still taken into consideration some of the major issues that had been plaguing the industry till now. It has tried to maintain a balance between the concerns of the investors as well as that of the promoters.

Methods of Financing :

Mergers are generally differentiated from acquisitions partly by the way in which they are financed and partly by the relative size of the companies. Various methods of financing an Mergers & Acquisition deals exist:

1. **Payment by cash:** Such transactions are usually termed acquisitions rather than mergers because the shareholders of the target company are removed from the picture and the target comes under the (indirect) control of the bidder's shareholders alone.

    A cash deal would make more sense during a downward trend in the interest rates. Another advantage of using cash for an acquisition is that there tends to be lesser chances of EPS dilution for the acquiring company. But a caveat in using cash is that it places constraints on the cash flow of the company.

2. **Ordinary Shares/Equity share Financing or exchange of shares:** It is one of the most commonly used methods of financing mergers. Under this method shareholders of the acquired company are given shares of the acquiring company. It results into sharing of benefits and earnings of merger between the shareholders of the acquired companies and the acquiring company. The determination of a rational exchange ratio is the most important factor in this form of financing merger. The actual net benefit to the shareholders of the two companies depends upon the exchange ratio and the price earning ratio of the companies. Usually, it is an ideal method of financing a merger in case of price earning ratio of the acquiring company is comparatively high as compared to that of the acquired company.

3. **Debt and Preference Share Financing:** A company may also finance a merger through issue of fixed instruct bearing convertible debentures and convertible preference share being a fixed rate of dividend. The shareholders of the acquired company sometimes prefer such a mode of payment because of security of income

along with an option of conversion into equity within a stated period. The acquiring company is also benefitted on account of lesser or on dilution of earnings per share as well as voting/ controlling power of its existing shareholders.

4. **Deferred Payment or earn- out plan:** Deferred payments also known as earn –out plan is a method of making payments to the target firm which is being acquired in such a manner that only a part of the payment is made initially either in cash or securities. In addition to the initial payment, the acquiring company undertakes to make additional payments in future years if it is able to increase the earning after the merger or acquisition. It is known as earn out plan because the future payments are linked with the firm's future earnings. This method helps the acquiring company to negotiate successfully with Target Company and also help in increasing the earning per share because of lesser number of shares being issued in the initial years. However, to make it successful, the acquiring company should be prepared to co-operate towards the growth and success of the target firm.

5. **Leverage buy-out:** A merger of a company which is substantially financed through debt is known as leveraged buy-out.

   Debt, usually, forms more than 70% of the purchase price. The shares of such a firm are concentrated in the hands of a few investors and are not generally, traded in the stock, exchange. It is known as leveraged buy –out because of the leverage provided by debt source of financing over equity. A leveraged buy-out is also called management buy-out (MBO). However, a leveraged buy-out may be possible only in case of a financially sound acquiring company which is viewed by the lenders as risk free.

6. **Tender offer:** Under this method, the purchaser, who has acquisitioned some company, approaches the shareholders of the target firm directly and offers them a price (which is usually more than the market price) to encourage them sell their shares to them. It is a method that results into hostile or forced take over. The management of the target firm may also tender a counter offer at still a higher price to avoid the takeover. It may also educate the shareholders by informing them that the acquisition offer is not in the interest of the shareholders in the long run.

7. **Hybrids:** An acquisition can involve a combination of cash and debt or of cash and stock of the purchasing entity.

3.2 Buy Back of Shares

The Provisions regulating buy back of shares are contained in Section 77A, 77AA and 77B of the companies Act, 1956. These were inserted by the Companies (Amendment) Act, 1999. The securities and exchange Board of India (SEBI) framed the SEBI (Buy Back of securities) Regulations 1999 and the Department of Company Affairs framed the Private Limited

Company and Unlisted Public company (Buy back of Securities) rules, 1999, pursuant to section 77A(2)(F) and (g) respectively.

Objectives of Buy Back: Shares may be bought back by the company on account of one or more of the following reasons

1. To increase the promoter's holding
2. Increase earnings per share
3. Rationalise the capital structure by writing off capital not represented by available assets.
4. Support share value
5. To thwart takeover bid
6. To pay surplus cash not required by business

In fact the best strategy to maintain the share price in a bear run is to buy-back the shares from the open market at premium over the prevailing market price.

Resources of Buy Back:

A company can purchase its own shares from

1. Free reserves; where a company purchases its own shares out of free reserves, then a sum equal to the nominal value of the share so purchased shall be transferred to the capital redemption reserve and details of such transfer shall be disclosed in the balance-sheet or
2. Securities premium account; or
3. Proceeds of any shares or other specified securities. A company cannot buy back its shares or other specified securities out of the proceeds of an earlier issue of the same kind of shares or specified securities.

Conditions of buy back:

1. The buyback is authorised by the Articles of Association of the company.
2. A special resolution has been passed in the general meeting of the company authorising the buy-back. In the case of a listed company, this approval is required by means of a postal ballot. Also, the shares for buy back should be free from lock in period/non transferability. The buy-back can be made by a Board resolution if the quantity of buy-back is or less than ten percent of the paid up capital and free reserves.
3. The buy-back is of less than twenty-five per cent of the total paid-up capital and fee reserves of the company and that the buy-back of equity shares in any financial year shall not exceed twenty-five per cent of its total paid-up equity capital in that financial year.

4. The ratio of the debt owed by the company is not more than twice the capital and its free reserves after such buy-back

5. There has been no default in any of the following
   (a) In repayment of deposit or interest payable there on
   (b) Redemption of debentures, or preference shares or
   (c) Payment of dividend, if declared, to all shareholders within the stipulated time of days from the date of declaration of dividend
   (d) Repayment of any term loan or interest payable thereon to any financial institution or bank.

6. There has been no default in complying with the provisions of filing of annual return, payment of dividend, and form and contents of annual accounts.

7. All the shares or other specified securities for buy-back are fully paid-up.

8. The buy-back of the shares or other specified securities listed on any recognised stock exchange shall be in accordance with the regulations made by the securities and exchange board of India in this behalf.

9. The buy-back in respect of shares or other specified securities of private and closely held companies is in accordance with the guidelines as may be prescribed.

Disclosures in the Explanatory Statement:

The notice of the meeting at which special resolution is proposed to be passed shall be accompanied by an explanatory statement stating –

1. A full and complete disclosure of all material fact
2. The necessity for the buy-back
3. The class of security intended to be purchased under the buy-back
4. The amount to be invested under the buy-back
5. The time-limit for completion of buy-back

Sources from where the shares will be purchased:

The securities can be bought buy from

1. Existing security-holders on a proportionate basis buy-back of shares may be made by a tender offer through a letter of offer from the holders of shares of the company or
2. The open market through
   (i) Book building process
   (ii) Stock exchanges

3. Odd lots, that is to say, where the lot of securities of a public company, whose shares are listed on a recognised stock exchange, is smaller than such marketable lot, as may be specified by the stock exchange
4. Purchasing the securities issued to employees of the company pursuant to a scheme of stock option or sweat equity.

Filing of Declaration of Solvency:

After the passing of resolution but before making buy-back, file with the registrar and the securities and exchange Board of India, a declaration of solvency in form 4A. The declaration must be verified by an affidavit to the effect that the Board has made a full inquiry into the affairs of the company as a result of which they have formed an opinion that it is capable of meeting its liabilities and will not be rendered insolvent within a period of one year of the date of declaration adopted by the board, and signed by at least two directors of the company, one of whom shall be the managing director, if any.

No declaration of solvency shall be filed with the securities and exchange board of India by a company whose shares are not listed on any recognised stock exchange.

Register of Securities Bought Back:

After completion of buy-back, a company shall maintain a register of the securities/shares so bought and enter therein the following particulars:
1. The consideration paid for the securities bought-back
2. The date of cancellation of securities
3. The date of extinguishing and physically destroying of securities and
4. Such other particulars as may be prescribed

Where companies buy-back its own securities, it shall extinguish and physically destroy the securities so bought-back within seven days of the last date of completion of buy-back

Issue of Further Shares after Buy-back:

Every buy-back shall be completed within twelve months from the date of passing the special resolution or board resolution as the provisions regulating buy-back of shares are contained in section

A company which has bought back any security cannot make any issue of the same kind of securities in any manner whether by way of public issue, rights issue up to six months from the date of completion of buy-back.

Filling of Return with the Regulator:

A company shall, after the completion of the buy-back file with the registrar and the securities and exchange Board of India, a return in form 4 c containing such particulars relating to the buy-back within thirty days of such completion.

No return shall be filed with the securities and exchange Board of India by an unlisted Company.

Prohibition of Buy-Back:

A company shall not directly or indirectly purchase its own shares or other specified securities

1. Through any subsidiary company including its own subsidiary companies
2. Through any investment company or group of investment companies

Procedure for Buy Back

1. Where a company proposes to buy-back its shares, it shall, after passing of the special/board resolution make a public announcement in at least one English National Daily, one Hindi National daily and Regional Language Daily at he place where the registered office of the company is situated.
2. The public announcement shall specify a date, which shall be "specified date" for the purpose of determining the names of shareholders to whom the letter of offer has to be sent.
3. A public notice shall be given containing disclosures as specified in schedule of the SEBI regulations.
4. A draft letter of the offer shall be filed with SEBI through a merchant banker. The letter of offer shall then be dispatched to the members of the company.
5. A copy of the board resolution authorising the buy-back shall be filed with the SEBI and stock exchanges.
6. The date of opening of the offer shall not be earlier than seven days or later than 30 days after the specified date.
7. The buy-back offer shall remain open for a period of not less than 15 days and not more than 30 days
8. A company opting for buy-back through the public offer or tender offer shall open an escrow account.

Penalty:

If a company makes default in complying with the provisions the company or any officer of the company who is in default shall be punishable with imprisonment for a term which may extend to two years, or with fine which may extend to fifty thousand rupees, with both. The offences are, of course compoundable under section 621A of the companies Act, 1956.

3.3 Delisting of Shares

Delisting refers to removing the listed securities of a company from the stock market. As per the SEBI Delisting Guidelines of Equity Shares, 2009, delisting can be of two types: "voluntary delisting: or "involuntary delisting/compulsory delisting.

1. **Voluntary Delisting and Economic Implications**

   Voluntary delisting refers to the company delisting its shares from the stock market on its own accord. It is typically done in case of economic losses incurred by the company. If the cost of enlisting exceeds the incurring losses, or where its securities are infrequently traded, the company would choose to delist its securities. Conversely, if the company is making huge profits then it could choose to remove its listing to consolidate its funds, rather than disperse it over the investors. Although it might seem unfair to the investors that they are losing out of profitable securities, it would be problematic to put barriers to the exit of firms (which might even lead to few firms listing in the stock exchange. In case of delisting, the Company is always given a fair hearing before proceeding with the formalities. There are certain guidelines for voluntary delisting. Firstly, the Company promoter is required to make the announcement for such an exit in a public hearing. The time frame and method of exit must be mentioned. Second, such delisting can proceed only if the decision has been approved by the investors. A postal ballot system has been formulated whereby the votes for such delisting must be more than twice the number of votes against delisting. Third, a mandatory exit price has to be given to the investors. This exit price strangely has to be paid by the promoter, not the Company. Thus, the 2009 Guidelines have strictly looked after the interests of the investors. It is clear that the consensus of the public is of essence. Moreover, the law penalizes the promoter for the delisting. Thus, while the company gets the profits, the loss of delisting has to be suffered by the promoter. This seems harsh and unfair.

2. **Compulsory Delisting And Economic Implications**

   Compulsory delisting happens usually in two types of scenarios:

   (a) The first scenario relates to the relationship of the stock exchange with listed companies. When certain rules are not adhered, the company is mandatorily delisted. For example, Schedule III of the Listing Agreement of the National Stock Exchange (NSE) codifies rules regarding the payment of listing fees to the exchange. If payment is not made to the stock exchange, it has no financial consideration to list the company. The listing fees is a major source of income for the Stock Exchanges. It would be costly for them to continue to list securities of such companies. Also, there is a requirement for a "minimum trading level" in the Schedule III of the SEBI Guidelines. It is submitted that delisting for the breach of such rules is economically justified for the stock exchange: the operation of the securities market must not result in a loss to the stock exchange.

   (b) The second kind of scenario relates to information disclosure by listed companies. Companies can get delisted when the rules regarding information disclosure is not adhered to. This is important as the aim of the secondary market is to ensure that material information is disclosed to the securities-holder, to enhance efficiency of the market.

The limitation period given to an aggrieved party for filing a suit in case of compulsory delisting is 15 days. This may be extended to a month, anyone can file a suit- the Company itself or even its investors. Also, an independent valuer values the fair price of shares in case of compulsory delisting. It is therefore seen that ample opportunity is given to the investors to claim against compulsory delisting. However, the interests of the stock exchange seem to be the primary aim of compulsory delisting.

3. Conclusion

There is a penalty of maximum ₹ 25 crores and/or a year of imprisonment, for violation of rules for listing and delisting procedures. Although some companies can afford such a loss, it seems like a deterrent factor to the players of the market. The process of listing securities is intended towards boosting trade volume in the securities market than removing its imperfections. This is particularly true in the case of voluntary delisting wherein the loss making companies can delist itselves to plug in further losses. However, investor protection in this area must be ensured to prevent companies from taking undue advantage and indulging in unfair practices. The practice of compulsory delisting also seems viable which protects the interests of the exchange itself and the investors in question. As a result, it is concluded that the SEBI Guidelines seem to strike a balance between investor sentiments and company regulation.

3.4 Issue of Debentures

3.4.1 SEBI Guidelines for Debentures

Debentures

A debenture is a document which either creates a debt or acknowledges it. Debenture issued by a company is in the form of a certificate acknowledging indebtedness. The debentures are issued under the Company's Common Seal. Debentures are one of a series issued to a number of lenders. The date of repayment is specified in the debentures. Debentures are issued against a charge on the assets of the Company. Debentures holders have no right to vote at the meetings of the companies.

Kinds of Debentures

    1. Bearer Debentures: They are registered and are payable to the bearer. They are negotiable instruments and are transferable by delivery.

    2. Registered Debentures: They are payable to the registered holder whose name appears both on the debentures and in the Register of Debenture Holders maintained by the company. Registered Debentures can be transferred but have to be registered again. Registered Debentures are not negotiable instruments. A registered debenture contains a commitment to pay the principal sum and interest. It also has a description of the charge and a statement that it is issued, subject to the conditions endorsed therein.

3. Secured Debentures: Debentures which create a change on the assets of the company which may be fixed or floating are known as secured Debentures. The term "bonds" and "debentures"(secured) are used interchangeably in common parlance. In USA, Bond is a long term contract which is secured, whereas a debentures is an unsecured one.

4. Unsecured or Naked Debentures: Debentures which are issued without any charge on assets are insecured or naked debentures. The holders are like unsecured creditors and may see the company for the recovery of debt.

5. Redeemable Debentures: Normally debentures are issued on the condition that they shall be redeemed after a certain period. They can however, be reissued after redemption.

6. Perpetual Debentures: When debentures are irredeemable they are called perpetual. Perpetual Debentures cannot be issued in India at present.

7. Convertible Debentures: If an option is given to convert debentures into equity shares at the stated rate of exchange after a specified period, they are called convertible debentures. Convertible Debentures have become very popular in India. On conversion, the holders cease to be lenders and become owners.

Debentures are usually issued in a series with a pari passu (at the same rate) clause which entitles them to be discharged rateably though issued at different times. New series of debentures cannot rank pari passu with the old series unless the old series provides so.

New debt instruments issued by public limited companies are participating debentures, convertible debentures with options, third party convertible debentures convertible debentures redeemable at premiums, debt equity swaps and zero coupon convertible notes. These are discussed below.

8. Participating Debentures: They are unsecured corporate debt securities which participate in the profits of the company. They might find investors if issued by existing dividend paying companies.

9. Convertible Debentures with options: They are a derivative of convertible debentures with an embedded option, providing flexibility to the issuer as well as the investor to exit from the terms of the issue. The coupon rate is specified at the time of issue.

10. Third Party Convertible Debentures: They are debt with a warrant allowing the investor to subscribe to the equity of third firm at a preferential price visa vis the market price. Interest rate on third party convertible debentures is lower than pure debt on account of the conversion option.

11. Convertible-Debentures Redeemable at a Premium: Convertible Debentures are issued at face value with 'an option entitling investors to sell the bond to the issuer at a premium. They are basically similar to convertible debentures but embody less risk.

12. Debt-Equity Swaps: Debt-Equity Swaps are an offer from an issuer of debt to swap it for equity. The instrument is quite risky for the investor because the anticipated capital appreciation may not materialise.

13. Deep discount Bonds: They are designed to meet the long term funds requirements of the issuer and investors who are not looking for immediate return and can be sold with a long maturity of 25-30 years at a deep discount on the face value of debentures. IDBI deep discount bonds for ₹ 1 lakh repayable after 25 years were sold at a discount price of ₹ 2,700.

14. Zero-Coupon Convertible Note: A zero-coupon convertible note can be converted into shares. If choice is exercised investors forego all accured and unpaid interest. The zero-coupon convertible notes are quite sensitive to changes in interest rates.

15. Secured Premium Notes (SPN) with Detachable Warrants: SPN which is issued along with a detachable warrant, is redeemable after a notice period, say four to seven years. The warrants attached to it ensures the holder the right to apply and get allotted equity shares; provided the SPN is fully paid.

There is a lock-in period for SPN during which no interest will be paid for an invested amount. The SPN holder has an option to sell back the SPN to the company at par value after the lock in period. If the holder exercises this option, no interest/ premium will be paid on redemption. In case the SPN holder holds its further, the holder wili be repaid the principal amount along with the additional amount of interest/ premium on redemption in instalments as decided by the company. The conversion of detachable warrants into equity shares will have to be done within the time limit notified by the company.

16. Floating Rate Bonds: The rate on the floating Rate Bond is linked to a benchmark interest rate like the prime rate in USA or LIBOR in eurocurrency market. The State Bank of India's floating rate bond was linked to maximum interest on term deposits which was 10 percent. Floating rate is quoted in terms of a margin above or below the bench mark rate. The-floor rate in the State Bank of India case was 12 per cent. Interest rates linked to the bench mark ensure that neither the borrower nor the lender suffer from the changes in interest rates. When rates are fixed, they are likely to be inequitable to the borrower when interest rates fall subsequently, and the same bonds are likely to be inequitable to the lender when interest rates rise subsequently.

Sebi Guidelines

Sebi Guidelines For Debentures

1. **Fully Convertible Debentures (FCD):**

SEBI restricts the conversion period to 36 months. Credit rating is required if the conversion is made after 18 months. Conversion beyond 36 months is permissible only if the conversion is made optional with "put" and "call" option. It may be noted that an option is merely an instrument that gives its owner the right to buy or sell shares of a company within a specified period of time. Options are a derivative instrument which have a beneficial impact all round. They stabilise share price by reducing its volatility and provide a hedge against risk for the investor. They are likely to be popular in this country.

Premium on Conversion of Debentures: Premium on conversion has to be predetermined and stated in the prospectus. The company is free to determine the rate of interest payable.

2. Debenture Redemption Reserve:

In the case of non-convertible debentures, a Debenture Redemption Reserve has to be created. A moratorium upto the date of commercial production is provided for the creation of the Debenture Redemption Reserve in respect of debenture raised for project finance. Debenture Redemption Reserve may be created either in equal instalments or with higher amounts in the remaining period, if profits permit. Companies are allowed to distribute dividends out of general reserves in certain years if the residual profits after transfer to the Debenture Redemption Reserve are inadequate to distribute reasonable dividend. The Debenture. Redemption Reserve will be treated as part of general reserve for consideration of bonus issue proposals and for price fixation related to post-tax return. In the case of new companies, distribution of dividend requires the approval of the trustees to the issue and the lead institution. Debenture redemption can be taken up only after 50 per cent of the amount of the debenture issue is created. Drawal from the Debenture Redemption Reserve is permissible only after 10 per cent of the debenture liability has been actually redeemed by the company. Dividends exceeding 20 per cent cannot be declared by existing companies without the prior permission of the lead institution or as per loan convenants if the cornpany does not-comply with institutional condition regarding interest and debt service coverage ratio. The company is free to redeem debentures in greater number of instalments. The first instalment may start from the fifth instead of the seventh year.

3. Debenture Trustees:

The names of the debenture trustees must be stated in the prospectus. The trust deed should be executed within six months of the close of the issue.

4. Conversion Option:

Any conversion in part or whole of the debenture will be optional at the hands of the debenture holder, if the conversion takes place at or after 18 months from the date of allotment but before 36 months.

5. Nonconvertible Debentures (NCDs) and Partly Convertible Debentures (PCDs) Debentures of less than 18 months duration:

If the maturity period of debentures is less than 18 months, it is not necessary to create a charge or appoint a trustee or create a Debenture Redemption Reserve. If no charge is created on such debentures they are unsecured and are treated as "deposits". The issuer has to comply with the requirements of the Companies (Acceptance of Deposits) Rules, 1975. The offer document should disclose this.

6. Prospectus and PCDs / NCDs:

In the case of PCDs, the premium amount at the time of conversion shall be predetermined and stated in the prospectus. Redemption amount, period of maturity, yield on redemption of PCDs/NCDs shall be indicated in the prospectus. The prospectus should indicate the discount on the non-convertible portion of the PCD in case they are traded and the procedure for their purchase on spot trading basis must be stated in the prospectus.

7. Roll-over of Non-convertible Portion:

Roll-over of non-convertible portion of PCD/NCD with or without change in interest rate can be done only on positive consent and not on passive consent. It is compulsory for companies to give an option to those debentures holders who want to withdraw and encash their debentures. Before roll-over, execution of fresh trust deed for non convertible debenture or non convertible portion of PCD is required. A company has to obtain credit rating six months prior to the date of redemption and communicate it to the debenture holder. A company desirous of roll-over of its NCD or non convertible portion of PCDs has to submit the letter of information containing credit rating, debenture holders resolution, option for conversion and such other items SEBI may prescribe from time to time to SEBI for vetting.

8. Disclosures for issue of Debentures:

The disclosures relating to raising of debentures should include, among others, existing and future debt equity ratios, servicing behaviour on existing debentures, payment of due interest on due dates on term loans and debentures, certificates from a financial institution or banker about their no objection for a second or pari passu charge being created in favour of the trustees to the proposed debevnture issue.

9. Protection of Debenture Holders' Interest:

Trustees to the debenture issue should be vested with requisite powers to protect the interest of debenture holders including a right to appoint a nominee director on the board of the company in consultation with the debenture holders. The progress in respect of debentures raised for project finance / modernisation / expansion / diversification / normal capital expenditure is to be monitored by the lead institution / investment institution. In regard to debentures issued for working capital, the lead bank for the company should do the monitoring. Institutional debenture holder and trustees should obtain a certificate from the company's auditors about the utilisation of funds during the period of implementation of the project.

In the case of debentures for working capital, a certificate has to be obtained at the end of each accounting year. Issues by companies belonging to the groups for replenishing funds or to acquire share holding in other companies is not permitted.

The company issuing debentures has to file with SEBI, certificates from its bankers that the assets on which security is to be created are free from encumbrances and the necessary permission to mortgage the assets have been obtained or a no objection certificate from the financial institution or bank'for a second or pari passu charge in cases where assets are encumbered. The security should be created within six months from the date of issue of the debentures. If the company, for any reason, is not in a position to create a security within 12 months from the date of issue of the debentures, a penal interest of 2 per cent has to be paid to debenture holders. If the security is not created even after 18 months, a meeting of debenture holders should be called within 21 days to explain the reason why, and.the date by which, the security would be created.

The trustees to the Debenture Issue will superwise the implementation of the conditions regarding the creation of security for the debentures, and regarding the Debenture Redemption Reserve.

10. Past Issues of FCDs and PCDs:

In the case of FCDs and PCDs issued in the past where conversion was to be made at a price to be determined by the Controller of Capital Issues at a later date, SEBI has laid down the procedure:- The price of conversion and the time of conversion should be determined bythe company in a duly organised meeting of the debentureholders and shareholders. The decision in the meeting has to be certified by the shareholders Such conversion will be optional. The dissenting shareholders shall have the right to continue as debentureholders if the terms of conversion are not acceptable to them. The letter of option should be vetted by SEBI.

11. New types of Debentures:

New types of Debentures mentioned by SEBI are deep discount bonds, debentures with warrants and secured premium notes. While making an issue of any new financial instrument, the issuer of capital shall make adequate disclosures regarding the terms and conditions, redemptions, security, conversion and any other relevant features of the instruments.

- (a) **Deep discount bonds:** They are designed to meet the long term funds requirements of the issuer and invest who are not looking for immediate return and can be sold with a long maturity of 25-30 years at a deep discount on the face value of debentures. IDBI deep discount bonds for ₹ 1 lakh repayable after 25 years were sold at a discount price of ₹ 2,700.
- (b) **Secured Premium Notes (SPN) with Detachable Warrants:** SPN which is issued along with a detachable warrant, is redeemable after a notice period, say four to

seven years. The warrants attached to it ensures the holder the right to apply and get allotted equity shares; provided the SPN is full paid.

There is a lock-in period for SPN during which no interest will be paid for an invested amount. The SPN holder has an option to sell back the SPN to the company at par value after the lock in period. If the holder exercises this option, no interest/premium will be paid on redemption. In case the SPN holder holds its further, the holder will be repaid the principal amount along with the additional amount of interest/ premium on redemption in instalments as decided by the company. The conversion of detachable warrants into equity shares will have to be done within the time limit notified by the company.

3.5 Portfolio Management Services (PMS)

Meaning

Portfolio is a collection of various assets. In portfolio management, these assets are of financial nature. A Portfolio Manager is a person who invest the money in a diverse assets with the aim of maximise the return and minimising the risk.

According to SEBI, portfolio means holding of securities belonging to one person and portfolio manager means any person who pursuant to a contract with a client undertake the management of portfolio of securities or funds of his client in order –

1. To frame investment strategy and select means of investment.
2. To provide a balance portfolio to hedge against the inflation and also to optimize the returns.
3. To take timely decisions for sale and purchase of securities.
4. To maximise after tax returns by investing part of the portfolio in tax saving instruments.

A portfolio management can also be of institutional nature.

Advantages of portfolio management for individuals:

1. Investment in capital market by an individual is a bit complicated. It is better if the same is handled by a professional.
2. Capital market over a longer period has always given better returns than any other investment options.

Types of Portfolio Management:

1. The Discretionary Portfolio Management Service (DPMS):

In this type of service, the client gives his money to the portfolio manager who handle the paper work, make all investment decisions and tries to give good returns to the investors and charges a fee for the services offered.

2. Non Discretionary Portfolio Management Service:

In this type of service, a portfolio manager act as a councilor and the investor is free to accept or reject his advice. A paper work is also done by portfolio manager for which he charges fee.

Essential for Portfolio Manager:

1. **Analytical ability:** He should have good knowledge and information about the financial market and should be good at predicting the future behavior of the market on the basis of analytical study about the industry and economy.
2. **Knowledge:** He should be well versed about the stock market and other financial market and should have sound general knowledge.
3. **Marketing skill:** He has to be a good salesman.
4. **Experience:** He should be an experienced person in financial market which will help him to take proper decision, based on past experience.

Steps in Portfolio Management:

Portfolio management is an ongoing process and accordingly following steps needs to be taken:

1. Specification and quantification of investor's objective, preference, constraints, risk appetite in the form of policy statement.
2. Determination and quantification of capital market expectation for economy, sector, industries and individual securities.
3. Allocation of assets and selection of individual securities.
4. Periodic performance review and evaluation of the portfolio so as to ensure that investor's objective are attained.
5. Rebalancing of portfolio as and when necessary.

Portfolio manager decisions depend upon investor's characteristics and liquidity need.

SEBI regulations for PMS (Portfolio Management Services):

1. Portfolio manager has to register with SEBI.
2. Must have adequate technology and infrastructure.
3. Must employ at least two people who are professionally qualified and experience to handle the PMS business.
4. The applicant must fulfill capital adequacy norms laid down by SEBI from time to time.
5. Applicant must not be involved in any litigation connected with Capital Market.
6. He must have professional qualification.
7. Applicant must pay registration fee as applicable.

8. Portfolio manager must enter into an agreement with his client clearly defining the inter-se relationship, mutual rights, liability and obligations.
9. Clients fund shall be kept in a separate account and should be maintained in a scheduled commercial bank.
10. He should charge an agreed fee to the client without guaranteeing or assuring either directly or indirectly about the returns and fee should be independent of the returns.
11. He should not accept money or securities from the client for the period less than one year.
12. Portfolio manager should purchase or sell securities separately for each client.

SEBI Code of conduct for the Portfolio Manager:
1. He shall observe high standard of integrity, fairness and transparency in all his business dealings.
2. Client's money should be deployed as early as possible and money due and payable to the Client should be paid forthwith.
3. He shall render at all time, high standards of services, exercise due diligence, ensure proper care and exercise independent professional judgment.
4. Shall not get involved in any unfair practices.
5. Clients information should be kept confidential.
6. Portfolio Manager should not be party to price rigging/ manipulation and passing of prize sensitive information to any participant in the market.

Registration of Portfolio Manager:

Following are the steps involved in the registration of portfolio managers:

Application for Grant of Certificate:

An application by a portfolio manager for grant of a certificate shall be made to the Board in 'Form A'. Any application made by a portfolio manager prior to coming into force of these regulations containing such particulars or as near thereto as mentioned in Form A shall be treated as an application made in pursuance of sub-regulation (1) and dealt with accordingly.

Conformance to Requirements:

Any application, which is not complete in all respects and does not conform to the instructions specified in the form, shall be rejected by the Board. Before rejecting any such application, the applicant shall be given an opportunity to remove within the time specified such objections as may be indicated by the Board.

Furnishing of Further Information, etc.:

The Board may require the applicant to furnish further information or clarification regarding matters relevant to his activity of a portfolio manager for the purposes of disposal of the application. The applicant or its principal officer shall, if so required, appear before the Board for personal representation.

Consideration of Application:

For considering the grant of certificate of registration to the applicant, the Board takes into account all matters which it deems relevant to the activities relating to portfolio management. The Board considers the following in this regard:

1. Whether the applicant is a body corporate.
2. Whether the applicant has the necessary infrastructure like adequate office space, equipments and the manpower to effectively discharge the activities of a portfolio manager.
3. Whether the principal officer of the applicant has the professional qualifications in finance, law, accountancy or business management from an institution recognised by the Government.
4. Whether the applicant has in its employment a minimum of two persons who, between them, have at least five years of experience as portfolio manager or stock broker or investment manager or in the areas related to fund management.
5. Whether any previous application for grant of certificate made by any person directly or indirectly connected with the applicant has been rejected by the Board.
6. Whether any disciplinary action has been taken by the Board against a person directly or indirectly connected with the applicant under the Act or the Rules or the Regulations made thereunder.
7. Whether the applicant fulfills the capital adequacy requirements as specified in regulation 7.
8. Whether the applicant, its director, principal officer or the employee as specified in clause (d) is involved in any litigation connected with the securities market which has an adverse bearing on the business of the applicant.
9. Whether the applicant, its director, principal officer or the employee as specified in clause (d) has at any time been convicted for any offence involving moral turpitude or has been found guilty of any economic offence.
10. Whether the applicant is a fit and proper person.
11. Whether the granting of certificate to the applicant is in the interests of investors.

Capital Adequacy Requirement:

The capital adequacy requirement shall not be less than the net worth of fifty lakhs rupees. For the purposes of this regulation, "net worth" means the "aggregate value of paid up equity capital plus free reserves (excluding reserves created out of revaluation) reduced by the aggregate value of accumulated losses and deferred expenditure not written off, including miscellaneous expenses not written off."

Procedure for Registration:

The Board on being satisfied that the applicant fulfils the requirements as specified, sends an intimation to the applicant and on receipt of the payment of fees as specified in Schedule II, then grants a certificate in 'Form B'.

Renewal of Certificate:

A portfolio manager may, three months before the expiry of the validity of the certificate, make an application for renewal in Form A. The application for renewal is dealt with in the same manner as if it were an application for grant of a certificate made under Regulation 3. The Board on being satisfied that the applicant fulfils the requirements specified in Regulation 6 for renewal of the certificate, grants a certificate in Form B and sends an intimation to the applicant.

Procedure where Registration is not Granted:

Where an application for grant of a certificate under Regulation 3 or of renewal under Regulation 9 does not satisfy the requirements set out in Regulation 6, the Board may reject the application, after giving an opportunity to the applicant of being heard. The refusal to grant registration is communicated by the Board within thirty days of such refusal to the applicant stating therein the grounds on which the application has been rejected.

Any applicant of, who is aggrieved by the decision of the Board, may apply within a period of thirty days from the date of receipt of such intimation, to the Board for reconsideration of its decision. The Board shall reconsider an application made under sub-regulation (3) and communicate its decision as soon as possible in writing to the applicant.

Effect of Refusal to Grant Certificate:

Any portfolio manager whose application for a certificate has been refused by the Board shall, on and from the date of the receipt of the communication under sub-regulation (2) of Regulation 10, cease to carry on any activity as portfolio manager.

Payment of Fees:

Every applicant eligible for grant of a certificate shall pay the required fees in such a manner and within the period as specified in Schedule II. Where a portfolio manager fails to pay the fees as provided Schedule II, the Board may suspend the certificate, whereupon the Portfolio Manager shall cease to carry on the activity as a portfolio manager for the period during which the suspension subsists.

No Person to Act as Portfolio Manager without Certificate:

No person shall carry on any activity as a portfolio manager unless he holds a certificate granted by the Board under these regulations, provided that such a person, who was engaged as portfolio manager, prior to the coming into force of the Act, may continue to carry on activity as portfolio manager, if he has made an application for such registration, till the disposal of such application. Nothing in this rule shall apply in case of a merchant banker holding a certificate granted by the Board under the Securities and Exchange Board of India (Merchant Banker) Regulations, 1992, as category I or category II merchant banker, as the case may be.

A merchant banker acting as a portfolio manager under the second proviso to this rule shall also be bound by the rules and regulations applicable to a portfolio manager.

Conditions for Grant or Renewal of Certificate to Portfolio Manager:

The Board may grant or renew a certificate to a portfolio manager subject to the following conditions:

1. The portfolio manager in case of any change in its status and constitution, shall obtain the prior permission of the Board to carry on its activities.
2. He shall pay the amount of fees for registration or renewal, as the case may be, in the manner provided in the regulations.
3. He shall take adequate steps for redressal of grievances of the clients within one month of the date of the receipt of the complaint and keep the Board informed about the number, nature and other particulars of the complaints received.
4. He shall abide by the rules and regulations made under the Act in respect of the activities carried on by the portfolio manager.

Period of Validity of the Certificate:

The certificate of registration or its renewal, as the case maybe, shall be valid for a period of three years from date of its issue to the portfolio manager.

Duties of Portfolio Manager:

Following are the general obligations of portfolio managers as enunciated by the SEBI:

1. Contract with Clients:

Every portfolio manager shall, before taking up an assignment of management of funds or portfolio of securities, on behalf of a client, enter into an agreement in writing with such client clearly defining the relationship, and setting out their mutual rights, liabilities and obligations relating to management of funds or portfolio of securities containing the details as specified in Schedule IV.

The funds of all clients shall be placed by the portfolio manager in a separate account to be maintained by him in a scheduled commercial bank [Any bank included in the Second Schedule to the Reserve Bank of India Act, 1934 (2 or 1934)].

The portfolio manager shall charge an agreed fee from the client for rendering portfolio management services without guaranteeing or assuring, either directly or indirectly any return and such fee shall be independent the return to the client and shall not be on a return-sharing basis.

The portfolio manager shall not pledge or give on loan securities held on behalf of clients to a third person without obtaining a written permission from his client'. The portfolio manager shall not accept money or securities from his client for a period of less than one year. In the case of placement of funds for portfolio management by the same client on more than one occasion or on a continual basis, each placement shall be for a minimum period of one year.

Notwithstanding anything contained in the agreement between a portfolio manager and his client referred to in regulation 14 hereof, the portfolio funds can be withdrawn or taken back by Portfolio client at his risk before the maturity date of the contract under the following circumstances:

1. Voluntary or compulsory, termination of Portfolio management services by the Portfolio manager;
2. Suspension or termination of registration of Portfolio manager by the Board;
3. Bankruptcy or liquidation in case the portfolio manager is a body corporate; and
4. Permanent disability, lunacy or insolvency in case the portfolio manager is an individual.

The portfolio manager shall not, while dealing with clients funds, indulge in speculative transactions, that is, he shall not enter into any transaction for purchase or sale of any security, which a transaction is periodically or ultimately settled otherwise than by actual delivery or transfer of security.

The portfolio manager may enter into transactions on behalf of a client for the specific purpose of meeting margin requirements only if the contract so provides and the client is made aware of the attendant risks of such transactions.

In the event of any dispute between the portfolio manager and his clients, the client shall have the right to obtain details of his portfolio from the portfolio manager.

2. Disclosures

The portfolio manager shall provide to the client the Disclosure Document as specified in Schedule V, along with a certificate in Form C as specified in Schedule I, at least two days prior to entering into an agreement with the client as referred to in sub-regulation (1). The Disclosure Document shall inter alia contain the following:

1. The quantum and manner of payment of fees payable by the client for each activity for which service is rendered by the portfolio manager directly or indirectly (where such service is outsourced);

2. Portfolio risks;
3. Complete disclosures in respect of transactions with related parties as per the accounting standards specified by the Institute of Chartered Accountants of India in this regard;
4. The performance of the portfolio manager; and
5. The audited financial statements of the portfolio manager for the immediately preceding three years.

The performance of a discretionary portfolio manager shall be evaluated using weighted average method taking each individual category of investments for the immediately preceding three years and in such cases performance indicators shall also be disclosed.

The contents of the Disclosure Document shall be certified by an independent chartered accountant. The portfolio manager shall file with the Board, a copy of the Disclosure Document before it is circulated or issued to any person and every six months thereafter or whenever any material change is effected therein-whichever is earlier, along with the certificate in Form C as specified in Schedule I.

The portfolio manager shall charge an agreed fee from the clients for rendering portfolio management services without guaranteeing or assuring, either directly or indirectly, any return and the fee so charged may be a fixed fee or a return based fee or a combination of both.

The portfolio manager may, subject to the disclosure in terms of the Disclosure Document and specific permission from the client, charge such fees from the client for each activity for which service is rendered by the portfolio manager directly or indirectly (where such service is out sourced).

Responsibilities of Portfolio Manager:

The general responsibilities of a portfolio manager are stated below:

1. **Independent Management:**

The discretionary portfolio manager shall individually and independently manage the funds of each client in accordance with the needs of the client in a manner which does not partake the character of a Mutual Fund, whereas the nondiscretionary portfolio manager shall manage the funds in accordance with the directions of the client.

2. **Fiduciary Position:**

The portfolio manager shall act in a fiduciary capacity with regard to the client's funds. The portfolio manager shall keep the funds of all clients in a separate account to be maintained by it in a Scheduled Commercial Bank [Any bank included in the Second Schedule to the Reserve Bank of India Act, 1934 (2 of 1934)].

3. **Transaction:**

The portfolio manager shall transact in securities within the limitation placed by the client himself with regard to dealing in securities under the provisions of the Reserve Bank of India Act, 1934 (2 of 1934).

4. **No personal Benefit:**

The portfolio manager shall not derive any direct or indirect benefit out of the client's funds or securities. The portfolio manager shall not borrow funds or securities on behalf of the client.

5. **Securities Lending:**

The portfolio manager shall not lend securities held on behalf of clients to a third person except as provided under these regulations.

6. **Handling Complaints:**

The portfolio manager shall ensure proper and timely handling of complaints from his clients and take appropriate action immediately.

Scope of Portfolio Management Services:

Portfolio management is a continuous process. It is a dynamic activity. The following are the basic operations of a portfolio management:

1. Monitoring the performance of portfolio by incorporating the latest market conditions.
2. Identification of the investor's objective, constraints and preferences.
3. Making an evaluation of portfolio income (comparison with targets and achievements)
4. Making revision in the portfolio.
5. Implementation of strategies in tune with the investment objectives.

Contents of Agreement between client and portfolio manager:

The following shall be mentioned in the agreement -

1. Appointment of portfolio manager.
2. Scope of services to be provided by the portfolio manager subject to the activities permitted under SEBI (Portfolio Managers) Regulations, 1993, viz, advisory, investment management, custody of securities, keeping track of corporate benefits associated with the securities. The Portfolio Manager shall act in a fiduciary capacity and as a trustee and agent of the clients' account.
3. Functions, obligations, duties and responsibilities (as discretionary and non discretionary to be given separately) with specific provisions regarding instructions for non discretionary portfolio manager, inter alia -

(a) terms in compliance with the Act, SEBI (Portfolio Managers) Regulations,1993, rules, regulations, guidelines made under the Act and any other laws/rules/ regulations / guidelines etc.;

(b) Providing reports to clients;

(c) Maintenance of client wise transaction and related books of accounts;

(d) provisions regarding audit of accounts as required under the SEBI (Portfolio Managers) Regulations, 1993;

(e) settlement of accounts and procedure therefore including the provisions for payment on maturity or early termination of the contract.

4. Investment objectives and guidelines :

   (a) Types of securities in which investment would be made specifying restrictions, if any.

   (b) Particulars regarding amount, period of management, repayment or withdrawal.

   (c) Taxation aspects such as Tax Deducted at Source etc., if any.

   (d) Condition that the portfolio manager shall not lend the securities of the client unless authorised by him in writing.

5. **Risk Factors:**

   (a) A detailed statement of risks associated with each type of investment including the standard risks associated with each type of investment.

   (b) Risk factors specific to the scheme as well as those attendant to specific investment policies and objectives of the scheme.

6. Period of agreement- minimum period if any, and provision for renewal, if any.

7. Conditions, under which agreement may be altered, terminated and implications thereof, such as settlement of amounts invested, repayment obligations etc. :

   (a) Voluntary/mandatory termination by the portfolio manager;

   (b) Voluntary/mandatory termination by the client;

   (c) Suspension by the Board or other regulatory authority.

8. **Maintenance of Accounts:** Maintenance of accounts separately in the name of the client as are necessary to account for the assets and any additions, income, receipts and disbursements in connection therewith, as provided under SEBI (Portfolio Managers) Regulations, 1993.

9. **Change in the quantum of funds to be managed:** The conditions under which the client may withdraw cash or securities from the portfolio account or bring in additional cash to be managed as per the terms and conditions that apply. The portfolio manager shall not change any terms of the agreement without prior consent of the client.

10. **Access to information: (Subject to the provisions of SEBI (Portfolio Managers) Regulations,1993):** Provisions enabling clients to get the books of accounts of the portfolio manager relating to his transactions audited by a chartered accountant appointed by him and permitting the client an access to relevant and material documents of portfolio manager, provisions listing the documents for inspection along with timings for such inspection, furnishing of reports to the client subject to furnishing atleast once in six months and the reports to be made available on the web site of the portfolio manager with restricted access to each client and other rights of clients etc. The provision that the statements / documents / report furnished by the portfolio manager to the client present a true and fair picture of the actual transactions.

11. **Terms of Fees:** The quantum and manner of payment of fees and charges for each activity for which services are rendered by the portfolio manager directly or indirectly (where such service is outsourced) such as investment management, advisory, transfer, registration and transaction costs with specific references to brokerage costs, custody charges, cost related to furnishing regular communication, account statement, miscellaneous expenses (individual expenses in excess of 5% to be indicated separately) etc. There is a provision that the portfolio manager shall take prior permission from the client in this respect.

12. **Billing:** Periodicity of billing, whether payments to be made in advance, manner of payment of fees, whether setting off against the account etc., type of documents evidencing receipt of payment of fees.

13. **Liability of Portfolio Manager:** Liability of Portfolio Manager in connection with recommendations made to cover errors of judgement, negligence, willful misfeasance in connection with discharge of duties, acts of other intermediaries, brokers, custodians etc.

14. **Liability of client:** Restricting the liability of the client to the extent of his investment.

15. **Death or Disability:** Providing for continuation /termination of the agreement in event of client's death/disability, succession, nomination , representation etc to be incorporated.

16. **Assignment:** Conditions for assignment of the agreement by client.

17. **Governing Law:** The law/jurisdiction of country/state which governs the agreement to be stated.

18. **Settlement of grievances/disputes and provision for arbitration:** (Provisions to cover protection of act done in good faith, risks and losses, redressal of grievances, dispute resolution mechanism, reference for arbitration and the situations under which such rights may arise, may be made).

Reports to be Furnished to Clients

The portfolio manager should furnish periodically a report to the client, agreed in the contract, but not exceeding a period of six months containing the following details:

1. The composition and the value of the portfolio, description of security, number of securities, value of each security held in portfolio, cash balances aggregate value of the portfolio as on the date of report.
2. Transactions undertaken during the period of report including the date of transaction and details of purchases and sales.
3. Beneficial interest received during that period in respect of interest, dividend, bonus shares, rights shares and debentures.
4. Expenses incurred in managing the portfolio of the client and details of risk relating to the securities recommended by the portfolio manager for investment or disinvestments.

3.6 Loan Syndication

Introduction

If a borrower requires a large or sophisticated facility or multiple types of facility this is commonly provided by a group of lenders known as a syndicate under a syndicated loan agreement. A syndicated loan agreement simplifies the borrowing process as the borrower uses one agreement covering the whole group of banks and different types of facility rather than entering into a series of separate bilateral loans, each with different terms and conditions.

3.6.1 Types of Loan Syndications

Two types of loan syndication facilities are viz.

(1) Term loan facilities and (2) Revolving loan facilities.

1. Term Loan Facility: Under a term loan facility the lenders provide a specified capital sum over a set period of time, known as the "term". Typically, the borrower is allowed a short period after executing the loan (the "availability" or "commitment" period), during which time it can draw loans up to a specified maximum facility limit. Repayment may be in installments (in which case the facility is commonly described as "amortising") or there may be one payment at the end of the facility (in which case the facility is commonly described as having "bullet" repayment terms). Once a term loan has been repaid by the borrower, it cannot be re-drawn

2. Revolving Loan Facility: A revolving loan facility provides a borrower with a maximum aggregate amount of capital, available over a specified period of time. However, unlike a term loan, the revolving loan facility allows the borrower to drawdown, repay and re-draw loans advanced to it out of the available capital during the term of the facility.

Each loan is borrowed for a set period of time, usually one, three or six months, after which time it is technically repayable. Repayment of a revolving loan is achieved either by scheduled reductions in the total amount of the facility over time, or by all outstanding loans being repaid on the date of termination. A revolving loan made to refinance another revolving loan which matures on the same date as the drawing of the second revolving loan is known as a "rollover loan", if made in the same currency and drawn by the same borrower as the first revolving loan. The conditions to be satisfied for drawing a rollover loan are typically less onerous than for other loans.

A revolving loan facility is a particularly flexible financing tool as it may be drawn by a borrower by way of straightforward loans, but it is also possible to incorporate different types of financial accommodation within it - for example, it is possible to incorporate a letter of credit facility, or overdraft facility within the terms of a revolving credit facility. This is often achieved by creating a sublimit within the overall revolving facility, allowing a certain amount of the lenders' commitment to be drawn in the form of these different facilities.

General: Syndicated loan agreements may contain only a term or revolving facility or they can contain a combination of both or several of each type (for example, multiple term loans in different currencies and with different maturity profiles are not uncommon). The facility may include a guarantor or guarantors and again provisions may be incorporated allowing for additional guarantors to accede to the agreement.

3.6.2 Parties to Syndicated Loan

The syndication process is initiated by the borrower, who appoints a lender through the grant of a mandate to act as the Arranger (also often called a Mandated Lead Arranger) of the deal.

The Arranger is responsible for advising the borrower as to the type of facilities it requires and then negotiating the broad terms of those facilities. By the very nature of this appointment, it is likely that the Arranger will be a lender with which the borrower already has an established relationship, although it does not have to be. At the same time the Arranger is negotiating the terms of the proposed facility. One of the Arrangers appointed by the Borrower to act as Bookrunner also starts to put together a syndicate of banks to provide that facility.

To facilitate the process of administering the loan on a daily basis, one bank from the syndicate is appointed as an Agent. The Agent who is appointed acts as the agent of the lenders not of the borrowers and has a number of important functions:

- **Point of Contact:** (maintaining contact with the borrower and representing the views of the syndicate)

- **Monitor:** (monitoring the compliance of the borrower with certain terms of the facility)
- **Postman and Record-keeper:** (it is the agent to whom the borrower is usually required to give notices)
- **Paying Agent:** (the borrower makes all payments of interest and repayments of principal and any other payments required under the Loan Agreement to the Agent. The Agent passes this money back to the banks to which they are due. Similarly the banks advance funds to the borrower through the Agent).

The terms of a syndicated loan agreement empower the Agent to undertake the roles described above in return for a fee. Any decisions of a material nature (for example, the granting of a waiver) must usually be taken by a majority, if not by the whole syndicate. Whilst the Agent carries the standard duties and responsibilities of any agent under English Law, the facility agreement will contain a number of exculpatory provisions to limit the scope of the Agent's relationship with the syndicate lenders and with the borrower.

If the syndicated loan is to be secured, a lender from the syndicate is usually appointed to act as Security Trustee to hold the security on trust for the benefit of all the lenders. The duties imposed upon the Security Trustee are typically more extensive than those of an agent.

In large syndicates, it is sometimes decided that some decision making power should be delegated to the majority from time to time (often referred to as the 'majority lenders' or 'instructing group'). This group usually consists of members of the syndicate at the relevant time that hold a specified percentage of the total commitments under the facility. By delegating some of the decision-making, the mechanics of the loan are able to work more effectively than if each and every member of the syndicate had to be consulted and subsequently reach unanimous agreement on every request from the borrower.

3.6.3 Documentation for Syndicated Loan

Mandate Letter: The borrower appoints the Arranger via a Mandate Letter (sometimes also called a Commitment Letter). The content of the Mandate Letter varies according to whether the Arranger is mandated to use its "best efforts" to arrange the required facility or if the Arranger is agreeing to "underwrite" the required facility. The provisions commonly covered in a Mandate Letter include:

1. an agreement to "underwrite" or use "best efforts to arrange";
2. titles of the arrangers, commitment amounts, exclusivity provisions;
3. conditions to lenders' obligations;
4. syndication issues (including preparation of an information memorandum, presentations to potential lenders, clear market provisions, market flex provisions and syndication strategy); and
5. costs cover and indemnity clauses.

Syndicated Loan Agreement: The Loan Agreement sets out the detailed terms and conditions on which the Facility is made available to the borrower.

Fee Letters: In addition to paying interest on the Loan and any related bank expenses, the borrower must pay fees to those banks in the syndicate who have performed additional work or taken on greater responsibility in the loan process, primarily the Arranger, the Agent and the Security Trustee. Details of these fees are usually put in separate side letters to ensure confidentiality. The Loan Agreement should refer to the Fee Letters and when such fees are payable to ensure that any non-payment by the borrower carries the remedies of default set out in the Loan Agreement.

Institutions offering Syndicate loans

Syndication as regards long-term loans is undertaken with the institutional lenders and the banks. The merchant bankers in India resort to syndicating loans, medium and long-term, granted by all-India and State-level financial institutions. The facility is provided to the clients by contacting, liaisoning and arranging loans. The institutions of finance with which the merchant bankers syndicate include Industrial Finance Corporation of India (IFCI), Industrial Development Bank of India (IDBI), Industrial Credit and Investment Corporation of India Ltd. (ICICI), Industrial Reconstruction Bank of India (IRBI), and Shipping Credit and Investment Company of India Ltd. (SCICI Ltd.), etc. The State level financial bodies such as State Financial Corporations (SFCs), State Industrial Development Corporations (SIDCs), and State Industrial and Investment Corporations (SIICs) and all-India investment institutions such as Life Insurance Corporation of India (LIC), Unit Trust of India (UTI), General. Insurance Corporation of India (GIC), and its subsidiary companies are also contacted for Syndicated loan arrangements.

In addition, commercial banks, mutual funds, and venture capital funds a also involved in the credit syndication for meeting the working capital requirements of trade and industry.

Procedure:

The merchant banker files the duly filled-in application in a manner as desired by the term-lending institution. While presenting the application, it is incumbent on the part of the merchant banker to ensure that all the required formalities have been complied with. For instance, it is important that necessary sanction is obtained from the Government for the proposed project. Loans are syndicated by developed financial institutions through the 'lead institution' especially in the case of 'consortium financing' or 'joint lending'. Where loans are sought in huge amounts consortium approach to lending is followed. The lead institution adopts 'single window scheme' while appraising, sanctioning and disbursing loans.

3.7 Project Appraisal

As part of credit syndication services, the merchant banker arranges for appraisal of the project by sufficiently interacting with the officials of the development financial institutions. The merchant banker holds formal discussions with the appraisal team of financial institutions. He helps the promoters/chief executive of the company by providing information to the appraisal team. He takes part in the site inspection with the appraisal team and provides information to them about the technical aspect of the project implementation. He also assists the appraisal team on matters connected with the choice of technique to be adopted for appraisal of the project. Merchant bankers provide advice in the preparation of project/feasibility report and the market survey report, and the financial projections relating to the project.

Appraisal of a project by the term lending institution happens by examining and ascertaining the technical, ecological, financial, organisational, managerial, commercial, economic and social aspects of the project.

1. Technical appraisal: Technical appraisal involves the assessment of technical and engineering soundness of the project. While carrying out the technical appraisal of a project, aspects such as competence of the experts preparing design of facilities and specifications; purchase arrangements of equipments; supervision of construction and installation; ability of consultants and their costs for services, are looked into. Attention is also paid to the aspects concerning the scale of operation, cost, of production and prospective demand. Similarly, attention is paid to understand the appropriateness of the methods and processes to be used for the project. Consideration is also given to the level of availability of latest technology, degree of obsolescence in technological process, etc.

Appraisal is also made from the viewpoint of appropriateness of location/layout design based on the advantages available by way of energy sources, skilled/unskilled labour, raw material and market. Further layout is looked into, from future expansion point of view.

In the event of the borrowing unit using or proposing to use non-conventional energy sources for the purpose of conserving and minimising energy and for ensuring better energy management, the lending agency would need to be provided with the following information:

(a) Nature of production process used or proposed to be used for making use of the alternative non-conventional energy sources.

(b) Steps initiated for improving energy efficiency and reducing energy losses thorough optimum power management.

(c) Steps proposed for monitoring the use of energy.

(d) Cost-benefit analysis and savings to be achieved by utilising the proposed alternative source of energy.

2. Ecological appraisal: Regarding the ecological aspects of the project, the merchant banker ensures that the borrowing company has taken all possible steps for preventing air, water and soil pollution arising out of the industrial project proposed to be undertaken. A certificate from the State Pollution Control Board has to be produced to the effect that the company has installed equipment adequate and appropriate to the requirement of meeting the environmental protection. Ecological appraisal is mandatory with respect to highly polluting industries such as zinc, lead, copper, aluminum, steel, paper, pesticides/insecticides, refineries, fertilizers, paints, dyes, leather tanning, rayon, sodium/potassium cyanide, basic drugs, foundry, batteries, acids/alkalis, plastics, rubber, cement, asbestos, fermentation, electro-plating, etc.

3. Financial appraisal: Financial appraisal involves analyzing the financial viability of the project under consideration. Analysis of the need for fixed capital and working capital is also carried out. Consideration is also given to the cost of the project as relating to acquisition of capital assets, interest cost on loans obtained for promotional, organisational, training, and other purposes.

The merchant banker should ensure that a forecast- of working capital funds is made with regard to the investment in inventory of raw material, WIP, finished goods, and receivables. Consideration must also be given to the possible fluctuations in payments and receipts due to seasonal variations in production and sales. As part of financial appraisal, efficiency of the project for generating revenue is to be examined. For this Purpose, data on funds utilisation, operating cost and revenue, liquidity, expected rate of return on investment, etc. are analyzed.

Financial statements are examined to ascertain the mode of valuation of fixed assets, inventories, receivables, etc. Attempt should also be made to find out the soundness of the depreciation policy adopted by the borrowing firm. Data is obtained on the sources and application of cash resources of the enterprise during the proposed operating period of the project. The sources of funding to be adopted by the firm should be enquired into to find out the proportion of debt and equity and proportion of short-term and long-term funding source. Besides, the merchant banker should analyze the balance sheet projections so as to glean the financial status of the firm.

4. Financial tools: The merchant banker uses the following tools of for appraising the financial efficacy of the project so as to determine the soundness of the proposed project:

(a) Break-even analysis
(b) Ratio analysis covering debt-equity ratio, current ratio, profitability ratio, output investment ratio, fixed assets coverage ratio, profit to sales, return on capitalisation, return on investment, return on equity.
(c) Debt service coverage ratio, servicing of debt and shareholders.
(d) Capital expenditure evaluation by both discounted and non-discounted cash flow techniques.
(e) Uncertainty or risk analysis/sensitivity analysis.

5. Promoters' contribution': Promoters' contribution for establishment and running of a project is vital. The important sources of promoters' contribution in the case of newly established companies include own equity, managed equity from special funds such as Risk Capital/Venture Capital Funds or Seed Capital from IDBI through SFCs, SIDCs, etc. and foreign equity, deposits contributed by promoters, etc. In the case of existing companies the sources of promoter contribution include internal accruals, right issues, divestment of shares, additional equity, unsecured loans, etc. The extent of promoters' contribution and debt-equity norms must be scrutinized by the merchant banker.

In addition, the merchant banker should also examine the extent of promoters' contribution in the event of administration of rehabilitation packages in the case of sick and weak industrial units. This is in tandem with the broad guidelines issued by the RBI.

6. Economic appraisal: Economic appraisal of the project involves making an analysis of the expected contribution of the project to the particular sector, besides its contribution to the development of the national economy. Particular attention is paid to the project's usefulness in terms of best possible utilisation of scarce resources. It is essential to consider the priority nature of the project. Accordingly, a project will be considered desirable if it has a tremendous impact on the balance of payment and the capacity to generate exchange surplus through new exports, import substitution and resultant savings in foreign exchange.

The economic viability of the project is determined in terms of less outgo of foreign exchange by way of continuous reduction in import of raw materials, spare parts, payment of technician fee, royalty, necessitating additional borrowings, etc. The competitive nature of the project is also evaluated by comparing the value added at domestic prices and value added at world prices. Further, the employment generating capacity of 6 project is also studied.

7. Commercial appraisal: Commercial appraisal involves the determination of commercial viability of the project in terms of arrangements for buying, transporting and marketing the product.

8. Managerial appraisal: Managerial appraisal is concerned with the evaluation of effectiveness and efficiency of the managerial personnel who are vested with the responsibility of organising the available resources of the project. The merchant banker checks the managerial competency both at construction and operation stages to ensure the success of the project.

Arrangement of Loan Sanction/Sanction of a Loan:

It is the function of a merchant banker to obtain the letter of intent/sanction from the lending institution/bank. The lending agency informs the merchant banker about the sanction of loan by the sanctioning authority. The, sanction letter invariably contains terms and conditions pertaining to the sanction of loan. Some these term include amount of loan, rate of interest applicable, commitment charge levied by the lender in order to motivate the borrowing unit to make efficient use of the loan, security for the loan, conversion option in the case of default and rehabilitation assistance, repayment terms of loan, and other terms and conditions.

Documentation and Creation of Security:

An important function of a merchant banker is to create an adequate documentation of security by working closely with the 'lead financial institution,' so as to ensure quicker disbursement of loan. The type of documents to be prepared and executed by the merchant banker will be as per the requirements of the lead financial institution. Depending on the loan type, the merchant banker executes bridge loan document or interim loan document.

The merchant banker provides the following details with regard to the security for the loan:

1. First mortgage and charge of all immovable properties both present and future of the borrower company in the form as may be indicated by lenders which is equitable mortgage by deposit of title deeds.
2. First charge by way of hypothecation (i) of all movables such as stocks of raw material, semi-finished and finished goods, consumable stores and such other movables as may be agreed to by the lead institution for securing the borrowings for working capital requirements in the ordinary course of the business, and (ii) on specific items of machinery as permitted by the lender purchased and/or to be purchased by the client company under the deferred payment facilities granted to the client company.
3. Security for bridge loan
4. Security for interim loan
5. Substantive security where the loan amount is being secured in terms of the loan agreement by first charge on the company's immovable and movable assets, present and future.
6. Personal guarantee where the borrowing is being secured by irrevocable and unconditional personal guarantee from its promoters/directors in favour of the lending institutions.

Points to Remember

- A merger refers to a combination of two or more companies, usually of not greatly disparate size, into one company.
- Acquisition refers to the acquiring of ownership right in the property and assets without any combination of companies.
- The Provisions regulating buy back of shares are contained in Section 77A, 77AA and 77B of the companies Act, 1956. These were inserted by the Companies (Amendment) Act, 1999. The securities and exchange Board of India (SEBI) framed the SEBI (Buy Back of securities) Regulations 1999 and the Department of Company Affairs framed the Private Limited Company and Unlisted Public company (Buy back of Securities) rules, 1999, pursuant to section 77A(2)(F) and (g) respectively.

- Delisting refers to removing the listed securities of a company from the stock market. As per the SEBI Delisting Guidelines of Equity Shares, 2009, delisting can be of two types: "voluntary delisting: or "involuntary delisting/compulsory delisting.
- A debenture is a document which either creates a debt or acknowledges it. Debenture issued by a company is in the form of a certificate acknowledging indebtedness. The debentures are issued under the Company's Common Seal.
- Portfolio is a collection of various assets. In portfolio management, these assets are of financial nature. A Portfolio Manager is a person who invest the money in a diverse assets with the aim of maximise the return and minimising the risk.
- A syndicated loan agreement simplifies the borrowing process as the borrower uses one agreement covering the whole group of banks and different types of facility rather than entering into a series of separate bilateral loans, each with different terms and conditions.
- As part of credit syndication services, the merchant banker arranges for appraisal of the project by sufficiently interacting with the officials of the development financial institutions.

Questions for Discussion

1. Define Merger, Amalgamation, Acquisition. State the types of Merger.
2. Define Buy Back of Shares. Explain the procedure of Buy Back of shares.
3. Define Delisting of shares. Explain the types of debentures.
4. Explain the Defensive Strategies to avoid Hoshle Merger.
5. Define Debentures. Explain the various kinds of debentures.
6. Discuss the SEBI Guidelines for Debentures.
7. Explain : Registration of Portfolio Manager.
8. Describe the Duties of Portfolio Manager.
9. Explain the contents of Agreement between Client and Portfolio Manager.
10. Write short notes on :
    (a) Methods of Financing Merger.
    (b) Valuation methods.
    (c) Step-wise Procedure for Amalgamation.
    (d) SEBI - Code of Conduct for the Portfolio Manager.
    (e) Credit Syndication Services.
    (f) Project Appraisal.
    (g) Sanction of a Loan.
    (h) Scope of Project Management Services.

Chapter 4...

Financial Services (Part - I)

Contents ...

- 4.1 Meaning, Scope and Evolution of Financial Services
- 4.2 Introduction of Various Financial Services
- 4.3 Leasing
  - 4.3.1 Definitions of Leasing
  - 4.3.2 Essential Elements of Leasing
  - 4.3.3 Types of Lease
  - 4.3.4 Advantages of Leasing
  - 4.3.5 Limitation/Disadvantages of Leasing
  - 4.3.6 Financial Implications of Leasing
- 4.4 Hire Purchase Finance
  - 4.4.1 Definitions of Hire Purchase Finance
  - 4.4.3 Scope of the Purchase
  - 4.4.4 Difference between Hire Purchase and Leasing
- 4.5 Factoring - Meaning, Definition, Scope, Advantages and Limitations
  - 4.5.1 Definitions of Factoring
  - 4.5.2 Features of Factoring
  - 4.5.3 Process or Mechanism of Factoring
  - 4.5.4 Scope of Factoring Services
  - 4.5.5 Types of Factoring
  - 4.5.6 Advantages of Factoring
  - 4.5.7 Limitations of Factoring
- 4.6 Forfaiting: Meaning, Scope, Advantages and Limitations
  - 4.6.1 Meaning and Scope of Forfaiting
  - 4.6.2 Essential Features of Forfaiting
  - 4.6.3 Process or Mechanism of a Forfaiting Transaction
  - 4.6.4 Advantages of Forfaiting
  - 4.6.5 Limitations of Forfaiting
  - 4.6.6 Difference between Factoring and Forfaiting

4.7 Discounting of Bills of Exchange

4.8 Insurance

    4.8.1 Meaning and Definition of Insurance

    4.8.2 Essential Features of Insurance Service

    4.8.3 Types of Insurance

- Points to Remember
- Questions for Discussion

Learning Objectives
- To examine the meaning, scope and evolution of financial services
- To study leasing
- To understand hire purchase finance
- To learn about factoring and forfaiting
- To be aware of discounting of bills of exchange and insurance

Introduction

The Government of a country makes plans for the growth and development of an economy. It is the financial sector or system of an economy that bridges the gap between the present economic status and the economic status planned. The financial sector operates with a network of financial markets, financial institutions, financial instruments and financial service providers. These terms are explained below:

1. **Financial institutions** are the intermediaries that mobilise the savings of individuals, firms, and institutions and facilitate its efficient allocation.

   Banking institutions create credit with the instrument of cheques whereas the non-banking institutions are purveyors of credit. Therefore, liabilities of banking institutions i.e. deposits are part of the money supply, but the liabilities of the non-banking institutions are not part of the money supply.

2. **Financial markets** facilitate the functioning of the financial system through financial instruments. They enable the participants to deal in financial claims. The investors, savers, and borrowers operate in the financial markets to attain their financial goals. Thus financial markets provide the platform for the financial institutions to operate with their financial instruments.

   Financial markets can be money market and capital market depending on the instruments dealt in the market. Money market caters to the need of short term funds and capital market for the medium and long term investments. Call money, treasury bill, trade bills are the instruments of money market. Primary market-issue of share, bonds etc., secondary markets - stock exchange, and derivative market- dealing in options and derivatives .

3. **Financial instruments** are the financial claims that are dealt in financial markets. These can be such documents as cheques, drafts, bonds, shares, bills of exchange, futures, options etc.

4. **Financial services** are provided by individuals and institutions to facilitate smooth trading of instruments in the financial market. The services include bill discounting, stock broking, insurance, credit rating, underwriting, hire purchase, leasing, merchant banking etc.

Illustration:

An individual with ₹ 10,00,000 as saving is looking for the best investment of the money, which would give him good return, increase in his wealth and make available his funds at the right time to meet contingencies. He is aware that there are large numbers of investment options available in the market right from bank fixed deposit to stock investment. Further investment may attract tax liability. He takes advice of a finance consultant in deciding the right mix of investment, to achieve his objective of liquidity, security and returns. Investment advisors or tax consultants will be in a position to provide services in return for fees. The service of the consultant is a case of financial service. The various investment options like Insurance policy, fixed deposits, equity share purchase etc. are financial instruments. Banks, insurance companies are examples of financial institutions. Stock exchange where the shares are traded is an example of financial market.

4.1 Meaning, Scope and Evolution of Financial Services

1. Meaning and Definition of Financial Services

Financial services are an important component of the financial system. It is broadly understood to include stock broking, insurance, housing finance, banking and investment service. Financial institutions and financial markets facilitate functioning of the financial system through financial instruments. In the process of functioning they require a number of services of financial nature. Financial services, through the network of financial institutions, financial markets and financial instruments, serve the needs of individuals, institutions and corporates.

The companies that provide financial services are grouped into:

(a) Asset Management companies, such as leasing companies, mutual funds, merchant bankers and issue or portfolio managers.

(b) Liability Management companies comprise of bill discounting and accepting houses.

2. Functions

The following functions are provided by the financial service companies:

(a) **Fund raising:** Financial services help to raise funds for corporate and individuals through various instruments.

(b) **Management of funds raised:** Financial services not only help in raising funds but also the effective use of the funds. Services such as credit rating, assisting in decisions regarding financing mix, parking of funds in the short term money market are some examples.

(c) Financial services include specialised services such as insurance, venture capital financing, lease financing, factoring, mutual funds, depository, credit card, housing finance, merchant banking etc.

(d) Financial services include the regulation of various aspects of the financial system in the interest of the investor and financial system. Agencies SEBI, RBI, department of Banking and Insurance, Board for Industrial and Financial Reconstruction are important regulatory bodies.

3. Scope of Financial Services

Financial services cover a wide range of activities. These services not only help to raise funds but also help in the efficient deployment of funds. Scope of their functions is determined by the need of financial services in the financial system and the rules framed by the various regulatory bodies in the interest of the investors and economy.

Financial services can broadly be grouped into

(a) Traditional activities; and

(b) Modern activities

(a) Traditional Activities

These are the activities which comprise of both capital and money market. These activities can be classified into the following:

(i) Fund based services

In fund based services, the service provider raises equity, debt and deposits and invests in securities or lends to those who are in need of capital.

The following services are examples:

- Underwriting or investment in shares, debenture, bonds etc. of new issues. Underwriting is a contract whereby the underwriters agree to buy securities of the client company if the public does not respond to the issue sufficiently.
- Dealing in secondary market activities ie. stock exchange

- Purchasing and selling money market instruments like commercial papers, certificate of deposits, Treasury bills, discounting of bills etc.
- Leasing plant and machinery, hire - purchase, providing venture capital, seed capital etc.
- Foreign exchange market activities.

(ii) Non-fund based services:

These services are fee based services. The financial service firms enable other entities to raise funds from the market and charge fees in return for their services. Such services include:

- Managing the capital issue of companies both pre-issue and post-issue activities in accordance with the SEBI guidelines and as per the Companies Act.
- Making arrangements for the placement of capital and debt instruments i.e. equity shares and debentures with the investment institutions.
- Arrangement of loans from financial institutions for the working capital needs of the client and for project cost.
- All activities required to obtain government clearance.

(b) Modern Activities:

Modern services are essentially fee based services. These include the following:

(i) **Project services:** Financial service providers provide services of identification of a new project, preparation of project report, obtaining capital for the project for their clients.

(ii) **Capital structure:** Capital structure is the debt equity mix of the capital. Financial service in this regard includes- advising the best source of funds, optimum debt-equity mix for the client's company.

(iii) **Risk management:** Businesses need to manage the various risks they are exposed to. Financial services include risk management services such as insurance services, buy-back options. Services of hedging risks such as exchange rate risk, interest rate risk, economic and political risk by use of swaps or other derivative instruments.

(iv) **Joint venture:** Finance services include assisting the clients with regard to decisions regarding financial collaboration with other companies and best joint venture arrangements.

(v) **Sick industries:** In order to revive sick industrial units, financial services are used.

(vi) **Credit rating:** Credit rating services before the public issue of debt is provided. Besides they act as trustees of debenture holders to protect their interest.

(vii) **Capital market services:** Capital market services include
- Clearing service,
- Safe custody of securities,
- Collection of income on securities,
- Registration and transfers etc.

4. Evolution of Financial Services

The evolution of financial services in India can be studied under various stages:

(a) 1960s to 1980s: During this period Banks were nationalised due to inefficiency and fraud. In 1969, 14 major Banks were nationalised and 1980, 6 more Banks were nationalised. This gave impetus to banking activities in India. Five year plans gave importance to industrialisation. Hence financial services such as merchant banking and leasing began to grow. Merchant bankers performed such functions as-

Identifying business opportunities, preparing project reports, underwriting, assisting companies in getting their securities listed, arranging working capital loans etc.

Life Insurance Corporation was formed way back in 1956 by merging over 250 life insurance corporations. It became a monopoly in the field. But general insurance business was in the private sector till 1970, when insurance was nationalised. In 1972 General Insurance Corporation of India was formed to handle general insurance business in India. This regulated the insurance business and added to investor confidence.

This period also witnessed the growth of a variety of investment institutions and banks. The investment companies include Unit Trust of India, which is the largest public sector mutual fund in the world. The Government of India established the UTI in 1964. This marked growth of the mutual fund industry in India which came up with innovative schemes for mobilising savings of people.

At the end of 1970s the leasing business also began to grow. The companies that were engaged in equipment lease financing, started financial, operating and wet leasing.

(b) 1980 – 1990 : A variety of financial products and services were launched during this period. The financial services included mutual funds, factoring, discounting, venture capital, credit rating etc. Besides during this period mutual fund started to grow. Unit Trust of India and other investment companies started mobilising the savings of people for investment. Innovative schemes were launched to encourage savings among the people. With the increase in investment needs and opportunities, credit rating became important as people need expert advice regarding the creditworthiness of the various debt securities to safeguard their investment. The system of credit rating was designed to boost investor's confidence and encourage their active participation in the capital market operation.

In 1988, SEBI was set up with regulatory powers for regulating the securities market and protecting the interest of the investors. SEBI also provides guidelines for some of the specific financial services like mutual funds, venture capital financing, portfolio management services, stock broking. The functioning of various intermediaries associated with management of public and rights issue of capital such as Merchant Bankers, Underwriters, Brokers, Market makers, Registrars, Advisors, Collection Bankers, Advertisement consultants, Debenture Trustees, Credit Rating Agencies etc. are regulated by the SEBI.

(c) 1990-2000: Following important events marked the growth of financial services in India.

(i) Depository system was introduced to promote the concept of paperless trading through dematerialisation of shares and bonds.

(ii) A separate corporation was set up to deal with the trading of Gilts.

(iii) Book-building was introduced.

(iv) The Bombay Stock Exchange introduced the concept of online trading.

(d) 2000 onwards:

1. Some of the important legislations of the period were – FERA replaced by FEMA. Amendments in the Companies Act and Income Tax Act to facilitate safe and orderly trading and settlement of transactions.

2. Foreign Institutional Investors permitted to operate in the Indian Capital Market.

3. The financial service firms in India are working to get capital from the international finance market.

4.2 Introduction of Various Financial Services

Some of the important financial services are briefly explained below:

1. **Leasing:** A firm in need of fixed assets like plant and machinery, equipment etc. may not have funds to make outright purchase of the asset or may not be sure if the asset would profit the firm, may go in for an alternative method called leasing of assets. Under the method, the firm enters into a legal agreement with the owner of the asset to use the asset for an agreed period of time by paying rent. On the expiry of the lease period, the lease contract may be renewed for a further period. The owner may sell the asset to the lessee.

2. **Hire Purchase:** It is a kind of credit sale, whereby a vendor enters into an agreement with the hire-purchaser, called 'Hire purchase agreement'. Under the method, the hire-purchaser is required to pay a certain amount called the down payment at the time of agreement and the balance of the cash price of the goods in periodical instalments including interest. The instalments paid are treated as hire charges by the vendor and the ownership of goods gets transferred in favour of the hire-purchaser

only on the payment of the final instalment. If the purchaser fails to pay the instalment the goods may be repossessed.

3. **Factoring:** Credit sale is an important marketing tool adopted by firms to protect their sale from competitors and to attract new customers for their products and services. The amount of credit sale is represented by 'Receivables', 'Book Debts' or 'Debtors'. Collection of receivables involves a lot of effort and time on the part of the firms. Factoring is a contract between the financial service provider and the firm whereby factor purchases the client's book debts for a price. Client thus, gets money on the book debts and is relieved from the effort of debt collection. The factor deducts the price and makes the balance payment. After the purchase of book debts the factor becomes responsible for collecting the debt and maintain records in this regard. Price includes interest on the money advanced, charges for the service and reserves for bad debt.

4. **Forfaiting:** Forfaiting is similar to bills discounting. It is a form of financing applicable to exporters. Under this arrangement the forfaiting agency discounts the bill of exchange or promissory notes, accepted by the importer and co-accepted by a bank. Forfaiting transfers the risk of non-payment by the importer, on to the forfaiting agency. The rate of discount charged by the agency is higher than the euro market interest rate.

5. **Bills Discounting:** A Trade Bill is a negotiable instrument. A person who has bought goods or services from another may agree to pay for it on a future date. The seller can draw a draft requiring the purchaser to pay the amount on the expiry of a specific period. The purchaser must accept and sign on the draft after which the bill becomes a bill of exchange. The owner of the bill will have to wait for the payment till the maturity period of the bill. Another option available to the drawer of the bill is to sell the bill at a discounted price to a commercial bank. The financial service provider, in this case a commercial bank may buy the bill and make the payment at a discounted price to the drawer. On the date of maturity of the bill, the bank would collect the amount from the acceptor of the bill. But if the acceptor of the bill fails to make the payment, the bank would get back to the drawer of the bill for payment.

6. **Consumer Finance:** It is a credit facility given to individuals who buy goods for their consumption and not for trade or manufacturing. Consumer goods such as Refrigerators, Scooters, Cars, Washing Machines, Televisions etc., require larger amount of funds than that is required for the day to day expenses. Consumers may find it difficult to pay the whole price at one go. Banks and finance companies may agree to give credit facilities to the consumers to enable them to own such goods. It is also called as credit merchandising, deferred payments, instalment buying, hire

purchase, pay-out of income scheme, etc. Typically, the consumer is required to pay a part of the cash price of the goods at the time of purchase and the balance in future along with interest.

7. **Housing Finance:** Housing is one of the basic needs and requires huge investment. Various institutions have come up with housing finance schemes to cater to the needs of people. The housing finance institutions check the loan repayment capacity of the individuals before granting loan. In most cases, personal guarantee and security of the house purchased is the main source of security to the financiers. The features of loans vary from scheme to scheme and from one housing finance company to another. But most commonly, loan repayment is done in instalment called EMIs (equated monthly instalments). The loan amount and the interest on it is calculated and spread over the period of loan equally, so that it becomes easy for the individuals to repay. In the initial years the EMIs have higher interest content and in the later years the instalments contain lesser interest amounts and higher principal amount.

8. **Insurance:** Insurance is an agreement whereby an insurance company agrees to indemnify the loss caused to the property of the insurer, and in case of life insurance to pay the assured amount on death of the policy holder, in return for a periodic or onetime payment called insurance premium. The periodic payment received from the clients is invested by the insurance company after keeping a certain percentage of the premium to meet claims.

9. **Credit Cards:** Credit cards also known as plastic money, are issued by Banks and financial institutions, to make the buying process convenient and safe for the consumers. The buyer of goods/services need not make payment immediately. The credit card has to be presented at the counter and the bill has to be signed. The traders would get the payment from the credit card issuer. The credit card company allows the customer to make the payment at their convenience. If the payment is made within the stated period, no interest is charged. Beyond the period, interest is charged for the delayed payment. Thus a customer can just pay the annual processing charge of the bank or financial institution concerned and avail around 15 days credit on all purchases.

10. **Credit Rating:** There are a large number of debt instruments i.e., bonds, debentures, etc. in the market for investment. It requires a lot of research to determine the worth of these instruments. An individual investor may not have the time nor the expertise to undertake such research. Credit rating institutions provide credit rating service to the investors. These institutions undertake systematic analysis of the risk of non-payment of interest and principal amount by the company and assign symbols to the

debt instruments denoting their credit worthiness. These symbols are easy to understand and normally are expressed with alphabetical or alpha-numeric symbols. A rating is an opinion on the future ability of the debt issuing company or authority, to make timely payment of principal and interest on the security. There is no guarantee given by the agency. It is for the investor to make a decision whether to buy, hold or sell the security.

11. **Mutual Funds:** A Mutual Fund is portfolio of investment. The funds of small investors are collected and invested on their behalf in various capital market securities by the mutual fund trust or company. For the purpose investors buy the units of the mutual fund and become its members. The fund managers of the trust manage the funds of the members and distribute the profits from the investment to the members.

12. **Venture Capital:** Venture capital is provided to entrepreneurs who want to start a high-tech untried project having risk and at the same time high potential of profits. It is also meant for those who do not have a long history of running businesses. Entrepreneurs who have new ideas of a promising business but don't have funds, or cannot borrow due to the risk involved in the project, or due to hesitation of banks to finance such ideas, may approach venture capital institutions for finance. Venture capitalist, if find the proposed business to be worthy, may provide equity i.e. invest in the proposal. They take part in the management of the business, provide guidance to the promoters and exit after 5 to 7 years by way of 'Initial Public Issue' (IPO). Thus they realise their investment and make capital gains if the company succeeds in the venture.

4.3 Leasing

Lease is one of the methods of financing the fixed assets of an enterprise. An enterprise with inadequate funds for financing the investment in plant and machinery may enter into lease agreement with the owners of the assets. The contract of lease allows the lessee to use the asset for a certain period in return for a periodical payment. After the expiry of the period the lease agreement may be renewed or the asset may be purchased by the lessee if so desired by the lessee.

4.3.1 Definitions of Leasing

1. **Herbert B. Mayo:** *"A contract for the use of an asset such as plant or equipment. The firm that owns the asset permits the lessee to use the goods. In return the lessor enters into a contract(the lease) to make specific payments for the use of the asset. The lease is usually for a specified time period and may be renewable."*

2. **Merriam Webster dictionary :** *"A legal agreement that lets someone use a car, house, shop etc., for a period of time in return for payment. It is a contract by which one conveys real estate, equipment, or facilities for a specified term and for a specified rent."*

3. **Raymond G. Schultz:** *"The user agrees to pay a rental charge and adhere to other conditions of a lease contract in return for the right to utilise property of the owner in his operations for a specified period."*

4. **Institute of Chartered Accountants of India:** *"A lease is an agreement whereby the lessor conveys to the lessee, in return for rent, the right to use an asset for an agreed period of time. Lessor is a person who carries to another person (lessee) the right to use an asset in consideration of a payment of periodical rental, under a lease agreement. Lessee is a person who obtains from the lessor, the right to use the asset for a periodical rental payment for an agreed period of time".*

4.3.2 Essential Elements of Leasing

The essential elements of leasing are:

1. **Parties to the contract of lease:** The owner of the asset to be leased and the user of the asset. The owner is called the lessor and user is called the lessee. Both of them can be individuals, firms, joint stock companies, or financial institutions. The parties to the lease agreement may come together due to the efforts of an intermediary called the lease broker, who charges commission from both the parties.

2. **Asset:** The asset is the subject matter of the contract of lease. It may be land and building, plant and machinery, or equipment etc.

3. **Term of lease:** The lease agreement is for a certain period of time. The period for which the lessee wants to use the asset, is called the term of lease. During the term rent is paid by the lessee. After the expiry of the term the asset may be taken over by the owner, or lease agreement may be renewed for a further period or the asset may be sold to the lessee.

4. **Lease rentals:** The consideration paid by the lessee to the owner of the asset, for its use is called the lease rentals. It may be a periodical payment or a single payment.

4.3.3 Types of Lease

Leases are classified into different types based on the variations in the elements of the lease agreement. Most popular classification of lease is – financial lease and operating lease. Apart from these, there are sale and lease back and direct lease, single investor lease and leveraged lease, and domestic and international lease. The variations can be in certain elements of the lease agreement as follows:

- the degree of ownership risk and rewards transferred to the lessee;
- location of the lessor, lessee and the equipment supplier;
- number of parties involved;

1. Financial Lease and Operating Lease

Financial lease is also called as Full Pay-out lease. Under this kind of lease agreement, the lessor transfers substantially all the risks and rewards associated with the asset to the lessee. The ownership gets transferred at the end of the economic life of the asset. Lease term is spread over the major part of the asset's life. It has the following features:

(a) It is for a long period of time, normally equal to the expected useful life of the asset;
(b) It is not cancellable;
(c) Usually the maintenance of the property, property taxes and insurance is provided by the lessee;
(d) The risk and rewards associated with the lease is transferred to the lessee;
(e) The burden of obsolescence falls on the lessee.

The companies that frequently update or replace equipment and want to use equipment for less than its economic life may not like to go for a financial lease. Operating lease does not run for full economic life of the asset, and the lessee is not liable for financing its full value. Lessor carries the risk associated with the asset. Maintenance, property taxes and insurance are usually provided by the lessor. Thus along with the right to use the property, the lessee obtains some services also. The main features of operating lease are:

(i) Normally leasing of the assets is the regular business of the lessor;
(ii) In most of the cases, the lease is cancellable at the instance of the lessor;
(iii) The lease period is relatively short, not exceeding 2 or 3 years;
(iv) The capital cost of the asset cannot be recovered from one such lease of the asset as the lease period is short. Hence the lessor leases the property a number of times either to the same lessee or to another lessee;
(v) The maintenance of the property, the payment of property taxes and insurance usually falls on the lessor.
(vi) The risk of obsolescence falls on the lesssor.

2. Sale and Lease Back

Under this method of lease the owner of an asset sells the asset to another person without giving away the possession of the asset. The purchaser of the asset now becomes owner of the property and enters into a lease agreement with the vendor of the asset who becomes the lessee after the contract of lease. The original owner pays rentals for use of the asset to the current owner of the asset. Thus under sale and lease back, the seller becomes the lessee and the buyer becomes the lessor of the property.

3. Leveraged Lease

Under leveraged leasing arrangement, the lessor borrows funds to buy the asset meant to be leased out. Around 80 per cent of the cost of the asset is borrowed from a third party on the security of the asset. The asset is leased out in the regular manner. The lease rental received from the lessee is used to repay the loan.

4. Direct Leasing

Under direct leasing, a firm acquires the right to use an asset from the manufacturer directly. The ownership of the asset remains with the manufacturer.

5. Big Ticket Leasing

This method of leasing is more popular for very expensive assets such as construction equipment, sophisticated computer systems, heavy machinery etc. The cost of asset is so huge that it may not be possible for one lessor to provide the asset on lease. Two or more lessor companies join hands in leasing. The asset may be funded by the lessors themselves or they might be financed partly by the lessors and partly lenders of it and the rest may be financed by borrowed funds.

6. Cross Border Leasing

When the lessor and the lessee belong to different countries the leasing arrangement is called as cross border leasing.

7. In House Leasing

When a group of companies promote a leasing company for the benefit of the companies in the group, the company is called an 'in house leasing company'. In house leasing company provides a lot of benefits to the group companies.

8. On the Basis of the Terms of Payment

(a) **Balloon rental leasing:** Here the initial rent amounts are lower and the rent amount increases during the later period of the lease.

(b) **Step rental leasing:** Under this arrangement the rent amount is not fixed for the whole of the period of lease. It depends upon the size of income flow of the lessee.

(c) **Front heavy type leasing:** According to this arrangement, larger rentals are collected in the initial period of the lease and lower amount of rent is charged during the later part of the lease.

(d) **Skipped payment leasing:** Under this arrangement, rentals of certain periods, when the equipment is not functioning, is skipped.

(e) **Trial period leasing:** Under this arrangement the lessee is allowed to take lease on a trial basis for sometime before deciding to take the asset on lease.

4.3.4 Advantages of Leasing

1. **Advantages to the Lessee:**
   (a) **Financing of capital goods:** Lessee can obtain the right to use capital goods without making any down payment and without any obligation to pay for the price of the asset in future.
   (b) **Availability of funds:** Lessee gets the benefit of use of the asset without making any payment towards the purchase of the asset. Funds thus saved can be used for working capital requirements.
   (c) **Flexibility:** The lease agreement can be made to suit the needs of the lessee and lessor. There is a lot of flexibility.
   (d) **Cheaper:** It is a cheaper source of financing when compared to debt financing.
   (e) **Tax advantage:** The rent paid is chargeable to the profit and loss account of the lessee. Thus the lessee gets tax advantage.
   (f) **Risk of obsolescence:** Due to technological developments there is a risk of obsolescence of assets especially with respect to machinery and equipment. This risk is averted by taking assets on lease. The business can use the latest technology in the business by not renewing the lease agreement. The risk of obsolescence is on the owner of the asset and not on the lessee.
   (g) **No change in the debt-equity mix:** Capital goods are taken on lease hence there is no need for the lessee company or firm to raise loan or ownership funds. Thus the ownership remains undiluted and the debt –equity mix is unchanged.

2. **Advantages to the Lessor:**
   (a) **Ownership of the asset:** The lessor remains the owner of the asset. If the lessee defaults in payment of lease rentals the lessor can repossess the asset.
   (b) **Depreciation and tax benefit:** Lessor being the owner of the asset, can charge deprecation on the asset to the profit and loss account and thereby enjoy tax benefit.

4.3.5 Limitations/Disadvantages of Leasing

1. **High rate:** The lessor usually charges higher rate of interest than the rate he pays on borrowings.
2. **Restriction on use:** The owner of the asset can impose some restriction on the use of the asset. The lessee cannot make alterations in the asset to suit his requirements.
3. **Residual value:** The residual value of the asset may accrue to the lessor. If the value of the asset appreciates after the lease period, which is normally spread over the working life of the asset, he does not get any share in the capital gain.
4. **Default:** If the lessee defaults, the owner can repossess the capital asset, and terminate the contract.

4.3.6 Financial Implications of Leasing

Financial implication of leasing can be studied for lessee and lessor separately.

1. Lessee:

Lease rental is a revenue expenditure and hence charged to the profit and loss account. This reduces the profit shown in the books of the lessee resulting in lesser tax liability and less cash outflow for tax payment. Effective rent is therefore lesser than the actual rent paid by the lessee.

For instance for a lease rent of ₹ 1,00,000 p.a., we can calculate the effective cash outflow. Say the business entity is in a tax bracket of 35%. By charging ₹ 1,00,000 to profit and loss account, the tax liability of the lessee is brought down by 35% of ₹ 1,00,000 i.e., ₹ 35,000. The cash outflow for lease is ₹ 1,00,000. The cash outflow in the form of tax payment saved is ₹ 35,000. That means the effective cash outflow is only ₹ 65,000 (1,00,000 – 35,000).

Had the asset been purchased by borrowing money from the Banks/Financial institutions, the cash outflow would have been the interest on the loan and a part of the principal amount. But the buyer could have charged depreciation of the asset as well as the interest on loan to the profit and loss account and would have reduced his tax liability and thereby his cash outflow.

The lesser must weigh the financial implication of lease financing and outright purchase of the asset in light of the tax implications and also consider such other factors as obsolescence of asset, legal formalities connected with borrowing, and the total debt equity ratio of the entity.

2. Lessor:

Lessor need to show the lease rent as income, but can claim depreciation of the asset as expenditure and thereby enjoy tax shield. Besides, the scrap value of the asset belongs to the lessor or the manufacturer which may give rise to capital gain or loss. If the residual asset after its life is sold at a price higher than the written down value, then there is a profit made by the lessor which would be considered as capital gain. Capital gain is taxable as per the Income Tax Act, but there are ways by which the tax can be avoided.

4.4 Hire Purchase Finance

Under this method of finance the purchaser acquires the possession of goods from the seller by making a part payment called down payment. The ownership of the goods remains with the seller. A hire purchase agreement is entered into between the hire-vendor and hire-purchaser, whereby the latter agrees to make payment towards the price of the goods in future, by way of periodic instalments along with interest. The periodic instalments are treated as hire charges by the hire-vendor. Hence the hire-vendor retains the ownership of the goods till the last instalment is paid by the purchaser. The hire-purchaser becomes the owner of the goods only after the payment of the last instalment.

4.4.1 Definitions of Hire Purchase Finance

1. According to **J. R. Batliboi**, *"under the Hire Purchase system, goods are delivered to a person who agrees to pay the owners by equal periodical instalments, such instalments are to be treated as hire of these goods, until a certain fixed amount has been paid, when these goods become the property of the hirer".*

2. According to **Hire Purchase Act 1972**, *"Hire purchase agreement means an agreement under which goods are let on hire and under which the hirer has an option to purchase them in accordance with the terms of the agreement* and includes an agreement under which –
   (a) Possession of goods is delivered by the owner thereof to a person on condition that such person pays the agreed amount in periodical instalments, and
   (b) The property in the goods is to pass on the payment of the last of such instalment.

Characteristics of Hire Purchase System:

1. **Possession of goods:** The hire-purchaser gets immediate possession of goods on signing the hire purchase agreement. He is entitled to use the goods.

2. **Ownership of goods:** The hire-purchaser does not get the ownership of the goods on signing the agreement. The hire-vendor retains the ownership till the last hire charge instalment is paid by the hire-purchaser.

3. **Payment of instalment:** Under the system the hire-purchaser is required to pay the hire purchase price which includes interest for the delayed payment, in periodic instalments. Each instalment is treated as hire charges and not as payment for ownership of goods.

4. **Hire purchase agreement:** As per the Hire Purchase Act of 1972, the hire-vendor and hire purchase must enter into a written agreement with the following contents:
   (a) The hire purchase price of the goods to which the agreement relates.
   (b) The cash price of the goods.
   (c) The date on which the agreement shall be deemed to have commenced.
   (d) The number of instalments by which the hire-purchase price is to be paid, the amount of each of those instalments, and the date, or the mode of determining the date, upon which it is payable, and the person to whom and the place where it is payable; and
   (e) The goods to which the agreement relates, in a manner sufficient to identify them.
   (f) The hire purchase agreement must be signed by the parties.

5. **Loss of goods:** The risk of loss to the goods is on the hire-vendor, provided hire-purchaser has taken care of goods.

6. **Liability of hire-purchaser:** The hire-purchaser is liable to keep the goods in good condition during the period when goods are in his possession. He has no right to sell or pledge the goods as he is not yet the owner of goods.

7. **Right of the hire-purchaser to buy at any time with rebate:** The hirer may, at any time during the continuance of the contract, can buy the goods, by giving 14 days notice, in writing to the vendor. The hirer is entitled to rebate calculated as per the following formula:

$$\text{Rebate} = \frac{2}{3} \times \frac{\text{Total hire purchase charges} \times \text{no. of instalment not yet due}}{\text{Total no. of instalment}}$$

The hirer shall pay the balance of the instalment amount less the rebate.

8. **Default by the hire-purchaser:** If the hire-purchaser fails to pay instalment the hire-vendor has a right to repossess the goods, as the ownership of goods is with the hire-vendor.

However if statutory proportion of the hire purchase price has been paid then repossession can take place only on the sanction of the court. Statutory proportion means one half of the price when the hire purchase price is less than ₹ 15,000 (in case of motor vehicles RS 5,000) and ¾th the price when the price is equal to or more than ₹ 15,000 (₹ 5,000 in case of motor vehicles).

9. **Refund to the hire-purchaser:** When the hire-vendor repossesses the goods for non-payment of instalment, he is not to refund the hire purchase price already received. But if the total amount of hire purchase price received so far plus the value of goods repossessed exceeds the amount paid by the hire-purchaser then the difference must be refunded to the hire-purchaser.

(Hire purchase price collected + value of good repossessed) – Hire purchase price of the goods = Refund.

4.4.3 Scope of the Purchase

(a) **Instalment Credit :** Many firms require large funds for purchase of plant and machinery or for constructions of factory-building. Hire-purchase financial institutions can provide finance for such purposes and arrange for repayments in equalised monthly or quarterly instalments. Such credit facilities are also required by merchants and especially, wholesalers.

Hire-purchase institutions can provide these facilities against hypothecation or against warehouse receipts.

(b) Financing of Purchase of Equipment, Vehicles etc. : A very important function of the Hire-purchase institution lies in this area. Many professionals like Doctors, especially Diagnostic specialists like Pathologists, Radiologists, Cardiologists, C. T. Scanners and Ultra-sound Testers, Architects and Interior designers, Engineers, Commercial artists, etc. require large investments on equipment, material and space. But they do not have any tangible security to offer to the lending institutions. The equipment etc. itself can, however, be hypothecated with the institution providing hire-purchase finance.

Similarly, many operators in the field of transport, plying heavy trunks, tankers, tempos, passenger buses, taxies, auto-rickshaws also need hire-purchase finance. Such finance is provided by Hire-Purchase Institutions or Commercial Banks doing such business.

(c) Purchase of Old Assets : Many times, people want to buy old buildings, second-hand or old vehicles. Banks and other term-lending institutions usually do not provide finance for such a purpose. Hire-Purchase Financial Institutions are bound to fill this gap.

(d) Consumer Credit : Hire-Purchase Institutions provide consumer credit for the purchase of residential houses/flats as well as for the purchase of durable consumer goods like Washing machines, Refrigerators, LCDs / LEDs, Smartphones and so on. Such schemes are, many times, operated through the dealers.

Rate of interest: The price quoted by the seller in the hire purchase system is higher than the price which he would have quoted for sale on cash basis. The excess of hire purchase price over the cash price is treated as payment for interest.

Hire purchase financer can adopt any of the following types of interest rates :

(i) Flat rate of interest: It is the discount rate at which future cash flows are discounted to arrive at the present value of money.

(ii) Add-on rate of interest: It refers to the rate of interest which is chargeable on the original cash price of the goods.

(iii) Effective rate of interest: It is also called as true rate of interest and is arrived at by a trial and error process. It is the rate at which present value of the stream of instalments is equal to the cash price of the asset bought on hire purchase.

Methods of Calculation of Interest (Annual):

The methods available are:
(i) Effective rate of interest or annual percentage method
(ii) Sum-of years digits method
(iii) Straight line method.

Effective rate of interest method: Under this method the rate of interest is determined by adopting the IRR technique. As per the technique the rate at which present value of all cash inflows is equal to cash price of the asset as deducted by the down payment.

For example, the asset price is ₹ 1,50,000. The hire-purchaser makes a down payment of ₹ 30,000 on the date of agreement. The balance to be paid is ₹ 1,20,000. Hire purchase agreement requires him to pay ₹ 50,000 p.a. for the next three years. That means he is still to pay ₹ 50,000 × 3 = ₹ 1,50,000. The total interest amount is ₹ 30,000. The rate of interest is the discount rate at which balance of ₹ 1,20,000 is equal to ₹ 1,50,000.

Sum of years digit method: Under this method the digits in the number of years is added up, and the proportion of total interest applicable to a particular instalment is calculated.

Illustration: A 3 year instalment would give rise to a sum of 6 ie. (3 + 2 + 1). The proportion applicable in the 1st year is 3/6. 3 is the total number of instalment remaining and 6 is the total no. of instalment. For the second year, two instalments are left in the beginning of the year hence the proportion applicable is 2/6. For the last instalment the interest proportion would be 1/6.

1st year interest = ₹ 30,000 × 3/6 = ₹ 15,000

2nd year interest = ₹ 30,000 × 2/6 = ₹ 10,000

3rd year interest = ₹ 30,000 × 1/6

Straight line method: Under the third method the total interest charged is divided equally over the number of instalments. In the example stated above the annual interest would be total of hire purchase interest divided by 3.

Annual interest amount = ₹ 30,000 / 3 = ₹ 10,000.

4.4.4 Difference between Hire Purchase and Leasing

Point of difference	Leasing	Hire purchase
1. Ownership	Under leasing the ownership of the asset lies with the lessor is never transferred to the lessee.	Under the hire purchase system the ownership of the asset gets transferred to the hire purchaser on payment of the last instalment.
2. Treatment in the profit and loss account	The entire lease payment is treated as rent and hence charged to profit and loss account of both the parties. Lessor shows it as income and lessee shows it as expenditure.	The entire hire amount cannot be charged to profit and loss account as a part of the hire charge is towards the capital value of the asset. Only the interest content of the hire charge is treated as revenue in nature and shown in the profit and loss account as income or expenditure as the case may be.

3.	Down payment	No down payment is required to be paid in case of leasing transaction since asset is not purchased.	On the other hand in case of hire purchase system there is an intention to trade and hence the hire-purchaser is required to pay a portion of cash price of the asset as down payment.
4.	Owner of asset	The leasing company need not necessarily be the owner of the asset leased. They may just be the financiers. Only when manufacturers of asset provide leasing facility, they remain the owners of the asset.	The hire-vendor is the owner of the goods dealt in.
5.	Maintenance expenses of the asset	In case of operating lease the maintenance cost is the responsibility of the lessor and in case of financial lease the lessee is responsible for the upkeep of the asset.	In case of hire purchase transaction, the hire purchaser is responsible for the maintenance of the asset.
6.	Salvage value of asset	The lessor has a right on the salvage value of the asset.	Hire-purchaser has a right on the salvage value of the asset as he becomes the owner of the asset on payment of the final instalment.
7.	Suitability	Leasing is used as a source of finance, for acquiring high cost asset such as plant and Machinery, Ships, Airplanes.	Hire purchase is used as a source of finance for acquiring relatively low cost assets such as automobiles, office equipment.
8.	Depreciation	Lessor, if owner of the asset is entitled to claim depreciation as a charge to profit and loss account and thereby get tax benefit (tax shield on depreciation)	Hire purchase being the prospective owner of the asset is entitled to tax shield on the depreciation of the asset.

4.5 Factoring - Meaning, Definition, Scope, Advantages and Limitations

Factoring is a unique financial service provided by factors which is both a financial as well as a management support to the client. It is a method whereby the book debts of a business are sold to a company that specialises in their collection and administration. The factor purchase the book debts at a discounted price and undertakes the collection of debts. The loss of bad debt is borne by the factor. Factoring is a unique financial innovation. It is both a financial as well as a management support to a client. It is a method of converting a non-productive, inactive asset (i.e. receivable) into a productive asset (viz. cash) by selling receivables to a company that specialises in their collection and administration.

4.5.1 Definitions of Factoring

1. **Biscoe P. N.:** Factoring can be defined as, *"a business involving a continuing legal relationship between a financial institution (factor) and a business concern (client) selling goods or providing services to trade customers, whereby the factor purchases the client's book debts and in relation thereto controls the credit, extended to customers and administers the sales ledger".*

2. **Westlake M.:** *Factoring is a contract between the suppliers of goods/services and the factor* under which: (a) The supplier and its customers other than those for the sale of goods bought primarily for their personal, family or household use; (b) The factor is to perform at least two of the following functions:
   (i) Finance for the supplier, including loans and advance payments
   (ii) Maintenance of accounts (ledger relating to the receivables)
   (iii) Collection of accounts, and
   (iv) Protection against default in payment by debtors.

3. **C. S. Kalyansundaram in his report (1988)** submitted to the RBI defines factoring as, *"continuing arrangement under which a financing institution assumes the credit and collection functions for its client, purchases receivables as they arise, maintains the sales ledger, attends to other book-keeping duties relating to such accounts, and performs other auxiliary functions."*

4.5.2 Features of Factoring

1. It is a contract between a factor and a client and buyer of goods.
2. The subject matter of contract is the book debts of the client which is purchased by the factor at a discounted price.
3. Realisation of debt is the main function of factor. The factor also provides the following three services to the client:

(a) Sales ledger administration and credit management
(b) Credit collection and protection against default and bad debt losses
(c) Financial assistance in the form of advance cash against book debts.

4.5.3 Process or Mechanism of Factoring

The agreement between the supplier and the factor specifies the factoring procedure. Usually the firm sends the customer an order to the factor for evaluating the creditworthiness of the customer and for approval. That means even before making a credit sale the firm consults the factor and only on receiving approval, makes the sale. Once the factor is satisfied with the creditworthiness of the customer, agrees to buy the receivables. The customer is informed that his account has been sold to the factor, and he is instructed to make payments directly to the factor.

The various activities performed by the three parties are stated below:

Factor:
1. Agreement is signed with the business firm to provide factor service.
2. On receiving copies of sale documents, advances a part of the receivable to the seller.
3. Provides credit administration service to the client.
4. Collects or receives payment from the buyer, and remits the due amount after deducting commission. Commission consists of interest for advance, reserve for bad debt and charge for administration cost.

Seller:
1. Signs Memorandum of Understanding with the buyer in the form of letter stating that the receivables will be assigned to a factor.
2. Sells goods to the buyer, after taking confirmation from the factor about the creditworthiness of the customer.
3. Delivers copies of invoice, delivery challan, instruction to make payment to the factor.
4. Sells the receivables to the factor and receives 80% or more of the debt as advance.
5. After the due date receives the balance of amount from the factor after deduction of factor's service charges.

4.5.4 Scope of Factoring Services

Factor services can be grouped under the following three categories:

1. Credit administration: A factor provides full credit administration services to the clients. From the stage of credit decision till the final stage of book debt collection.

On receiving order from the customers for goods, the seller sends the copy of the order to the factor and factor undertakes the necessary steps to determine the creditworthiness of the customer. The factor helps the client decide whether or not and how much credit to extend to the customer. If satisfied by the capacity of the customer, agrees to buy the book debt. The factor maintains a ledger of all customers and monitors debt collection.

2. **Credit collection:** When any payment becomes due from the customer, the factor undertakes all collection activity that is necessary. He also provides full or partial protection against debts. Since factor is an expert in debt collection, he can take necessary steps to guard against losses.

3. **Financial assistance:** Often factors pay advance cash against book debts to their clients. In such a case the customer of the client become debtors of the factor and are required to pay directly to the factor their dues.

4. **Other services:** In developed countries factors provide the following other services also:
   (a) Providing information on prospective buyers
   (b) Providing financial counselling
   (c) Assisting in managing liquidity
   (d) Financing acquisition of inventories
   (e) Providing facilities for letters of credit

4.5.5 Types of Factoring

On the basis of the arrangement between the client and factor, there can be different types of factoring. The important forms of factoring arrangements are :

1. **Recourse factoring:** Under this arrangement the factor does not bear the loss due to default in payment by the customer of the client. In other words, the factor does not bear the bad debt loss.

2. **Non-recourse factoring:** Under this arrangement factor has to bear the loss due to bad debt, hence in such an arrangement the factor charges are higher.

3. **Advanced factoring:** Under this arrangement the factor makes advance payment against the book debt. Even before collection of debt the factor makes payment to the client. The factor charges in such case include any interest from the date of advance till the due date of the book debt.

4. **Maturity factoring:** This is also called as collection factoring. The payment is made only after collection from the customer of the client.

5. **Disclosed factoring:** The name of the factor is disclosed in the invoice of sale instructing the buyer to make payment to the factor.

6. **Undisclosed factoring:** The name of the factor is not disclosed, hence the factor carries out the entire activity of collection in the name of the supplier company.

7. **Domestic factoring:** The three parties to the factoring arrangement belong to the same country.
8. **Export factoring:** There are four parties involved in export factoring- exporter, importer, export factor and import factor. It is also called as Two-Factor System of Factoring.

4.5.6 Advantages of Factoring

1. The client's cost of administration of debtors reduces.
2. There is improvement in liquidity as the factors often advance cash against book debts.
3. There is reduction in loss due to bad debts as factors are specialised in the job of debt collection.
4. It regulates the credit management of the clients business as creditworthiness of the customer is systematically analysed before granting credit. Besides for determining the period and amount of credit, the approval of factor is sought. Thus there is better credit discipline in the client's business.
5. It serves as a form of short term credit to the client.

4.5.7 Limitations of Factoring

1. Factoring may not be effective if the clients have their customers spread all over the nation.
2. Factors would interfere in the credit policy of the client.
3. The clients cannot maintain secrecy about the large customers.
4. It may reduce the scope for other borrowing - book debts will not be available as security.
5. How the factor deals with customers with affect what customers think of the organisation.

4.6 Forfaiting: Meaning, Scope, Advantages and Limitations

Forfaiting is a financial service provided by banks and financial institutions by way of purchasing the trade bill or promissory notes of an international buyer from the exporter, at a discounted price. Forfaiting thus converts a credit sale into a cash sale. The forfaiter takes all the the risks associated with the receivables but earns a margin.

4.6.1 Meaning and Scope of Forfaiting

Forfaiting is a method of trade finance that allows exporters to obtain cash by selling their medium and long-term foreign accounts receivable at a discount on a "without recourse" basis.

A forfaiter is a specialised finance firm or a department in a bank that performs non-recourse export financing through the purchase of medium and long-term trade receivables. "Without recourse" or "non-recourse" means that the forfaiter assumes and accepts the risk of non-payment. Similar to factoring, forfaiting virtually eliminates the risk of non-payment, once the goods have been delivered to the foreign buyer in accordance with the terms of sale.

Forfaiting as a financing concept has been in use across the world since the 1960s. The word forfait means to forgo one's right to something. In the context of export finance, the exporter forgoes his right to receive payment from the importer at later date and surrenders the right to collect payment to a third party or agency (known as forfaiter). Instead the exporter receives an immediate reimbursement of his payment less certain discounts from the forfaiter. Normally, these payments are due at a later date, forcing the exporter to bear the cost for the intervening period, as well as being exposed to the risks of exchange rate fluctuations, political situations etc. These are risks which expose a small or medium exporter to significant erosion of profits. With forfaiting finance, the exporter passes on his debts as well as attendant risks to the forfaiting agency. This form of financing is referred to as without recourse financing (in case the debt cannot be recovered there is no risk for the exporter). Forfaiting is a medium term financing option typically for the three to seven year time frame.

Forfaiting comes with the following terms and conditions:
- there is a discounting of the amount to be received from the importer
- discounting is on a fixed rate
- debt is in the form of bills of exchange or promissory notes guaranteed by a bank
- such financing is without recourse to the seller
- 100% of the amount receivable can be financed in this manner

Forfaiting – The Modus Operandi

The parties/agencies involved in a forfaiting transaction include the exporter, the importer, a forfaiting agency, a bank that stands guarantee (aval) for the bills of exchange or promissory notes (this is normally the importers bank) and the Exim bank in India acts as the facilitating agency between the Indian exporter and the forfaiting agency …Typically the exporter negotiates terms like price, payment currency, credit period and the like with their overseas buyer. The exporter then approaches the Exim Bank with these terms. The Exim Bank obtains a tentative forfaiting quotation from a forfaiting agency. Armed with this quote the exporter can now finalise the contract with the buyer. The exporter should ensure that most of the forfaiting charges are passed on to the buyer. Once the terms have been settled with the buyer, a final forfeiting quote is obtained by the Exim Bank. If this quote is acceptable, the exporter signs the contract with the buyer as well as a separate one with the forfaiting agency. Once shipment of goods has taken place the exporter obtains availed (guaranteed) bills of exchange from the importer (through an bank) or availed promissory notes. These bills of exchange or promissory notes are endorsed by the exporter and are routed to the forfaiting agency through the Exim Bank. The forfaiting agency will then remit the payment due to the exporter to an account of the exporter's bank in the country where the forfaiting agency is based. This bank then transfers the amount to the exporter in India, and the exporter will be provided with a Certificate of Foreign Inward Remittance as proof. When the promissory notes/bills of exchange reach maturity, the forfaiting agency collects the payment from the aval (the bank or agency that stands guarantee irrespective of whether the importer has paid the aval).

Forfaiting Costs

In a forfaiting transaction the exporter has to bears the following costs:

A commitment fee has to be paid to the forfaiter for the period of time from when the commitment is entered into upto the date of discounting or date of expiry of the contract. The commitment fee typically ranges between 0.5 to 1.5 per cent per annum of the utilised portion of the forfait amount. This fee has to be paid irrespective of whether the export takes place or not. The second, is the actual discount fee which is the interest on the receivable amount for the entire period of credit as well as a premium for the various risks involved. This fee is based on prevailing market interest rates including LIBOR (London Inter Bank Offered Rate). These are the two main costs involved. In addition there could be documentation costs in case of a lot of paperwork, penalties, handling charges etc. The Exim Bank which acts as the facilitator also charges a service fee which can be paid in Indian rupees.

As per RBI regulations it is mandatory that the discount fees and any documentation fees charged by the forfaiter should be passed on to the overseas buyer. During shipping, it is not necessary that any of the forfaiting fees be shown separately, they can be included in the FOB value indicated in the invoice. The export contract can be executed in any of the major convertible currencies of the world, in order to be eligible for forfeiting.

Forfaiting in India - Regulatory Aspects

Forfaiting as an export financing option in India has been approved by the Reserve Bank of India vide its circular A.D. (G.P. Series) No. 3 dated February 13, 1992. The Forfaiting facility is to be provided by an international forfaiting agency through an Authorised Dealer (see RBI Circular No. 42 A. D. (M.A.) series dated October 27, 1997).

Forfaiting proceeds, on a without recourse basis, are to be received in India as soon as possible after shipment but definitely within the 180 day period specified by RBI for all exports. A Forfaiting transaction is to be routed through an Authorised Dealer, who apart from handling documentation will also provide Customs Certification for GR Form purposes.

Definitions of Forfaiting:

1. **Investopedia:** "the purchasing of an exporter's receivbles (the amount importers owe the exporter) at a discount by paying cash".

2. **Business Dictionary:** "type of export financing (practiced largely in Europe) in which a forfaitor (usually a bank or a finance company) purchases freely negotiable instruments (such as unconditionally guaranteed letters of credit and order, bill of exchange) at a discount from an exporter. This arrangement is without recourse to the exporter who is relieved of all (commercial, political, exchange rate, and interest rate) risks, but is liable for the payment for the payment's legal validity and any defect resulting from the underlying transaction.

4.6.2 Essential Features of Forfaiting

1. Forfaiting is a financial service available in international trade.
2. The parties to forfeiting transaction are : forfaitor, exporter, importer and bank of the importer.
3. It is a contract between forfaitor and exporter whereby the former commits to buy the bill of exchange or promissory not of the importer at a discounted price. Thus on a credit sale exporter realises cash immediately.
4. It is without recourse to seller contract, which means the loss of non-payment by the buyer is borne by the forfaitor and not the exporter.

4.6.3 Process or Mechanism of a Forfaiting Transaction

1. The exporter and importer take a decision to enter into a trading transaction and decide about the terms and conditions of sale. The sale is to be a credit sale and the importer is ready to accept a bill of exchange for the amount due or the make a promissory note.

2. The exporter needs cash for the transaction earlier than the period of the negotiable instrument of the importer. He can approach a forfaitor to buy the instrument. The forfaitor would demand certain details of the transactions, importer and bank of the importer, and about the goods to be transacted, in order to decide whether to buy the bill of exchange or not.

3. After scruitiny of the details the forfaitor may agree to purchase the bill and would state his charges for the same. At this stage he may give his commitment.

4. On receiving commitment from the forfaitor the exporter would sign the trading transaction with the importer and furnish the details if transaction to the forfaitor so that the later can assess the validity of the transaction.

5. The exporter would deliver the goods and importer in return would sign the bill of exchange.
6. The bill of exchange would be purchased by the forfaitor at a discounted price. the transaction between the forfaitor and exorter is without recourse to hence exporter would not be interested in the transaction between the importer and forfaitor.
7. Forfaitor would collect the money on the receivable on maturity.

4.6.4 Advantages of Forfaiting

1. **Risk cover:** Forfaitor fully covers all the risks such as - country risk , currency risk like exchange rate fluctuations, interest rate risk. Thus an exporter is freed from risks associated with export trade.
2. Instant cash is received by the exporter. Thus the exporter is relived from liquidity crunch. Credit sale is converted into cash sale.
3. Loss due to non-payment by the importer or his guarantor is averted as forfaiting is non recourse facility.
4. A large range of instruments are covered by forfaiting like bill of exchange, promissory note, letter of guarantee, discounter receivables in the balance sheet.

4.6.5 Limitations of Forfaiting

1. The forfaitor has to bear the risk of default by the importer and importer, bank.
2. Forfaitor may interfere in the export trade due to the risk involved.
3. The risk of exchange rate fluctuation falls on the forfaitor.
4. It is an expensive arrangement since risk is high. The forfaitors charge premium charge.
5. Importer may not agree for forfaiting since the cost of forfaiting is to be borne by the importer.

4.6.6 Difference between Factoring and Forfaiting

Points of difference	Forfaiting	Factoring
1. Type of transaction:	Forfaiting is a finance service available for export trade.	Factoring is available for domestic trade.
2. Parties involved:	The parties involved in forfaiting are – importer, exporter, bank and exporters forfaitor.	The parties involved in factoring are the seller, the buyer and the factor.

3. Recourse to seller:	Forfaiting service is usually a non-recourse to seller service. The loss due to default by the bank of the importer is borne by the forfaitor.	Factoring can be a non-recourse to arrangement or recourse to arrangement.
4. Cost of financial service:	Cost of forfeiting is borne by the importer.	Cost of factoring is borne by the seller.
5. Suitability:	Forfaiting is suitable for transaction with medium term maturity period i.e. more than 6 months.	Factoring is suitable for transaction with short term maturity.
6. Finance:	The whole amount of the bill, promissory note etc. is paid as advance by the forfaitor after deducting the discount.	Only a certain part of the book debt is available as advance to the seller.

4.7 Discounting of Bills of Exchange

Bills of exchange is a negotiable instrument created against credit sales. The seller of credit sales makes the bill stating the amount due from the buyer, the time period within which the amount is payable, the date of drawing of the bill, and asks the buyer to sign it. Once it is signed as accepted by the buyer, it becomes a bill of exchange. It is bills receivable for the seller and bill payable for the buyer. The drawer of the bill i.e., the seller can do the following ;

1. retain the bill till the due date and present it for payment to the acceptor,
2. transfer the ownership of the bill in favour of his creditors during any time before the maturity of the bill
3. or sell the bill to a bank or financial institution before the due date and obtain discounted amount on the bill.

The last option is technically called as 'discounting of bill'. This makes available the amount of the bill before the maturity of the bill. The seller gets the advantage of higher liquidity. The margin between the face value of the bill and the net cash given on discounting is called discount. A part of the discount is the 'interest' on the advance made by the discounting agency and the balance is charged for the discounting.

Advantages:
1. It is like a short term finance made available to the trader.
2. In the presence of discounting facility buyers are likely to get credit sales facility.
3. The process is simple.
4. For banks and financial institutions it is a source of income.
5. The loss due to bad debt is not to be borne by the bank but by the drawer of the bill. Thus banks would not hesitate to discount bill.

Disadvantages:
1. In case of default by the acceptor of the bill, bank reverts to drawer for the amount of the bill.
2. The drawer will have to show the discounted bill as a contingent liability in his balance sheet till the bill is paid by the acceptor to the bank or the discounting agency.

4.8 Insurance

4.8.1 Meaning and Definition of Insurance

Insurance is a financial service for collecting the savings of the people and providing them risk coverage. Risk may be death, retirement, pension, education, or uncertain events like accident, theft, fire, ill-health etc. Some examples of insurance are life insurance, voyage insurance, vehicle insurance, crop insurance and building insurance.

1. According to **Chambers Dictionary**, the word 'insure' means *"to make arrangement for the payment of a sum of money in the event of loss or injury"* and Insurance means *"act or system of insuring".*
2. *"Insurance is a co-operative device to spread the loss caused by a particular risk over a number of persons, who are exposed to it and who agree to insure themselves against the risk".*

Insurance is a contract between two parties, the insurer and insured. Insurer agrees to indemnify insured against a loss which may be caused by the happening of an event or pay an assured sum on the death of the person whose life has been insured. The contract is embodied in a document called the policy. The maximum amount payable on the happening of the stated event, is called the policy amount. The consideration payable by the insured is called the premium. The contingency insured against is called risk.

4.8.2 Essential Features of Insurance Service

1. It is contract between two parties hence must have all the essentials of a valid contract. The contract is called 'Insurance Policy'.

2. The parties to the contract are the insurer and the insured. Insurer is the company which has agreed to compensate in case of loss. Insured is the party whose loss is going to be indemnified. In case of life insurance the loss of life cannot be indemnified hence these contracts are contracts of assurance.
3. The consideration for the agreement is premium which may be a periodic amount or single payment. The amount of premium depends on the policy amount along with other factors.
4. The maximum compensation for loss is limited to the policy amount. The rule is –'loss or the policy amount whichever is low'. In case of life insurance, the whole policy amount becomes payable on the death of the assured.
5. There are some insurance policies, where the policy amount becomes payable after a certain period. In other words it is like a saving for the insured.
6. Insurance companies are able to make good the losses, as all those who have taken policy do not suffer loss at the same time. By pooling the small resources of people they are able to meet the claims of those who have suffered losses and at the same time invest the balance of funds in productive activities and make profit out of it.

4.8.3 Types of Insurance

1. Life insurance/assurance: Life insurance policies are for long periods ranging between 25 to 30 years. The insured is to pay premium up to a certain year. On the death of the assured the policy amount is paid to the nominee. Some policies allow one to discontinue payment of premium after a certain minimum number of payments without losing all the money paid. In such cases a proportionate amount of the policy amount is payable on maturity.

As per Oxford Dictionary of Business and Management, "it is an insurance policy that pays specified amount of money on the death of the life assured or in the case of an endowment assurance policy, on the death of the life assured or at the end of an agreed period whichever is the earlier". The various life insurance policies are:

(a) In life insurance contract, the insurer agrees to pay a fixed sum called sum assured to the nominee of the insured in the event of the death of the persons whose life has been insured. Such policies are called the whole life policy. There is a variation to this policy called as endowment policy. These contracts make the payment of the policy amount either on the death of the policy holder or on the expiry of the stated period to the assured, whichever occurs earlier. Thus it allows the insured to enjoy the amount during his life time.

(b) The life insurance policies can be with profit policies or without profit policies. Under with profit policies the insured gets a share in the profits of the insurer called 'Bonus'. On the other hand under without profit policies, the insure does not get any profit share.

(c) Annuity policies provide a certain sum of money regularly to the insured from a certain age till death. Under the contract the insured is required to pay a lump sum amount to the insurer called as 'consideration for annuities granted'.

Advantages of Life Insurance Contracts:

(a) The most important benefit of life cover is it provides funds to the dependants on the death of the assured.

(b) Endowment policies give dual advantage of risk cover due to death as well as a source of investment.

(c) During the continuance of the life insurance contracts the needy can borrow money against their life insurance policies. Thus the policy is a security fro loan.

(d) The premium paid on life insurance policy can be deducted from the total income of the assured for calculation of tax liability. Further the amount realised on the policy on maturity is not taxable.

(e) In case of partnership firms insurance policies provide financial stability. On the death of a partner, his capital and interest in the partnership firm has to be settled. Insurance policy takes care of the need for funds.

(f) Insurance encourages thrift among the people which is not only good for the individuals but also for the economy. The premium paid by the policy holders is invested in productive activities, after keeping a part of it for claim settlement.

2. **General Insurance Contracts:**

General insurance contracts are meant to cover loss for short period of time, normally a year. Fire insurance, marine insurance, Building insurance, vehicle insurance are some examples. The insured enters into agreement with the insurer stating clearly the subject matter of insurance, the amount of policy which must be equal to the money value of the asset insured or else all the loss cannot be recovered from the insurance company, the risks to be covered, the period of insurance etc. in these policies, the rule is loss or the actual policy amount whichever is lower is paid by the insurer. These policies may have average clause, in which case if the asset is underinsured ie, the policy amount is less than the value of the asset, only proportionate amount of loss shall be indemnified by the insurer.

The risks that are covered by general insurance are:
- Property loss, for example, stolen car or burnt house
- Liability arising from damage caused by yourself to a third party
- Accidental death or injury

The main products of general insurance include:
- Motor insurance
- Fire/ Houseowners/ Householders insurance

- Personal accident insurance
- Medical and health insurance
- Travel insurance

Advantages of General Insurance:

1. The greatest advantage of general insurance is the risk cover to property and goods of the insured. For example fire insurance, accident insurance, theft insurance etc.
2. It is a short term contract. Hence can be taken when necessary.
3. The premium paid on the policy is chargeable to profit and loss account of the business and hence provides tax shield.

Scope of Growth of Insurance in India:

The business of life insurance was in the hands of the private players till 1956, when Life Insurance Corporation was established in the public sector by merging over 250 insurance companies. The general insurance was brought under the government in 1972 after the formation of General Insurance Corporation of India. After the Implementation of Insurance (Amendment) Act, 2002, private players have been allowed to conduct insurance business in India.

India's insurance market is growing but is yet to reach the majority of population. Privatisation of insurance is a good measure to increase the reach of the insurance sector, but then in India, this is a unique case where traditional players in the public sector are dominating and the private sector is not growing as is required.

The good thing is insurance companies are coming up with innovative products to attract customers. The related segments like health insurance, fidelity insurance etc. are growing.

The Indian insurance industry has undergone transformational changes since 2000 when the industry was liberalised. With a one-player MARKET to 24 in 13 years, the industry has witnessed phases of rapid growth along with extent of growth moderation and intensifying competition.

There have also been a number of product and operational innovations necessitated by consumer need and increased competition among the players. Changes in the regulatory environment also had a path-breaking impact on the development of the industry. While the insurance industry still struggles to move out of the shadows cast by the challenges posed by economic uncertainties of the last few years, the strong fundamentals of the industry augur well for a roadmap to be drawn for sustainable long-term growth.

The decade 2001-10 was characterised by a period of high growth (compound annual growth rate of 31 percent in new business premium) and a flat growth (CAGR of around two percent in new business premium between 2010-12), according to KPMG.

There was exponential growth in the first decade of insurance industry liberalization. Backed by innovative products and aggressive expansion of distribution, the life insurance industry grew at jet speed. However, this frenzied growth also brought in its wake issues related to product design, market conduct, complaints of management and the necessity to make course correction for the long term health of the industry.

Regulatory changes were introduced during the past two years and life insurance companies adopted many new customer-centric practices in this period. Product-related changes, first in ULIPs (Unit Linked Insurance Plans) in September 2011 and now in traditional products, will have the biggest impact on the industry.

New Product Guidelines

The new guidelines for both linked and non-linked products will now come into force from the beginning of year 2014, an extension of three months from earlier specified date. This additional period will ensure that life insurers enter the crucial quarter of Jan-March with a full bouquet of products and the sellers are well trained in the nuances of all these new products.

These product guidelines are in line with the IRDA's regulatory theme of customer orientation and long-term nature of the life insurance business. The guidelines follow two overarching themes of providing Guarantee and enhancing Transparency. The major changes introduced include - Higher Death Benefit, Guaranteed Surrender Value and mandatory Benefit Illustration for all life insurance products.

The changes related to death benefit and surrender value may marginally reduce the customers' overall maturity benefit, i.e., policy IRR, especially at higher ages but will ensure that life insurance serves the purpose of providing life cover which no other financial instrument offers.

All ULIPs are currently sold mandatorily with a personalised Benefit Illustration. This requirement is now being extended to other product forms. The new guidelines have also provided for setting up a "With Profit Committee" at the board level.

While personalized benefit illustration will provide for greater transparency in the pre-sales discussion, the With Profit Committee is likely to lead to greater governance in the administration of Participating policies. Premium paying term linked distributors' commission will promote the long-term nature of insurance products.

Future Looks Good

India continues to be a country of savers though we have witnessed a decline in the household savings rate in the past couple of years. In India, the problem lies in household savings lying idle or getting invested in saving instruments that do not help them achieve their life stage goals. There is a worrying trend of larger portion of household savings getting into non-productive physical assets such as real estate and gold.

But even then, the future looks interesting for the life insurance industry with several changes in regulatory framework which will lead to further change in the way the industry conducts its business and engages with its customers. World over it has been observed that the life insurance industry does behave in a counter cyclical manner in many cases, e.g., in a situation where the economic growth is slowing down, due to other factors such as high current account and fiscal deficits, currency depreciation, high interest rates, savings rate will continue to be high, leading to higher demand for life insurance.

Life insurance is a big savings vehicle along with banking in such uncertain economic environment and so we expect the industry to fare reasonably well. Demographic factors such as growing middle class, young insurable population and growing awareness of the need for protection and retirement planning will also support the growth of Indian life insurance.

For life insurance, it is time to re-commit itself to customer-centric behaviour, product solutions based on consumer needs, ethical market conduct, transparency and governance. The growth will be the natural outcome for now and years to come.

Points to Remember

- Financial services are an important component of the financial system. It is broadly understood to include stock broking, insurance, housing finance, banking and investment service.
- Financial services cover a wide range of activities. These services not only help to raise funds but also help in the efficient deployment of funds.
- Lease is one of the methods of financing the fixed assets of an enterprise. An enterprise with inadequate funds for financing the investment in plant and machinery may enter into lease agreement with the owners of the assets.
- "Under the Hire Purchase system, goods are delivered to a person who agrees to pay the owners by equal periodical instalments, such instalments are to be treated as hire of these goods, until a certain fixed amount has been paid, when these goods become the property of the hirer".
- Factoring is a unique financial service provided by factors which is both a financial as well as a management support to the client.
- Forfaiting is a financial service provided by banks and financial institutions by way of purchasing the trade bill or promissory notes of an international buyer from the exporter, at a discounted price. Forfaiting thus converts a credit sale into a cash sale.
- Insurance is a financial service for collecting the savings of the people and providing them risk coverage.

Questions for Discussion

1. What is Lease contract? Explain its financial implications.
2. Differentiate between Hire Purchase and Leasing.
3. Explain the essential elements of hire purchase financing.
4. What is Bills Discounting? What are the advantages and disadvantages of bill discounting as a source of short term finance.
5. Define Insurance. Justify insurance contract as a source of investment.
6. What are the differences between factoring and forfaiting?
7. Explain the methods of calculating interest in case of a hire purchase transaction?
8. What are the advantages of factoring?
9. What is the evolution and scope of financial services in India?
10. What is Forfaiting? Explain the mechanism of forfeiting.
11. Define Insurance. Explain the types of insurance and their advantages.
12. Describe the various financial services.
13. State the meaning, scope and evolution of financial services.
14. Write short notes on :
    (a) Types of Lease.
    (b) Hire Purchase Finance.
    (c) Forfaiting.
    (d) Discounting of Bill of Exchange.

Chapter 5...

Financial Services (Part - II)

Contents ...
5.1 Consumer Finance
5.2 Housing Finance
5.3 Credit Rating
5.4 Mutual Fund
5.5 Venture Capital
• Points to Remember
• Questions for Discussions

Learning Objectives
- To define the merchant banking and its scope
- To understand the different services, types of Housing Finance
- To understand the different types of Credit Rating and the Rating symbols and Implications

5.1 Consumer Finance

Meaning

Consumer Finance refers to the provision of credit to consumers to enable them to possess goods for everyday use such as cars, scooters, televisions, refrigerators, washing machines etc. it is also called as credit merchandising, deferred payments, installment buying. Typically in consumer finance, the individual pay a fraction of the cash purchase price at the time of the delivery of the asset and pays the balance with interest over a specified period of time. The main suppliers of consumer credit are – commercial banks, foreign and multinational banks, and finance companies.

Definitions

1. **Investor Dictionary:** The dictionary of retail banking that deals with lending money to consumers. This includes a variety of loans, including credit cards, mortgage loans, and auto loans.

2. **E. R. A. Seligman:** *"The term consumer credit refers to a transfer of wealth, the payment of which is deferred in whole or in part, to future, and is liquidated piecemeal or in successive fraction under a plan agreed upon at the time of the transfer"*

3. **Reavis Cax:** *"Business procedure through which the consumers purchase semi-durables and durables other than real estate, in order to obtain from them a series of payments extending over a period of three months to five years, and obtain possession of them when only a fraction of the total price has been paid."*

Essential Features of Consumer Finance:

1. **Parties to the transaction:** In a typical consumer finance there can be two to three parties – borrower i.e., the consumer, and financier / borrower, dealer and financier. In a Bipartite arrangement the parties are- borrower / consumer and dealer who is also the financier. On the other hand in a Tripartite arrangement the parties are customer/ borrower, dealer/seller and Financier (Bank, non-banking financial company).

2. **Modes of consumer finance:** The consumer finance can be arranged in the following ways:

   (a) **Hire purchase system:** Under this system the customer enters into a hire purchase agreement with the dealer. As per the agreement, the customer gets the possession of the goods on making the down payment. The balance of the cash price of the goods is payable in installments together with interest. But the consumer does not get the right to make outright purchase during the continuance of the arrangement, which is normally allowed in a hire purchase sale. The ownership of the goods is not transferred to the customer until the total purchase price including the credit charge is paid. The customer cannot terminate the agreement before the payment of full price.

   (b) **Installment sale:** The ownership is transferred to the customer on payment of the first installment. The customer may be asked to pay a part of the price of goods as down payment and the balance in periodic installments with interest. He cannot cancel the agreement.

   (c) **Overdraft or demand loan:** Commercial banks grant overdraft facility against the security of insurance policies, fixed deposit receipt, government securities etc. under the arrangement which is an ongoing one, the customer is allowed to draw more than the balance in his account but upto a limit. Interest is charged on the overdrawn amount.

   (d) **Credit loan:** Loan is provided against security of some asset of the customer, such as Life Insurance Policy (80% to 95% of the surrender value of the policy), Fixed deposit receipt, RBI relief bonds, Shares and Debentures etc. Loan may be sanctioned against equitable mortgage of immovable property.

3. **Period:** The period of finance range between 1 year to 5 years.

4. **Products covered:** Consumer finance in India covers a wide range of products such as cars, TVs, washing machines, refrigerators, geysers, air conditioners, computers etc.

Types of Consumer Credit or Finance

Types of consumer finance can be studies under the following heads:

1. **On the basis of period involved, consumer finance can be:**

   (a) **Revolving credit:** It is an on-going credit arrangement with the like overdraft facility with banker. This credit is not restricted to one specific purchase of goods. The financiers sanction a certain amount of credit and consumer is allowed to avail the facility till the limit is reached. Once the loan is repaid fresh credit of the same amount is available.

   (b) **Fixed Credit:** It is like a term loan. Consumer is sanctioned credit for a fixed period of time. The consumer has to settle the credit with interest within the stipulated time. Hire purchase is an example of such type of consumer credit.

2. **On the basis of security:**

   (a) **Secured loan:** As the name suggest the credit is granted on the security of an asset which may be a real property or a liquid asset like gold or claims like Fixed Deposit Receipt, LIC policy, NSC, KVP etc. In the event of default by the consumer the financial institution would seize the security.

   (b) **Unsecured loan:** These loans are not secured by asset of the consumer and hence the interest rate is higher and the amount sanctioned is small.

3. **On the basis of institution extending credit, consumer finance can be:**

   (a) **In house credit:** One of the popular methods of consumer finance is a credit by the trader from who consumer is buying goods. There is neither a down payment, nor any interest charged on such credit. Under this method retailer allows the customer to make any number of purchases during a month not exceeding a certain value.

   (b) **Finance by banks, non-banking financial institution, co-operative banks:** The finance from banks, etc. may be in the form of cash loan or credit payment facility. In the former case loan is given to the consumer and he is allowed to use the loan for purchasing any good or service.

   Under credit facility cash loan is not granted, rather credit is allowed after the purchase is made by the consumer and he is allowed to repay in installment or to make the payment within a stipulated time with interest. Credit card companies allow the repayment without any interest if the customer makes the payment within few days of the purchase of goods or service. In case of delay interest is levied.

Procedure

The procedure for sanction and operation of consumer finance can be grouped into two categories:

1. Pre-sanction stage
2. Post-sanction stage

1. **Pre – sanction stage:** Before sanction of loan or credit to the consumer the following activities are undertaken by the financier:
   (a) Receiving application for credit from the customer.
   (b) **Collecting credit information and evaluating the credit worthiness:** The credit worthiness of the consumer is established before sanctioning credit. The important information collected for the purpose are -the monthly income of the consumer, the nature of employment, the age, previous payment record, asset owned, borrower's equity in purchase, type of collateral offered. These details are collected from the customer, employer, local credit rating agency and any other third party.
   (c) **Accepting or rejecting the application:** If the customer is found to be credit worthy, and if there is no other legal or practical problem, then credit is sanctioned by the fancier and the terms of finance is discussed.
   (d) **Entering into contract:** The financier enters into contract with the customer. The following details must be mentioned in the contract, i.e., terms of financing:
   - amount of loan
   - details of security
   - period of finance
   - rate of interest applicable-fixed or floating
   - fees and charges
   - mode of payment and repayment.
2. **Post-sanction stage:** after the sanction of the loan/credit the following steps are undertaken
   (a) Submission of documents – documents include (i) Delivery letter (ii) Transfer deed. (iii) Security related documents.
   (b) Payment of credit/ finance or sanction of loan by opening loan account.
   (c) Payment of installment by the consumer.

Documents

As per the NHB guidelines housing loans processing is as follows:
1. **Credit Appraisal:** Objective of credit appraisal is to assess the applicant and his repaying capacity over the period. The appraisal should consider mainly the following points:
   (a) Income
   (b) Age
   (c) Employment details / business details

(d) Family background

   (e) Assets and liabilities

   (f) Track record of previous borrowing, if any (CIBIL report).

   (g) Income and Expenditure details.

2. **Documents required:**

   (a) Salary slips and forms 16 for last 3 years for salaried person and Balance sheet and profit and loss statement for last 3 years and income tax return copy, assessment order, shop act license in case of businessmen.

   (b) Residence proof.

   (c) Pan Card.

   (d) Latest photo.

   (e) Agreement with builder / contractor.

   (f) Copy of the approved plan.

   (g) Commencement certificate from local authorities.

Players in the Market of Consumer Finance:

The various institutions that are providing consumer finance are-

1. Commercial Banks
2. Non-Banking Financial institutions
3. Co-operative Banks

1. Commercial Banks: Commercial banks are the institution that accept deposits of money from people and lend the same to the needy. The rate of interest allowed on deposit is less than that charged on the money lent by them, thus they make profit. The money lent for consumer finance is of two types – (i) Direct finance and (ii) Indirect finance.

Under direct financing, the banks lend to the consumers directly by way of personal loan, meant to purchase consumer durables. Personal loans are granted without security.

Banks lend to commercial finance companies, hire purchase concerns and other such financial intermediaries, who in turn provide finance to consumer. Large sums of money are lent to these intermediaries at lower rate of interest. This is indirect finance.

2. Non Banking Financial Companies: A non banking financial company is a company registered under the company's Act, 1956 engaged in the business of loans and advances, acquisition of share/stock/bond/debenture/securities issued by Govt. or local authority or other marketable securities of a like nature, in leasing, hire purchase, insurance business, chit fund business.

NBFCs constitute another important source of consumer finance. Consumer finance companies also known as small loan companies, personal finance companies or licensed lenders, are non-saving institutions whose prime assets business receivables, personal cash loans, etc. they charge high rates of interest.

3. Co-operative banks: Co-operative bank is a co-operative society, which is doing the business of banking as defined in the Banking Companies Act 1949. A cooperative society is an association of persons united voluntarily to meet their common economic, social and cultural needs and aspiration through a jointly owned and democratically controlled enterprise. These banks lend money to their members.

Role of Consumer Finance in the Growth of the Economy:

In order to know the role of consumer finance in the growth of the economy, we may analyse the benefits of consumer finance:

Advantages to Consumer

1. **Increase in the demand for physical goods:** The availability of easy credit increases the demand for physical goods in the country. A consumer whose earning is not enough to buy a car would buy it under installment system because he can pay installment and enjoy the facility of a car. In the same way other consumer durables like LED televisions, washing machines, dishwashers etc. can be bought.

2. **Standard of living:** Availability of finance increases the demand for goods and services. The purchase of goods increases the comforts of people and leads to better standard of living.

3. **Forced savings:** When consumers buy goods under installment system or by availing consumer loan, they are to pay for the installment, which amounts to forced savings. Had there been savings first and purchase of goods after the needed funds saved, probably consumer wouldn't have saved in a systematic way.

4. **Emergency expenditure:** Consumer finance helps the consumer meet their emergency needs.

Benefits to the Trader:

1. **Increase in sales of goods:** Easy finance whether by the trader or by the financier, increase the total turnover of the trade, thereby increase his profits. But it increases the default risk if the trader is the financier as well.

2. **Increased goodwill:** Goodwill helps the trader in the long run as well. It increases the life of business.

3. **Increase in business of manufacture:** Increase in the sales of trader increases the demand for goods of the manufacturer.

Thus three parties directly engaged in consumer finance viz consumer, financier and trader, benefited. There are others also who are benefitted by the consumer finance:

1. There is a general increase in the demand for loans and advances in the economy. Manufacturer would need more of long term funds to invest in fixed assets to meet increased demand for goods. Thus banks and financial institutions start lending more. This increases their revenue.

2. Increase in demand for goods increases the demand for capital goods like plant and machinery, equipment etc. Thus the sale of capital goods increases, thereby generating more revenue to the producers of such goods. Further, this adds to the increase in demand for finance from banks and financial institutions.

3. Increased investment in machinery, equipment to meet increased demand increase the demand for labour – skilled, unskilled and semi-skilled. There is more employment generated in the economy.

4. The increased employment increases the purchasing power of the people who demand further goods and services and also save a part of their earnings for future, leading to increased deposits in banks and purchase of instruments like share, debenture, bonds, mutual funds, pension funds etc.

5. Banks and financial institutions get deposits which are lent by them to the needy and a part invested in bonds, gold bullion, government bonds etc.

Thus there is overall growth of all the sectors of the economy leading to economic growth.

5.2 Housing Finance

Housing finance refers to the provision of finance to individuals or group of individuals for the purchase, construction or related activities, of house, flat etc. Housing loan is a type of installment credit which forms the largest single source of housing finance.

1. Housing loan can be availed for the following purposes:
    (a) Construction of house,
    (b) Extension of existing house,
    (c) Purchase of house/ apartment,
    (d) Both for the purchase of plot and for construction of house,
    (e) Acquire house through co-operative society.

2. **Sources of housing finance:** Individuals and groups in need of finance for housing may depend on their own savings and their properties or else borrow from friends, relative etc. There are formal agencies which finance housing requirements. Such as commercial banks, housing finance banks, co-operative banks, Non banking financial companies, non banking housing finance companies and specialised institutions set

up to provide housing finance. The various institutions providing housing finance in India include-

(a) Industrial Development Bank of India (IDBI)
(b) Housing Development Finance Corporation ltd (HDFC)
(c) State Bank of India (SBI)
(d) Life Insurance Corporation of India (LIC)
(e) Tata Home Finance etc.

3. **Rate of Interest**

    (a) **Fixed rate:** The interest charged on the housing loan can be a fixed rate of interest or a floating/variable rate of interest. Under fixed rate of interest method, the rate of interest over the period of loan (say 10 years) will not change even if the market rate of interest changes. If the market rate of interest falls, the loan has to be paid at the higher rate of interest agreed upon at the time of agreement.

    (b) **Floating rate:** Under variable rate of interest arrangement the loan repayment is made at the rate of interest prevalent at the time of repayment ie., Prime Lending rate (PLR). In India it is the average rate of interest charged by commercial banks to private individuals and companies. Floating rates are better in a falling rate scenario, but expensive in an increasing rate scenario.

    (c) **Fixed and Floating Rate:** Some housing financers allow shifting from fixed rate to fluctuating rate. Sometimes the customers are on charged fixed rate of interest in the initial years and thereafter floating rate of interest.

4. **Charges and Fees payable:** The charges payable for availing loan facility include the following:

    Processing fees, search report charges by the advocate at the time of sanction and insurance charges are the charges payable at the time of sanction of loan. The housing finance institution may deduct this amount out of the total loan sanctioned. During the continuation of loan period fine for non-repayment or late payment of installment has to be paid if non-payment or late payment is made by the customer.

5. **Security for the Loan:** According to Oxford Dictionary of Business and Management, "Security is an asset or assets to which a lender can have recourse if the borrower defaults on the loan repayment. In case of loans by banks and other money lenders the security is sometimes referred to as 'collateral'."

    Security given can be a physical asset or a financial asset like shares, bonds, LIC policy etc. it may be a Primary Security, Collateral Security or Interim Security.

Primary security is the asset itself that is created or bought out of the loan granted, and collateral security is any other security offered for the said facility. For example in case of housing finance, the house itself is the primary security and any other additional security given such hypothecation of jewellery, mortgage of land etc. is a collateral security. Primary security is given by way of deposit of title deeds.

Interim security may be additionally required, if the property is under construction. Collateral or interim security could be assignment of life insurance policies, the surrender value of which is at least equal to the loan amount, guarantees from sound and solvent guarantors, pledge of share and such other investments that are acceptable to the financer.

Types of Housing Finance

Major Housing Finance Institutions in India:

A number of institutions provide housing finance in India. The major institutions operating are as follows:

1. National Housing Bank (NHB): The National Housing Bank was established in July 1988 under an Act of Parliament, to function as the apex institution in the housing sector. It is wholly owned by RBI. The NHB was set up to perform promotion function, regulatory function, and financing function.

Home loan account scheme of NHB: Home loan account scheme of the NHB was initiated with a view to encourage people to save for housing. The basic features of the scheme are:

(a) **Eligibility:** Any Indian citizen who is not owning any house in his or her name can open an account under this scheme.

(b) **Contribution:** The individual has to save a minimum amount in the account up to a period of 5 years, every month to be eligible for housing loan.

(c) **Interest:** The deposit under the scheme is eligible for 10% interest.

(d) **Default:** If the depositor fails to deposit for a continuous period of 12 months, then the original date of opening the home loan account is shifted forward by the period of default.

(e) **Withdrawals:** The amount can be withdrawn only after 5 years for construction or buying house.

(f) **Loan eligibility:** On completion of the saving period an account holder is eligible for loan as under-

For a built up area of 430 sq ft.	4 times the accumulated saving
Upto 860 sq ft	3 times the savings
Above 860 sq ft	2 times the savings

(g) Interest on Loan:

For a loan up to ₹ 50,000	10.5%
From ₹ 50,001 to ₹ 1,00,000	12.0%
From 1,00,001 to ₹ 2,00,000	13.5%
Above 2,00,001	14.5%.

2. **Housing Development Finance Corporation Ltd. (HDFC Ltd.):** It is a leading private sector housing finance company in India. It was set up in 1977 by the ICICI. The two important schemes offered by the HDFC are:

   (a) Home Saving Plan
   (b) Home Loans

   (a) Home saving Plan: It is similar to the Home Loan Account Scheme of NHB. Under the scheme an individual can open a saving account singly or along with spouse and a child. The minimum period of saving is 25 months with a maximum period of 7 years. The amount of loan will be equal to 70% of the cost of the property and the balance 30% would be financed from the borrower's savings.

   (b) Home loan (individuals): In order to provide housing finance, HDFC offers the following types of loan:

   (i) **For dwelling house:** These loans are given to individuals, base on their income. They are repayable over a period of 20 years.

   (ii) **Extension of existing houses:** Loans are provided for either vertical or horizontal extension of existing houses.

   (iii) **Purchase of land or plots:** It provides loans for the purchase of land or plots for construction of house.

   (iv) **Repair and renovation:** Loans are available for repairs and modernisation of existing houses.

   (v) **Large housing loan:** It is provided to group of individuals or employees of an organisation, on the basis of collective responsibility.

3. **Life Insurance Corporation Housing Finance Ltd (LICHFL):** The corporation was set up under the Companies Act 1956, incorporated in 1989. It is recognised by the NHB. The housing loan of LICHFL can be grouped under:

   (a) Loan to individuals: Loan assistance is provided to individuals for purchase/construction/extension of residential house including for second residential house.

   (b) Loan to corporate: Loan assistance is available to public sector undertakings and public limited companies for construction of 'Staff Quarters', for Office premises, and also to the employees of these institution on the guarantee of the company.

(c) **Loan to co-operative societies:** Loans to individual members of co-operative housing societies formed by employees of public sector undertakings with the guarantee of the undertaking.

(d) **Loan to public agencies:** Loan is provided to public agencies like housing boards, for residential housing projects.

(e) Bridge loans to reputed developers for housing projects.

The various schemes of LIC Housing Finance Ltd. are – Griha Pravesh, Griha Shubh, Griha Dhara, Griha Lakshmi, Griha Jyothi, Jeewan Niwas, Jeewan Kutir.

4. GIC Housing Finance: It was set up in 1989 by the General Insurance Corporation as its subsidiary company. The various schemes are – Apna Ghar Yojna, Repais/Renovation, Line of Credit to Company, Line of Credit through company, Employees Housing Scheme, Construction Finance Scheme.

5. Housing and Urban Development Corporation of India (HUDCO): It was incorporated in 1970, established by the central government. The main objective was to meet the housing need of the low-income group and economically weaker sections of the society. HUDCO undertakes the following housing finance.

Urban and rural housing, cooperative housing, night shelter for pavement dwellers, working women ownership condominium, staff rental house, repairs renewals and up gradation, housing through NGO's and individual housing loans through 'HUDCO' Niwas.

6. SBI Home Finance: It was established in 1988 as a subsidiary of the State Bank of India, to provide financial assistance for housing. The loan is granted for construction of houses, purchase of house/flat, repairs and renovation, extension, and alteration of the existing houses. The rate of interest varies from time to time depending upon the amount of loan, term of loan and purpose of loan.

Types of Housing Loans: Some popular types of Home loans are discussed below:

1. **Land Purchase Loans:** These loans are meant to assist the applicant in buying plot for the construction of house. The loan granted is normally 85% of the price of the plot. Banks like ICICI bank (land loan), Axis Bank (loan for Land purchase) etc., lend for this purpose.

2. **Home Purchase Loans:** These loans are granted to purchase a new residential property or an old one. Up to 85% of the market value of house is granted as loan.

3. **Home Construction Loan:** The loan is given for construction of house, the application and processing of such loan is different from those for the purchase of house. The applicant has to make a rough estimate of the cost that will be incurred for the construction of the house and then apply for loan. The loan amount may be disbursed at one go or in several installments according to the progress of the work of construction of the house. Banks like SBI, Canara Bank, Corporation Bank etc. lend this type of loan.

4. **Home Expansion/Extension Loan:** This loan is available for the vertical or horizontal extension of an existing house. Example of extension are – construction of additional room, a floor, a bigger bathroom, or enclosing bathroom.

5. **Home Improvement Loan:** Renovation and repair works such as internal and external painting, electrical work, construction of underground or overhead water tank etc. can also be financed through loans and such loans are called home improvement loans.

6. **Home Conversion Loan:** An existing loan can be transferred to a new house. HDFC provides such loans.

7. **NRI Loan:** Housing loan to non-resident Indians is called NRI loans. The paper work is elaborate in the case. Almost all public and private banks provide this kind of loan.

8. **Balance Transfer Loan:** This is a transfer of loan from one bank to the other. The reasons may be to avail better service or to avail lower rate of interest on the housing loan. Deutshe Bank, ICICI Bank and Kotak Mahendra are some examples of the banks giving such housing loans.

9. **Stamp Duty Loan:** This loan is granted exclusively to meet the expenses of stamp duty while registering a house in one own name. This loan is to be used for the said purpose only.

10. **Bridged Loan:** It is short term loan given to those who already have a house but want to buy another house by selling the previous one. They may need loan for the new house till the time their old house is realised. Vijaya bank is one of the banks that provides this kind of loan.

Housing Finance Scenario in India: Housing loans are an attractive means of owning a dream house for most of the people in India. The demand for housing finance has increased manifold in the last decade. India is highly populated country. Housing needs are increasing, hence there is a great need and scope for the development of this sector. Some important points with regard to housing finance in India can be-

1. There is tax benefit available for house purchase or construction. Tax benefits are available for both interest and principal amount paid towards housing loan.

2. There are large number of players in the sector. This has lead to high level of competition among the lenders. Therefore the interest rates are almost uniform for housing loans.

3. The companies and institutions are providing special services to attract higher market share. Almost all the big players offer standard services. Hence the banks like ICICI, LIC, HDFC etc. are dominant players.

5.3 Credit Rating

1. According to Webster's new world Finance and Investment Dictionary:

"Credit rating is a formal evaluation of an individual's or company's credit history and ability to repay obligations. Many firms investigate, analyse, and maintain records on the credit responsibility of individuals and business. A credit rating is based on the number of outstanding debts and whether debts have been repaid in a timely manner in the past."

2. According to Oxford Dictionary for Business and Management:

"Credit Rating is an assessment of the creditworthiness of an individual or firm i.e., the extent to which they can safely be granted credit. Traditionally, banks have provided confidential trade references, but recently credit reference agencies also known as credit rating agencies have grown up, which gather information from wide range of sources like court, bankruptcy proceedings, hire-purchase companies and professional debt-collectors. This information used to be then provided as credit reference for a fee to interested parties. There are also agencies that specialise in the corporate sector, giving details of a company's long-term and short term debt".

Credit rating is a grading service. It is a technique in which relative ranking is provided to different instruments of a company on the basis of systematic analysis of the strengths and weaknesses of them. The credit ranking is done on the basis of analysis of financial statements, project analysis, credit worthiness of the company, past history of repayment of debt and future prospects of the concerned project.

Definitions of Credit Rating:

According to **L. M. Bhole** *"it can be defined as an act of assigning values to credit instruments by estimating or assessing the solvency, ie. the ability of the borrower to repay debt, and expressing them through pre-determined symbols".*

Essential Features

1. Credit rating is done by independent agency.
2. It is more popular with debt instruments like debenture, bond etc. through the issue of which, companies borrow money from the investors. There are other credit ratings too, like equity rating, commercial paper rating, borrowers rating, and sovereign rating.
3. It is a service to evaluate the debt servicing capacity of a company ie., its capacity to pay interest to the creditors as per agreement and its capacity to repay the principal amount of the debt.
4. Rating is done by analysing the Financial statements of the business, the prospects of the project for which debt instruments were issued, past history of the company, and credit worthiness of the company.

5. Rating is expressed by way of pre-determined symbols like triple A ie., AAA would imply highest security, AA would mean high safety etc.
6. It is an advisory service. Hence an instrument given high credit, if proves to be otherwise, the investor cannot make the credit agency liable for loss.
7. Credit rating is not a permanent rate given to an instrument. With the change in the liquidity, profitability of company and concerned project, the rating should be upgraded or downgraded.
8. In India credit rating is not obligatory in case of equity shares. It is only the debt instruments for which credit rating is obligatory. The instruments include convertible and non-convertible debentures/bonds, fixed deposits issued by non-banking financial companies and commercial paper. If the size of the issue is more than ₹ 100 crore, the issue is to be rated by at least two credit rating agencies.

Origin: The origin of credit rating can be traced to 1840s when the first mercantile credit agency was set up in New York by Louis Tappan. The objective was to rate the ability of the merchants to pay their financial obligation. In 1849, John Bradstreet set up a rating agency. These two agencies merged in 1933 under the name Dum and Bradstreet. In 1900 John Moody founded Moody's Investors Service. It published 'Manual of Railroad Securities in 1909. Several companies such as Poor Publishing Company in 1916, the standard Statistics Company in 1992, and Fitch Publishing Company further published credit ratings in 1924. Then a number of credit rating institutions started commercial operations all over the world- Duff and Phelps Credit Rating Company, Japanese Bond Rating Institution, Thomson and Phelps etc.

As capital markets grew, more and more companies made public issue of their debt instruments for their capital requirement. Investor's interest grew in the debt instrument due to definite returns and return of the principal amount of investment after the stipulated period. But many companies had failed in the past to meet their debt servicing obligation. A study of the company's history regarding debt repayment and interest payment as well as its present capacity to pay interest and principal amount, was needed by the investors. The study requires a lot of research and expertise to analyse the financial and non-financial information about the issuer, which not possible for the investors. Therefore independent agencies have come up to assess the debt servicing capacity of different companies. In India the CRISIL was set up as the first credit rating agency in 1987 followed by ICRA, CARE and so on.

Types of Credit Rating: The different types of credit ratings are:
1. **Bond Rating:** Rating of the bond or debt securities issued by a company, Government or Quasi-government body is called bond. This type of rating occupies the major share in the business of credit rating agencies.

2. **Equity Rating:** The rating of equity shares in the capital market is called equity rating and it occupies the minimum share in the business of credit rating agencies.
3. **Commercial Paper rating:** It is mandatory on the part of a corporate body to obtain rating from credit rating agency before issuing commercial paper in the market.
4. **Borrower's rating:** This a rating to establish the credit worthiness of a prospective borrower- an individual or a firm. Rating agencies collect information about individual or firms from various sources like court, bankcruptcy proceedings, hire purchase traders etc. Banks would like to get the ratings before lending money to customers.
5. **Sovereign rating:** This is a rating done by international credit agencies assessing the creditworthiness of a country. Sometimes the central government may get such rating done for the states of the country.

Advantages of Credit Rating:
1. Credit rating helps investors to invest in best available investments and reduce their risk. Funds of the investors are directed towards more productive investment, the possibility of investment failing is comparatively less.
2. A company can float its instruments at less cost if the credit rating is favourable. Besides it would be easier for such companies to raise funds from the market.
3. It works as a motivator for companies to improve their performance.
4. The savings of the people is directed towards productive investment. Thus the resources of the country is put to best use.

Limitations of Credit Rating
1. The rating depends upon the information available to the rating agencies. Further the business world is dynamic. The rating hence may not be correct sometimes.
2. It is compulsory for companies to get ratings done for some instruments under certain circumstances. But companies may not publish such rating.
3. The rating by different agencies, for the same instrument of a company may be different.
4. Subjectivity of the rating agencies may creep in defeating the whole purpose of rating.

Credit Rating symbols: The credit rating symbols of different credit rating agencies are given below. The basic description for the use of symbols is same as used by CRISIL.

Credit rating agencies in India and symbols used:

Credit Rating Information Services of India Ltd. (CRISIL): It is the first credit rating agency in India. It was promoted in the year 1987 by the ICICI and Unit Trust of India along with other institutions- Asian Development Bank, Life Insurance Corporation, HDFC Ltd,

General Insurance Corporation and several Indian and foreign banks. It provides the following services:

(a) Credit rating of debentures, deposits, preference shares, chit funds and commercial paper.

(b) It provides information services.
- 'Crisil card' provides corporate and balance sheet data for analysis.
- 'CRISIL view' highlights the outlook and solvency of the concerned companies on the basis of published data.
- 'CRISIL judge' provides data as well as analysis of Indian companies.
- CRISIL 500 Equity Index' is an index of equity shares of 500 companies representing 74% of the market capitalisation of the BSE.

(c) Advisory services: it provides advisory services to the Government, banks and financial institutions etc. it also provides training facilities.

Rating Symbols: The ratings and symbols used by CRISIL for debenture, fixed deposit and short term instruments is given below.

Debenture rating:

Rating	Implication
Triple A –AAA	Highest security
Double a – AA	High safety
Single A – A	Adequate Safety
Triple B –BBB	Moderate safety
Double B –	Inadequate Safety
B	High risk
C	Substantial Risk
D	Default

Fixed Deposit Rating:

Rating	Implication
FAAA	Highest Safety
FAA	High Safety
FA	Adequate safety
FB	Inadequate safety
FC	High risk
FD	Default

Short Term Instruments

Rating	Implication
P-1	Highest Safety
P-2	High Safety
P-3	Adequate Safety
P-4	Inadequate safety
P-5	Default

2. **Investment Information and Credit Rating Agency of India Ltd. (ICRA):**

ICRA was incorporated on January 16, 1991 and launched its services on August 31, 1991. The main promoter is IFCI Ltd. and other promoters are Unit Trust of India. LIC, HDFC, ILFS, GIC, and Exim bank. It offers credit rating services for rating debentures/bonds, preference shares, medium term debts including certificates of deposits as well as short term instrument including commercial paper and also credit rating of LPG firms or dealers and banks. Besides credit rating services ICRA also provides advisory and information services.

Rating Symbols

Long Term Instruments – Bonds, Debentures, Preference Shares:

Rating Symbols	Implication
LAAA	Highest Safety
LAA +, LAA	High safety
LA +, LA	Adequate Safety
LBBB	Moderate Safety
LBB+, LBB	Inadequate Safety
LB+, LB	Risk prone
LC+, LC	Substantial risk
LD	Default extremely speculative

3. **Credit Analysis and Research Ltd. (CARE)**

The CARE Ltd is promoted by the Industrial Development Bank of India jointly with financial institutions, private and public sector banks and private finance companies. It commenced its credit rating in October 1993 and provides besides credit rating services, advisory services, information services, equity research etc.

Rating symbols	Implication
CAR-1	Excellent debt management capability
CAR-2	Very good management capability
CAR-3	Good capability in debt management
CAR-4	Barely satisfactory capability for debt management
CAR-5	Poor capability for debt management

4. FITCH Ratings India Ltd: It is an international agency that provides global capital market investors with highest quality ratings and research. It provided ratings for financial institutions, insurance corporate, sovereigns and public finance markets worldwide. FITCH India is a 100% subsidiary of FITCH group. It is the only rating agency in India with the ability to issue ratings o both domestic and international debt iuues.

Rating symbols

Long term Investment (12 months and above)

AAA (ind)	Highest Credit quality
AA (ind)	High Credit quality
A (ind)	Adequate Credit Quality
BBB(ind)	Moderate Credit Quality
BB (ind)	Speculative
B (ind)	Highly speculative
C (ind)	High default risk
D (ind)	Default

Time Deposits (Bank Deposits and Fixed Deposits)

tAAA (ind)	Highest Credit Quality
tAA+(ind)	High Credit Quality
tA+(ind)	Adequate Credit Quality
tB+(ind)	Speculative
tC(ind)	High Default Risk
tD (ind)	Default

Global Credit Rating Agencies: A brief account of some important global rating agencies is given below:

1. **Moody's investors service:** The agency was founded in the 1909 by John Moody of the US. It was the first agency to introduce rating system in the US. The agency offers rating coverage for a wide range of debt related securities, both in the US and

international markets. It also offers sovereign ratings. It has network of offices in other countries.

2. **Standard and Poor's Corporation (S&P)**: It is a premier international rating agency, which began its operations with a publication containing financial information on US industrial companies. It offers ratings on a wide range of debt securities, both in the US and overseas markets, US corporate, Municipalities and states, and sovereign nations. It publishes ratings of common stocks and mutual funds.

3. **Duff and Phelps Credit Ratings Co (DCR):** DCR is a major international source of credit information. It rates all major types of fixed-income securities, long-term and short-term debt of corporations, sovereign nations and financial institutions. It also rates insurance companies. It has joint venture with Asian countries and Latin American countries.

4. **Japan Credit Rating Agency (JCR)**: It was established in 1985 and was promoted by financial institutions, banks and insurance companies in Japan. It provides ratings to domestic and foreign debt issues.

CIBIL

The CIBIL TransUnion Score is a 3 digit numeric summary of a prospective borrower's credit history which indicates his/her financial & credit health. The Score is derived from ones credit history as detailed in the Credit Information Report [CIR] and ranges from 300 to 900 points. The credit score tells the lender how likely the borrower is to pay back loan or credit card dues based on the past repayment behaviour. The higher the score, the more the chance of loan application getting approved.

Equity rating: An evaluation of stocks of a company and assigning rates is called equity rating. Equity share is ownership based security which entitles the holder to residual profits. Equity can be purchased from the primary market or from the secondary market. Primary market is the company itself which is floating it's shares and secondary markets are the stock exchanges where the concerned security is listed. In case of debts the investor get interest at a fixed rate over a period of time and repayment of principal amount on the maturity of the bond/debenture etc. but equity is different. It is a risky investment. Company may pay or may not depending upon the profitability or otherwise of its projects. The source of income for equity shareholder can be:

1. **Dividend:** It is a share in the residual profits of the company. After the claims of bond holders, income-tax liability, transfer to reserve and preference dividend is settled, the equity shareholders are paid a share in the profits. It is thus very risky. There is no obligation on the part of the company to pay dividend.

2. **Capital gains:** Most of investors are interested in making capital gain on their holdings. They buy the shares at lower prices than at which they sell and thus make profits out of the transaction.
3. **Profit from trading:** Another most important source of income is making profits by trading in the shares of companies. Many investors buy and sell shares many number of times in a short period to make profits. The intention here is not to hold the shares as co-owner in the company.

Need for Equity Rating:
1. Credit rating by reliable agencies would result in quality information about the companies and their stocks, helping the investors in making right choice.
2. Lesser known entrepreneurs also would be able to raise funds by issue of equity in the market on the basis of profitability of the project as reflected in the credit rating of credit rating agencies.
3. Credit rating is done for each security of a company. Thus if a company is profit making but a particular project has no profit prospects then the stock associated with that particular project would not get a good rate. Investor can decide which particular stock of a company is worth purchasing and not blindly purchasing any stock of an efficient company.

Grading: For the purpose of rating stocks fundamentals of the company is analysed. Benchmarks are set for certain key performance parameters. The performance of a company is then measured against these benchmarks.

Fair value of stock is calculated by an objective evaluation of the company. If the Fair value exceeds the market value of a share, then the share may be bought as its value is more than its price and the market price is likely to move up to match the fair value in which situation those bought the share would make profits. On the other hand if Market value of a stock is higher than the fair value, then the investors may sell the stocks held by them as any time market price will fall to match the fair value.

Equity grades of ICRA

ERA 1 : Excellent earning prospect and low risk
ERA 2 : Excellent earning prospect and moderate risk
ERA 3 : Excellent earning prospect and high risk
ERB 1 : Good earning prospect and low risk
ERB 2 : Good earning prospect and moderate risk
ERB 3 : Good earning prospect and high risk
ERC 1 : Moderate earning prospect and low risk
ERC 2 : Moderate earning prospect and moderate risk

ERC 3 : Moderate earning prospect and high risk

ERD 1 : Poor earning prospect and low risk

ERD 2 : Poor earning prospect and moderate risk

ERD 3 : Poor earning prospect and high risk.

5.4 Mutual Fund

Meaning of Mutual Funds

Investors like to maximise their returns and minimise their risk. Diversified portfolio can help achieve this objective. But all investors may not have the time or the expertise to take decisions regarding diversification of investment. Mutual fund investment caters to the needs of such investors. By participating in a scheme of mutual fund, the investor becomes a part owner of all the investments held under the scheme, in the same proportion as the scheme. Every unit will have the same proportion of debt and equity as is the scheme.

Mutual funds are investment companies that invest the funds collected from the sale of their units or shares, in different classes of assets, on behalf of their unit holders or share holders. Mutual fund is a portfolio of investment. Small investors who don't possess knowledge and are not ready to take risk may depend on mutual funds. Investors can buy the units of mutual fund and become its member. The fund managers would manage the funds of the members and make investment on behalf of the investors and distribute the profits from the investments to its members.

Types of Mutual Funds

1. Mutual Funds Schemes on the Basis of Asset Mix

Mutual fund schemes can be classified on the basis of asset-mix into three broad categories:

(a) Equity schemes;

(b) Debt schemes; and

(c) Hybrid schemes.

(a) Equity Schemes:

These schemes invest around 85% to 95% of the funds in equity shares or equity linked instruments and the balance in cash. Equity schemes can be:

(i) **Diversified equity scheme:** Under this scheme, wide range of industries are chosen for investment. It invests in the equity of diversed industries. For example the portfolio may consist of investment in FMCG, Petroleum and oil, agro based industries, pharmaceutical, automotive industries, banks etc.

(ii) **Index schemes:** This scheme invest in the equities that are listed in a stock exchange. For example if 30 stocks are listed in sensex, then in those 30 stocks investment will be made by the mutual fund in the same proportion as the respective equity base of the 30 companies. The index scheme appreciates or depreciates in the same way as the concerned index.

(iii) **Sectoral schemes:** These schemes invest in the equity stocks of a given sector, for example : steel sector, banking sector, power sector etc.

(iv) **Tax planning schemes:** These schemes invest in such equity stocks that reduce the tax liability of the investor. For example the unit linked schemes of Reliance Tax saver (ELSS).

(v) **Arbitrage schemes:** These schemes purchase securities in the spot market and sell them in the futures market. There is a difference in the price of spot market and futures market. Spot market prices are typically lower than the prices in the futures market. On or before the expiry date of the futures contract, the difference between the two market prices disappears. At that time the position is unwound to book the profit.

(b) Debt Schemes

As the name suggest these schemes invest in the debt instruments viz; bonds and cash. Debt schemes may assume any of the following schemes:

(i) **Gilt schemes:** Under the scheme investment is made only in the government bonds and 10 to 15 percent of pooled funds in cash. Examples are UTI G-sec. Tata GSF

(ii) **Mixed Debt schemes:** These schemes invest in government bonds, corporate bonds and cash. 30 to 40 percent of funds are invested in Government Bonds, 40 to 55 percent in corporate bonds and balance is invested in cash. For example UTI bond.

(iii) **Floating rate debt scheme:** These funds invest in a portfolio comprising substantially of floating rate debt and bonds. For example Grindlays Floating rate schemes.

(iv) **Cash schemes:** These schemes are also called as liquid schemes. These schemes invest in the money markets instruments like treasury bills, commercial paper, certificate of deposits, call money, reverse repos and deposits with banks. They also have around 25% of their fund investment in short-term bonds.

(v) **Fixed maturity Plan:** It is an important debt scheme. It is a closed ended scheme that has a fixed maturity. The maturity period ranges between three months to three years. The funds of the scheme are invested primarily in corporate bonds.

Hybrid Schemes

These schemes invest in both equity and debt instruments. A hybrid scheme may be equity oriented or debt oriented or have a variable ratio of the two instruments. A hybrid scheme where the proportion of equity investment is more is called the equity oriented scheme and where debt proportion is more is termed as debt- oriented scheme.

A hybrid scheme may vary the proportion of debt and equity based on the market conditions. The equity proportion in such schemes increase when the market falls and decrease when market price rise. It is good to buy/invest in equity when the price is low and is better to sell when the market price is high.

2. Mutual Fund Schemes on the Basis of Trading Possibility

On the basis of trading possibility, mutual fund can be classified into:

(a) Open-ended schemes

(b) Closed-ended schemes

(a) Open Ended Schemes:

These schemes allow the investors to subscribe and sell the units of the fund on a continuous basis. There is no fixed maturity period for the units. These schemes are not listed in a secondary market. The Net Asset Value (NAV) is declared on a daily basis. The investors can purchase units on a continuous basis and sell or withdraw their funds under a re-purchase arrangement. The subscribers to the scheme get a value closer to the NAV.

(b) Closed Ended Schemes:

These schemes are open for the investors only for a limited period of time, usually one month to three months. The investors can not withdraw their investment as and when they want. These schemes have a maturity period ranging between 5 to 15 years. These schemes are listed on stock exchange. Investors can withdraw from the scheme by selling their units in the secondary market. The price quoted on the stock exchange is much less than the NAV of the units.

Difference between Open-ended and closed-ended Schemes:

(a) **Period:** The subscription to a closed ended scheme is kept open only for a limited period, usually one month to three months. The subscription to an open-ended scheme is allowed on a continuous basis.

(b) **Withdrawal of funds:** A closed ended scheme does not allow its investors to withdraw funds as and when they like. An open-ended scheme on the other hand allows the investors to withdraw funds under re-purchase arrangement.

(c) **Maturity period:** A closed ended scheme has a specific maturity period say 5 to 15 years. An open-ended scheme does not have a maturity period.

(d) **Listing on stock exchange:** The units of closed-ended scheme are listed on stock exchange. The open-ended schemes are not listed on stock exchanges.

(e) **Net asset value(NAV):** In the secondary market, the shares of closed-ended schemes sell at a discount (5% to 20%) over their NAV. On the other hand, the subscriber to a closed ended scheme gets a value close to (0 to 2 percent) NAV on withdrawal.

(f) **Performance:** The fund managers of closed-ended scheme can perform better as the funds are available for use for the entire period of the scheme.

The performance of an open-ended scheme gets adversely affected due to sharp inflow and outflow of funds ie., changing amount of funds may cause difficulty in its management.

3. **Advantages and Disadvantages of Mutual Funds:**

Advantages:

(a) **Diversification:** Mutual funds usually spread their investment across various industries and asset classes like banking companies, food industries, land, gold, government bonds etc. diversification reduces risk. An investor of mutual fund thus gets the benefits of diversification.

(b) **Professional management:** Mutual funds are managed by professionals who are experienced in the field. They have education, skill and resources to know about the investment opportunities. Mutual fund investors get benefit of their expertise.

(c) **Liquidity:** An open-ended scheme, allows the unit holders to redeem their units by paying a fee called exit-load. On the other hand closed-ended schemes are listed on the stock exchange, that allows the investors to sell off their units in the stock markets whenever they want to withdraw their funds. Thus both the schemes provide liquidity to the investment.

(d) **Return potential:** Equity oriented schemes have potential for higher returns.

(e) **Tax benefits:** Dividend received from equity-oriented mutual funds is tax free. Besides investment in certain mutual funds is deductible from the total income of individual assesses.

(f) **Regulations:** Mutual funds in India are regulated and monitored by the Securities and Exchange Board of India (SEBI). The interest of the investors is well protected.

Disadvantages:

(a) **Dependence on manager's skill:** The investor in mutual funds places his money in the hands of the managers of the fund. The return on the investment depends on the skill and judgments of the manager.

(b) **Cost:** Mutual funds charge fees for management and various administrative services. The fees can reduce the return on investment.

(c) Redemption of mutual funds: Although redemption of mutual funds is allowed but the return could get adversely affected due to sales commission and redemption fees.

4. SEBI Requirements of AMC

The department of company affairs, ministry of law, justice and company affair has issued guidelines in respect of registration of AMC in consultation with SEBI. A brief account of the areas in which SEBI has issued guidelines is as follows:

(a) The memorandum and articles of association of AMC must be approved by SEBI.

(b) SEBI has tightened the disclosure norms for the mutual funds to help investors take better informed decisions.

(c) It has laid down detailed investment and disclosure norms for employees of the mutual fund and trustee companies, in order to avoid any conflict of interest.

(d) It has allowed the mutual fund to invest in the listed and unlisted securities or units of venture capital funds within the overall ceiling, for such investment.

(e) For investment in foreign securities, detailed guidelines on the disclosure and reporting requirements were issued to mutual funds.

(f) For improving professional standard for management of mutual funds, SEBI has made it mandatory for all mutual funds to appoint agents/distributors who have obtained Association of Mutual Funds of India certification.

5. Association of Mutual Funds of India (AMFI):

The association was set up in 1995 as a non-profit organisation as a regulating association of AMCs. It is the chief governing body of all mutual funds in India. It is registered under SEBI. The main functions are:

(a) To define and maintain high professional and ethical standards in all areas of operation of mutual fund industry.

(b) To recommend and promote best business practices and code of conduct to be followed by members and others engaged in the activities of mutual fund and asset management including agencies connected or involved in the field of capital markets and financial services.

(c) To interact with the Securities and Exchange Board of India (SEBI) and to represent to SEBI on all matters concerning the mutual.

(d) To represent to the Government, Reserve Bank of India and other bodies on all matters relating to the Mutual Fund Industry.

(e) To develop a cadre of well trained Agent distributors and to implement a programme of training and certification for all intermediaries and other engaged in the industry.

(f) To undertake nationwide investor awareness programme so as to promote proper understanding of the concept and working of mutual funds.

(g) To disseminate information on Mutual Fund Industry and to undertake studies and research directly and/or in association with other bodies.

6. Mutual Fund Growth in India

Mutual fund industry in India started to grow in India with the setting up of Unit Trust of India (UTI) in 1964. It is a world's largest mutual fund in the public sector. The basic object was to mobilise small savings and to channelise the savings to productive sectors of the economy.

UTI came up with "US-64" the first unit. Thereafter host of other mutual fund schemes were introduced by it.

In 1987, the Government of India permitted commercial banks in the public sector to set up subsidiaries, to operate as trust and perform functions of mutual fund. It was done through amendment of the Banking Regulation Act. State Bank of India set up the first mutual fund followed by Canara Bank. Later many large financial institutions under the government control also came up with mutual funds.

On the basis of recommendations of Abid Hussain Committee, foreign companies were allowed to start mutual funds in India.

Government has taken many regulatory measures through SEBI for the growth of mutual fund industry in India.

5.5 Venture Capital

Meaning of Venture Capital

Venture capital is provided to entrepreneurs who want to start a high-tech untried project having risk and at the same time high potential of profits. It is also meant for those who do not have long history of running businesses. Entrepreneurs who have new ideas of promising business but don't have funds, or cannot borrow due to the risk involved in the project, or due to hesitation of banks to finance such ideas, may approach venture capital institutions for finance. Venture capitalist, if find the proposed business to be worthy, may provide equity i.e. invest in the proposal. They take part in the management of the business, provide guidance to the promoters and exit after 5 to 7 years by way of 'Initial Public Issue' (IPO). Thus they realise their investment and make capital gain if the company succeeds in the venture.

Definitions of Venture Capital

1. **According to Investopedia:** *"Money provided by investors to startup firms and small businesses with perceived long-term growth potential. This is a very important source of funding for start ups that do not have access to capital markets. It typically entails high risk for the investor, but it has the potential for above-average returns"*

2. **According to Oxford Dictionary of Business and Management:** *"Capital invested in a project in which there is a substantial element of risk, especially money invested in a new venture or an expanding business. Risk capital is normally invested in the equity of the company in the hope of high returns, it is not a loan."*

3. **According to Webster's New World Finance and Investment Dictionary:** *"Money that is given to entrepreneurs to invest in a start-up business or to develop a product. Venture capital is very risky investment and those investing money may lose their entire investment. However, if the business or the product becomes successful, the return can be huge. Venture capital is raised by venture capital firms who solicit investment from institutional investors, such as banks, private equity units, pension funds, or other investment management firms, as well as from wealthy individuals. Venture capital investments are made at different stages, with some venture capitalists focussing only on seed or initial investments, others on middle stages firms and others on later stage companies that have a viable product that is producing revenue."*

4. **The 1995 Finance Bill, defines Venture Capital as:** *"Long-term equity investment in novel technology, based projects with display potential for significant growth and financial returns".*

New business ideas or untried ideas are very risky. The ideas may turn out to be a success and generate huge profits or may fail in which case the capitalist would lose everything invested. Firm of investors or wealthy individuals may be interested in taking the risk of providing funds for such business ideas in the form of equity and may exit after few years when their capital appreciates.

Characteristic Features of Venture Capital:

1. Capital investment may be in the form of either equity or debt or both as a derivative instrument.
2. It is made in hi-tech projects involving high risk and strong potential of high profitability.
3. Venture capitalist finance the projects and wait for 5 to 7 years to reap the benefits of capital appreciation.
4. Venture capital funds is not repaid rather is realised through exit route.
5. The exit route may be any of the following:
   (i) Public issue of shares,
   (ii) Sale of share to entrepreneurs,
   (iii) Sale of company to another company,
   (iv) Finding new investor, or
   (v) Liquidation.

6. Venture capital organisation may be wholly owned subsidiaries of financial institutions, or owned by Government, or may be a group of individual venture capitalists.
7. The financing of high-tech projects in the form of venture capital is done in various stages.
8. Venture capitalists become member of the board in order to closely watch the performance of the business unit. The claim over management is decided on the basis of proportion of investment.

Venture Capital Investment Process/Stages in Venture Capital Process

Financing of novel high-tech project under venture capital has following process:

1. Contact between entrepreneur and venture capitalist: The prospective entrepreneur prepares project report and makes a formal application to venture capital investor. This can be done with the help of auditor, banker or professionals. It consists of five important feasibility report – technical, financial, managerial, marketing, and socio-economic feasibility.

2. Preliminary evaluation: After receiving the application the venture capitalist go through the project report and if find the deal worthwhile they may establish contact with the management to make a detailed appraisal of the project. The management team of the venture is required to present the detailed model of the company, unique aspects of the proposed business, future prospects, investment proposal. During the interaction with the management team the venture capitalist assess the quality and competence of management team. If the venture capitalist find the proposal investible proposition, a document containing terms of proposed investment is devised and negotiated with promoter. This is called term sheet.

3. Detailed analysis: After getting the approval of the promoters on the terms of proposed investment, the detailed analysis of the project is carried out. During this stage the business, financial and legal aspects of the project is examined. The risk is assessed through sensitivity analysis. The requirement of funds, stages and quantum of investment is also assessed. On successful completion of the analysis, the venture capitalist may modify or stipulate such other conditions as are considered by them for investment in the company, and negotiate changes in the term sheet with the entrepreneurs. In case the revised terms are agreeable to the entrepreneurs, venture capitalist funds issue 'Letter of Intent' for investment in the venture and require the investee company to complete formalities for availing the investment. These formalities include- execution of the legal agreement by promoter, passing of requisite Board resolution, obtaining approval of the government and other statutory approvals for investment.

4. Investment: On getting a formal request from the company for release of investment the venture capitalist make investment in the company as per the agreement.

5. Monitoring the project: The progress of the project shall be monitored by the venture capitalist. An executive director is appointed for the purpose by the venture capitalist. The venture capitalist give inputs on strategic plans and guide the company for optimising its performance.

Exit Route of Venture Capitalist:

The aim of venture capitalist is to realise huge profit on exiting the venture after some period of functioning of the venture. The venture capitalist may exit the company by adopting any of the following modes-

(a) **Going public:** Most of the venture capital firms prefer to go in for public issue to recover their investment with profits. The company makes public issue of its shares. The shares are listed on stock exchange. By selling the shares at premiums the venture capital firms make profit on their investment and exit the company.

(b) **Sale of shares to entrepreneurs/companies:** Instead of selling shares in the primary market, may sold to entrepreneurs or to other companies, who may be interested in taking over the venture due to its high profit potential.

(c) **Liquidation:** If the project performs badly, it may be closed down.

Venture capital in India: History of venture capital in India dates back to the early 70s when Government of India appointed a committee headed by R. S. Bhatt to find out new methods of funding start-up companies that are ready to bring innovative technologies. The committee recommended starting of venture capital Industry in India. The committee emphasised the need for providing such capital to help new entrepreneurs and technologists in setting up industries.

1. In 70s and 80's financial institutions like ICICI, IDBI, IFCI came forward to fund small technological companies. In 1975, Industrial Finance Corporation of India (IFCI) launched the first venture capital fund 'Risk Capital Fund'. The objective was to encourage technologists and professionals to promote new business, by supplementing the promoter's equity. IDBI launched venture capital fund in 1976, to provide seed capital. This fund was converted into Risk Capital and Technology Finance Corporation Ltd (RCTFC) in 1988.

2. In 1983, the Central Government announced the 'Technology Policy Statement', which prescribed guidelines for achieving technological self reliance.

3. ICICI, a financial institution in the financial sector set up a 'venture capital scheme' in 1986. The object was to provide venture capital to risky but high profit potential projects. In 1988, ICICI sponsored company viz., Technologies Development and

Information Company of India Ltd. (TDICI) was set up for taking up the venture capital operation of the ICICI.

4. In 1989, VECAUS-1, in 1990 VECAUS-II and in 1991 VECAUS III, the UTI sponsored venture capital schemes were launched. TDICI was appointed as the manager of VECAUS I and II. RCTFC was appointed as the fund manager of VECAUS III.
5. The IDBI administers the venture capital fund created by the central government from 1st April 1986.
6. The government imposes a 'research and development' levy on all payments made for the purchase of technologies from abroad, so that technologies developed in India is cheaper from 1986.
7. Venture capital institutions are regulated by guidelines issued by the 'Controller of Capital Issues" (CCI) in India.
8. In 1995 Government of India permitted Foreign finance companies to make investment in India. Many foreign venture capital firms entered India. Government has been issuing guidelines to regulate the venture capital industry.

Points to Remember

- **Essential Features of Consumer Finance:**
    1. Parties to the transaction
    2. Modes of consumer finance
    3. Period
    4. Products covered
- **Types of Consumer Credit or Finance:**
    1. On the basis of period involved
    2. On the basis of security
    3. On the basis of institution extending credit
- **Players in the Market of Consumer Finance:**
    1. Commercial Banks
    2. Non Banking Financial Companies
    3. Co-operative banks
- **Types of Housing Finance:**
    1. National Housing Bank (NHB)
    2. Housing Development Finance Corporation Ltd. (HDFC Ltd.)
    3. Life Insurance Corporation Housing Finance Ltd (LICHFL)
    4. GIC Housing Finance

- **Types of Housing Loans:**
    1. Land Purchase Loans
    2. Home Purchase Loans
    3. Home Construction Loan
    4. Home Expansion/Extension Loan
    5. Home Improvement Loan
    6. Home Conversion Loan
    7. NRI Loan
    8. Balance Transfer Loan
    9. Stamp Duty Loan
    10. Bridged Loan
- **Mutual Fund:**
    1. Mutual Funds Schemes on the Basis of Asset Mix
    2. Mutual Fund Schemes on the Basis of Trading Possibility
    3. Advantages and Disadvantages of Mutual Funds
    4. SEBI Requirements of AMC
    5. Association of Mutual Funds of India (AMFI)
    6. Mutual Fund Growth in India
- **Venture Capital Investment Process**
    1. Contact between entrepreneur and venture capitalist
    2. Preliminary evaluation
    3. Detailed analysis
    4. Investment
    5. Monitoring the project

Questions for Discussion

1. What is Consumer Finance ? State the various types of Consumer Finance.
2. Define Credit Rating. State the Features and Types of Credit Rating.
3. What is Mutual Funds ? Explain the Types of Mutual Funds.
4. State the Advantages and Disadvantages of Mutual Funds.
5. What is Venture Capital ? State the Feature of Venture Capital.

6. Write short notes on :
   (a) Players in the Market of Consumer Finance.
   (b) Types of Housing Finance.
   (c) Equity Rating.
   (d) CRISIL.
   (e) ICAA
   (f) AMFI
   (g) Venture Capital in India.

Case Studies

Case Study - 1

Industrial Credit and Investment Corporation of India Ltd (ICICI) yesterday stepped in to rescue beleaguered non-bank finance company ITC Classic Finance Ltd, announcing a merger between the two companies.

The respective boards of the two companies will meet on December 1 to consider the merger. Market sources are speculating that the swap ratio will range between 10: 1 and 15:1, that is, one share of ICICI for every 10-15 shares of ITC Classic.

After the announcement of the merger, ITC Classics share price declined to ₹ 19.45 against Tuesdays close of ₹ 21.50. ICICIs scrip rose marginally on the news from Tuesdays close of ₹ 72.50 to ₹ 73.25.

The merger appears to be a win-win situation for ICICI, said analysts. Not only does the merger with ITC Classic provide a tax shelter for ICICI, ITC Ltd has also agreed to pump in long term funds, said one analyst.

ITC Classic had posted a net loss of ₹ 285 crore for the year ended 1996-97. In order to avail of the tax shelter, it was decided to merge ITC Classic with ICICI and not with I-Credit, the non-bank finance company promoted by ICICI, ICICI officials told Business Standard.

As part of the revival package, ITC Ltd has agreed to infuse funds amounting to ₹ 350 crore into ITC Classic by way of preference capital of 20-year maturity, carrying a nominal dividend of 0.01 per cent.

In addition, ITC has undertaken to ensure that ITC Classic disengages its intra-group assets. The sale of these assets either to ITC or to any other investors will infuse ₹ 220 crore into ITC Classic.

On the asset side, ICICI officials said it would acquire leased and other assets which have been carefully assessed while evaluating the condition of ITC Classic.

An ICICI press release said given the size constraint and the high finance cost inherent in non-banking finance companies, the viable option for ITC Classic was to a merge with a strong and healthy financial intermediary which is geared to take advantage of the opportunities in the financial sector. While this infusion of long-term capital will restore the financial health of ITC Classic, the rapidly changing financial sector makes it imperative to develop a long term strategic plan for ITC Classic, said the ICICI press release.

We expect to consolidate our position in the financial market through the acquisition of ITC Classic, said an ICICI official. Synergy would also be achieved on account of the common clientele between the two companies.

The merger is expected to provide comfort to ITC Classics seven lakh retail depositors. At the same time, the merger will add 10 branches and 12 franchisees to ICICIs retail network.

Case Study 2

Should an insurance claim be paid to insured or financer? Inder Singh Chauhan had purchased a bus by taking a loan from Swami Financers. The bus was being used as a private service vehicle, and not as a public transport one. It was insured under a comprehensive insurance policy issued by United India Insurance. The bus met with an accident, for which insurance was claimed. The insurance company appointed its surveyor, who assessed the loss at ₹ 1,26,500. However, the company deducted ₹ 33,125 from the assessed amount, on the ground that the driver did not have an endorsement on his licence to drive a transport vehicle. Even this amount was not paid to Chauhan, but was directly paid to the financer.

Aggrieved, Chauhan filed a consumer complaint that ultimately reached the National Commission. It was held that once a person had a licence to drive a heavy goods carriage vehicle, it would mean that he/she was entitled to drive a transport vehicle, including a public service vehicle. Accordingly, the insurance company was directed to pay the balance amount, along with 12 per cent interest and costs of ₹ 5,000.

The commission also ruled that the practice adopted by insurance companies of directly paying to the financer, without informing the insured or without his consent, cannot be justified. If the insurance policy is taken in the name of the vehicle purchaser, there is no question of paying the amount straightaway to the financier. [United India Insurance Co Ltd v/s Inder Singh Chauhan – IV (2006) CPJ 15 (NC)]

Case Study 3

Can an insurance company independently challenge the award under a professional indemnity policy?

During a gall bladder surgery, Mohinder Kaur developed ventricular tachycardia, followed by ventricular fibrillation. She suffered cardiac dysrhythmia and went into coma due to medical negligence, becoming bedridden at the age of 45. A case was filed against the surgeon, the anaesthetist and the hospital. The insurance company was a party to the proceedings. The District Forum awarded a compensation of ₹ 2 lakh, payable by the insurance company on behalf of the doctors under the professional indemnity policy. This was challenged in appeal before the State Commission, which upheld the Forum's order. The doctors did not continue further litigation, but the insurance company filed a revision petition before the National Commission.

Observing that it was incumbent on the insurance company to indemnify doctors under the professional indemnity policy by paying the amount awarded by the consumer forum, the commission stated the challenging of the order by the insurance company without rhyme or reason is neither proper nor desirable. The commission expressed deep anguish that such petitions were being filed. It observed that such cases are not meant to be fodder for the legal department and the insurance company cannot go on a spree in filing such petitions.

The commission stated it was restraining itself this time, but warned that if such petitions are filed in future, heavy cost would be imposed. The agony of a consumer must end at some stage. It is the duty of the insurance company to see that frivolous cases were not filed so as to clog the wheels of justice, which result in wastage of time. While dismissing the revision petition, the commission directed the order be sent to the chairman-cum-managing directors of all insurance companies. [New India Assurance Co Ltd v/s Hardip Singh & Others – II (2003) CPJ 103 (NC)]

Case Study - 4

Mutual Fund Settlement Processing & Data Management

Market Timing/Late Trading Settlement

A major mutual fund company was ordered to pay restitution to its shareholders in the matter of improper trading by a small number of shareholders.

The Challenge

This was a project of extraordinary magnitude and complexity. Improper transactions conducted over the course of 5 years affected millions of shareholder accounts.

As a result, hundreds of millions of transactions required analysis to determine when the trades were executed and the harm that was caused.

Colbent was chosen as the systems provider for the mutual fund settlement.

The Colbent Solution

In the first project phase, Colbent worked with the administrators to gather millions of records from not only the fund company but also hundreds of brokers - in dozens of different electronic and paper formats. Applying our robust hardware and programming capabilities, and leveraging the skills and experience of our project managers, Colbent effectively converted and assimilated this data into our system for processing.

In the next phase, our analysts scrutinized every transaction to determine where and when harm occurred as a result of improper trading to determine the amount of harm to allocate to each shareholder. We aggregated these amounts, performed de minimus calculations and prorated individual settlements within the allotted damage pool.

Before distributing the settlement to shareholders, Colbent performed list maintenance to ensure mailing addresses were accurate. When payments were undeliverable, we marshaled the necessary resources to find and pay those shareholders. Colbent also provided the system for shareholder phone support and correspondence services.

The Result

Interfacing with all parties involved in the Fair Fund Settlement Process, Colbent supported the administration of the settlement, paying all affected shareholders in a speedy and accurate manner.

Case Study - 5

Fleet financing for added employee benefits

Alcatel-Lucent is a global leader in mobile, fixed, IP and opticstechnologies and a pioneer in applications and services. In India, Alcatel-Lucent is engaged in R&D, Sales, Marketing, Customer Support, Services, Operations and Development of Embedded as well as Application Software for Telecom Networks.

Alcatel-Lucent is the single largest supplier of digital switching in India for both Fixed and CDMA wireless lines with over 50% market share. The company believes in recruiting, retaining and developing the best talent with a professional work environment and employee best practices.

Alcatel-Lucent's Challenge

Alcatel-Lucent was looking to assist its employees in India with vehicle financing and acquisition as part of an efficient employee compensation structure. The company wanted to provide to its 600+ eligible employees a lease solution with transparent pricing and an easy buying option at the end of the term.

At the same time, it wanted the leased vehicles to be completely off-balance-sheet with no capital allocation.

The Solution

As an Auto Lease partner, GE Capital India understood Alcatel-Lucent's needs. Our innovative operating lease structure offered a consolidated solution that met the company's requirements while providing unparalleled levels of employee engagement. By educating the employees about the lease product and its advantages, our exceptional customer service helped manage their employee expectations.

GE Capital's Strategy

GE Capital India offered Alcatel-Lucent operating & finance lease options as a part of its Employee Auto Lease program at flexible terms.

GE Capital India offered Alcatel-Lucent's employees fixed residual value for buy-back without the mandatory add-ons like insurance, maintenance, accident management etc.

The Results

Since the launch of the program, over 100 Alcatel-Lucent employees have enrolled for the Auto Lease program. GE Capital India's portfolio management team carried out employee engagement campaigns in Gurgaon, Delhi, Mumbai and Bangalore by conducting helpdesk sessions, test drive campaigns and arranging spot dealer discounts. The high employee take-off was the result of our sincere efforts in dealing with employee enquiries in a uniform and transparent manner.

Our vehicle-acquisition process, dedicated team and world-class operational practices have made GE Capital India Alcatel-Lucent's preferred partner. The company is now in a long-term relationship with GE Capital for its product enhancement program.

www.ingramcontent.com/pod-product-compliance
Lightning Source LLC
Chambersburg PA
CBHW062134160426
43191CB00013B/2296